The Magic Daughter

Jane Phillips

The Magic Daughter

A MEMOIR OF LIVING WITH

MULTIPLE PERSONALITY

DISORDER

Viking

VIKING
Published by the Penguin Group
Penguin Books USA Inc., 375 Hudson Street,
New York, New York 10014, U.S.A.
Penguin Books Ltd, 27 Wrights Lane, London W8 5TZ, England
Penguin Books Australia Ltd, Ringwood, Victoria, Australia
Penguin Books Canada Ltd, 10 Alcorn Avenue,
Toronto, Ontario, Canada M4V 3B2
Penguin Books (N.Z.) Ltd, 182–190 Wairau Road,
Auckland 10, New Zealand

Penguin Books Ltd, Registered Offices:
Harmondsworth, Middlesex, England

First published in 1995 by Viking Penguin,
a division of Penguin Books USA Inc.

1 3 5 7 9 10 8 6 4 2

LIBRARY OF CONGRESS CATALOGING IN PUBLICATION DATA
Phillips, Jane.
The magic daughter : a memoir of living with multiple personality
disorder / Jane Phillips.
p   cm.
ISBN 0-670-85970-2
1. Phillips, Jane—Mental health.   2. Multiple personality—Patients—
United States—Biography.   I. Title.
RC569.5M8P48   1995
616.85'236'0092—dc20   95-7604
[B]

This book is printed on acid-free paper.

Printed in the United States of America
Set in Garamond No. 3
Designed by Francesca Belanger

For my therapist—

with gratitude and affection

Author's Note

I SUFFERED SOME MISGIVINGS while writing this book because I have no wish to hurt those who loved me, and love me still, or those who hurt me, or dismissed my hurts, when I was very young. Although all multiples come from families where there has been much violence and fear, I like to think that sooner or later such violence should draw to a close. Since exposing my family in the pages of this book would only cause more anguish, I have changed many external facts. Names, events, characters, and identities have been disguised, combined, or altered altogether.

What has not been changed in this account are the details and workings of my disorder. I have written as forthrightly as possible about the odd disjointedness of living as a multiple in a world of "ordinaries," about the nature of my therapeutic process, and about the harrowing joys of integration. These, I believe, are what matter most: the internal truths of what it has meant to live my life as a multiple.

Contents

Prologue

THIS BOOK BEGAN as a suicide note. On a clear, sunny day in April 1993, I sat down at my desk with the intention of leaving behind a document that would explain why I could no longer bear to be alive. As a multiple, the wish for my own death is never far from my consciousness: even now, life sometimes seems too difficult, too meaningless, or too painful to make it worth the effort to live as much as one more hour. On that particular April morning, I decided to leave behind some record of what it had been like to live with a disorder I was required to keep secret from nearly everyone I knew.

Scheherazade stayed alive because she was an artful storyteller. I stayed alive because the business of writing about my multiplicity took a whole lot longer than I had imagined, and because within days of beginning this project, I soon grew interested in the task that I had set for myself.

When I began this book, I was host to a range of selves. Each knew some share of what was to become my history. Each had its own quirks, its own voice, and its own vulnerabilities. As the drafts progressed, so did my integration. Still, I took great care to write about my disorder in ways that were acceptable to my various selves. They have been a remarkably forthright and generous group; their cooperation was crucial to the early stages of this project. One especially fragile part did not wish to be included; I respected that request.

The Magic Daughter was not written as part of my therapeutic process. As a college professor, I am sometimes asked to read writings whose sole purpose is to make the writer feel better. Such writing has value, but it belongs in journals or among private papers. Instead, I wrote in order to pass along what one person thought about what it was like to live with this disorder. Sometimes I felt a little like a journalist who, by sheer dumb luck, had found herself smack in the middle of an important story.

The original text of this book was in some ways extraordinarily different from the final version. Most significantly, the original version ended with the wish, perhaps even the desperate longing, for the deep integrative process to begin. But then I began to revise and, to my surprise, the book and the therapeutic process became one and the same thing during the summer of 1994. "How's the book?" and "How are you?" became nearly synonymous questions.

Two of my editor's requests were particularly disconcerting: Could I wrestle what had been a collection of essays into a chronology? And, could I do something about the relentless repetition?

"Of course," I told her, trying to sound calm.

"Chronology?" I wailed to my therapist. "I haven't had a chronological thought in my life."

He nodded and smiled. "Let me know if you need help," he said.

For the next few weeks, I muttered and I sulked. I wrote the events of my life on index cards and laboriously shuffled them into sequence. I cut chapters apart. One day I told my therapist I was ready to throw up. "You know," I told him, "it's a little horrifying the way this fits together."

He grinned. "Does that mean the book's in order?"

"Yes, damn it," I said.

"And just think—you left out ninety percent of the horror stories."

Dizziness washed over me. I put my head down between my knees. "Thanks a lot," I muttered. "I needed the reminder."

Once the text was in some kind of sequence—one that at least made sense to me—the real fireworks began. As a multiple, my thoughts are quite repetitive. Because various selves were often present at, or aware of, any given event, each had its own take, opinion, or slice of memory, each had a vested interest in being heard, and none had much interest in whether *their* view matched the view of any other part in the system. In the original manuscript, facts, events, and perceptions showed up again and again. The wording differed slightly from one paragraph or chapter to the next, and vantage points shifted everywhere. Following along behind my editor's notations, I tried to convince my selves that their views were still represented in the more streamlined text, although not quite so laboriously as before. Once in a while, when I sensed too much fear and too much resistance—"If she's getting rid of my idea, then she's getting rid of me"—I simply let the repetition stand with the full intention of letting my editor be the bad guy.

Then an abrupt change took place. "Repetition! Duplication!" seemed like brand-new concepts among my selves, and barriers within the system began to open. I was sometimes reminded of an icebreaker at a cocktail party, my parts eagerly playing some absurd matching game, frantically putting this idea together with that event, or this sensation with that memory. A significant flush of integration thus began—although the process was so relentless and so tumultuous that I certainly don't recommend revising a memoir as a therapeutic technique.

In 1980, Multiple Personality Disorder appeared in the *American Psychiatric Association's Diagnostic and Statistic Manual*. When I was diagnosed in the fall of 1990, I was glad the disorder had been included. I felt a little less crazy somehow, knowing MPD had been declared both real and legitimate, although I also knew it was, and remains, a source of controversy.

In 1994, Multiple Personality Disorder disappeared from

DSM IV. And, four years into my treatment for MPD, I was glad to see it go. "Personality" conjures too many false images in the minds of the general public, as well as, perhaps, in the minds of patients and clinicians. Language is a powerful thing; it creates images and conjures expectations. One close friend, for instance, has steadily teased me because I have none of the flamboyant, dramatic, or even bizarre selves that the old term suggests.

MPD is now called Dissociative Identity Disorder, and the change is very much for the good. The diagnostic criteria are more accurate, and the emphasis now falls where it should: on the dissociative process and on "identities" which can be far more subtle and far more fragmented than our vernacular ear expects from "personalities."

Still, because I have worked and lived with the old terminology, I have retained it within this text. Although I do not see myself as having personalities so much as I have selves, parts, or even force fields, I think of myself as "a multiple," and I think of my disorder as multiplicity. I am not sure what kind of nomenclature the next generation of patients will come to use. Sadly, because of the large incidence of childhood violence, there will be a next generation of patients; my wish is that they find a vocabulary that seems accurate to them.

My one great sorrow in writing this book has been that, in order to maintain my privacy and the privacy of my family, I cannot thank or acknowledge the many people who have been kind to me over the years and the many people who have cheered me on in my efforts to write. I would, however, like to thank two close friends who read this book in manuscript. They accepted my disorder with tact and with compassion.

I have also been quite lucky in my editor, who has had the good grace to laugh over my general inability to remember my pseudonym. Her questions edited not only this text but, whether she intended to or not, some of the workings of my mind. Whatever leaps and gaps remain in this narrative are due to my rather recent acquaintance with chronology.

Special thanks go to my agent, whose responses both to my initial proposal for this book and to the chapters as they were written have been marked by kindness, enthusiasm, and understanding.

And of course, there is my psychologist, who, like me, must unfortunately remain anonymous. His belief in the value of this project and his enduring faith in me have meant more than I can say.

The Magic Daughter

THE URGE TO TELL

A YOUNG WOMAN SITS at the head of the table. She is short, round-faced, chubby. Her blonde hair is elaborately shingled, and she sports a black beret and an antique coat with a dramatic cape. She smiles and tells us that she really, honestly, truly has *no* recollection—none whatsoever—of the window-smashing spree that has brought her here before us.

Questioned, she does admit that yes, there *were* witnesses, and that no, she can think of no reason they would lie about her actions.

Well, someone asks, does that mean she *did* break all those windows? Every single window in the lounge of Newton Hall?

Her brow furrows briefly. She looks at us, then at the dean of students. Isn't there a letter, she asks, from her psychologist that explains all this? She had been told there would be.

For several years, I have been a member of my college's disciplinary appeals board. Hearings held by student boards settle the majority of campus problems; the staff and faculty board convenes only for especially sensitive cases. We read the case notes, interview the perpetrator, then confer behind closed doors. Sometimes we expel the students who come before us; sometimes we allow them to remain on campus, but only if they will sign a contract of behavior that includes various activities and tasks we believe they should participate in or undertake. Because the safety and integrity of the entire college is at stake, one requirement we have is that the student must, from the start, accept responsibility for the action that brings her here before us. This young woman, in order to remain a student, must admit her guilt.

And she, therefore, presents a problem. Like me, she is a dissociator. Although she does not deny the actions that have brought her here before us, she also clearly cannot remember them.

I sit at the far end of the table. My palms sweat. Beneath the table, I weave my fingers together and I concentrate on the cadence of my pulse as it rebounds back and forth. I listen to the questions: Would she describe her family? Does she have friends? What does she do for fun? How are her grades? What does she plan to do when she graduates? Again and again, however, the questioning returns to her lack of memory.

Leave her alone! I want to shout. *She's telling the truth!*

But, usually an active participant, I am quiet. I will either shout or cry, and neither will help the young woman sitting at the far end of the table.

Someone double-checks that she's in counselling. Is there someone helping her with this, um, problem?

Her smile broadens. She beams around the table, literally grows taller by three inches. Yes, she tells us. She has the most wonderful psychologist. His name is . . .

And she says the name of my own psychologist, a professional I have been consulting for three years now, beginning the summer I was thirty, when I seemed to be going mad.

Beneath the table, I dig a thumbnail into the fleshy part of my other hand.

It occurs to me that I should excuse myself from the hearing. But I am too frightened to move, and I fear that if I try to stand I will black out. Wonderful, I think, and grind my teeth. Dissociators at both ends of the table. Then, terrified of being found out, terrified that people will match her range of odd affects with my own pale, slack face, I inhale deeply and straighten up.

Eventually, the young woman is dismissed from the room. The door is closed behind her so that we can discuss her case.

The dean passes my therapist's letter around the table. We are a mixed but competent group: the director of residential life, a board-certified therapist from our counseling staff, the director of security, a student representative, and faculty from the departments of psychology, education, nursing, and economics. And me, an associate professor of French.

I take the letter when it comes to me. I read it quickly, having no real need to read my own therapist's description of my disorder. I pass it on.

"Good Lord, that was fast," remarks the security director, who sits next to me.

"I've had a lot of experience," I say.

"All those translations she corrects," says the psych professor, and smiles at me.

The letter continues to be passed around the table. People talk quietly, waiting as each board member reads it in turn. Discreetly I blot a little sweat off my upper lip.

Discussion begins. I am quiet at first, because to me it is a given that the young woman be allowed to stay, that she be offered the chance it is so desperately clear she needs.

To the others, it is not so obvious.

"So," asks the security director, "what's the story on this counselor? Any good?"

I hold my breath.

The dean hesitates, looks around the table. "Yes," she says. "As far as I know."

The professors of nursing and psychology nod.

"But if these cases are so uncommon," says the economics professor, "how can he be sure that's her problem? Couldn't she just be faking? I mean, what's his background, after all?"

I shudder. My vision narrows and my eyes blur. What I would give for the safety of his office right this minute. What I would give to be in the presence of someone who does not wield doubt and disbelief like a weapon.

"Yes," the dean says, perhaps a little irritated, "I believe he's had prior experience."

The nurse checks the letter. "It does say he's a PsyD."

"What's that?" the education professor asks.

"A clinical degree. Not just theory or research."

Everyone nods. My therapist—or at least his credentials—has met with their approval. I exhale.

The discussion turns to the student. Can we allow her to stay at the college? Isn't she too sick? She seems a little weird. And, of course, she's obviously in denial.

The director of residential life quietly shuffles his papers and lays them neat and straight on the table. The economics professor leans back in his chair and says, "Forget it. She's a real sicko."

"A psycho maybe," someone else chimes in.

There is a quiet, nervous laugh around the table.

I freeze.

"Right," says the economics prof, nodding doggedly. "Psycho."

The woman from the counseling department begins to pontificate on trauma and dissociation. She speaks as if reciting from a textbook. There is no compassion in her voice.

The security director turns his fact sheets facedown. "Too sick for us," he says. "I say no."

Around the table, arms fold across chests. Chairs push back an inch or so from the table. Heads shake.

I clear my throat, moisten my mouth. I cannot believe what is happening.

Before I can speak, the student representative says, her words a little clipped, "I don't believe a word of this." She waves dismissively at her case notes. "Can we bring her back? And ask her some good hard questions? Let's just *force* her to tell the truth."

I clear my throat again and blink hard. I've never heard this tone among these people. We listen to cases, hear young people talk about their hopes and their mistakes; we do not interrogate.

The nurse seconds the motion to bring the student back. And then she adds that, for a person of her age, the student seems utterly lacking in direction. She glances at her fact sheet and purses her lips. "Just look at these courses: Painting, math, writing, ancient history."

"And clothes," someone jokes.

I blow up.

"For God's sake," I say. "There's not that much difference between her and me at that age. I had even more interests than *that*," I say. "And I turned out okay."

The education professor looks away, seeming suddenly a little torn, embarrassed maybe.

But I am off and running, nearly deaf to my own words and scared as hell: What secrets of mine am I giving away? But I seem to be arguing that we accept her. I argue that her psychologist, who knows more than we do, is very much in favor of her staying in school. I argue that yes, she's a little different, but that she can be helped, that she deserves a chance, that she's something of a special case. I move for her acceptance. After all, we've accepted other special cases in the past.

"How do *you* know so much about this?" the security director asks with a sharp look and a laugh that softens the look just a little.

All eyes turn toward me: My colleagues, whom I admired for the volunteering of their time and for their interest and compassion. My colleagues, with whom I have worked, sometimes in tension and sometimes in camaraderie, to hammer out our recommendations. My colleagues, whose diversity and diverging viewpoints I have respected. Until today.

They look down the table at me, and at this moment I both hate and fear them. Neither I nor the young woman who has left the room deserves this treatment.

"How do I know so much?" I echo.

My mouth glues briefly shut. Under the table, my hands cling to one another.

I lie. Sort of. I tell them I know a dissociator. As if on cue, I assume a warm, kindly adult voice. Privately I am surprised. "I know a dissociator," I repeat, "and while I'm not skilled enough to lecture on the subject, I can tell you that everything the psychologist wrote is sound. There's a continuum to the disorder, with multiples at the most severe end and post-traumatic stress and so forth at the other." I wave to the student's empty chair. "At her age, the problem is nearly always the result of severe abuse—in her case probably repeated abuse, probably beginning when she was very young. It's not her fault and she isn't playing games. She really *can't* remember certain things, because her memory simply isn't structured like yours." I falter. *Or like mine,* I desperately wish to add.

After a long pause, I see the psychology professor, the nurse, then the counselor nod, and I wonder why it has to be me—not one of these trained professionals—who speaks out on her behalf.

I gulp some air and plunge on: "I move that we allow her to stay and that we require continued work with her therapist and whatever else she is capable of performing."

The room is silent for a moment, then a low murmur sweeps around the table. Shoulders shrug. Postures shift. Fingers touch fact sheets, most already facedown on the table.

Then the education professor sighs, looks up at the ceiling, sighs again, glances at me and then away. "Okay," he says. "I'll go along with Jane. I say we give the girl a chance."

There is some dissension, some muttering, the words "psycho" and "sicko" are hazarded again, but in the end my motion passes.

The economics professor shoves his chair back and shoots his fact sheet angrily across the table toward the dean. "I still say it's impossible to break all those windows and not know it."

Board members look back and forth between him and me. I say nothing.

We hammer out our recommendations. They include counseling, an apology to the residents of Newton Hall, restitution, community service, and educational goal-setting. I think it's overkill, but I say very little. I believe I have done all I can for her.

After the contract recommendations are finalized, I look at my watch. We've spent a long time on this case, and claiming that I am late for another meeting, I excuse myself from the rest of the hearing. Everyone calls good-bye, see you next time.

In the hall, I pass the student as she returns to hear the board's decision. She gives me a vague and fearful smile.

"Good luck," I tell her.

She gives me a puzzled look.

I pause. "I mean it," I say, desperate to make some kind of contact, to convey something to her, anything that might someday help her.

She shakes her head, and passes by without answering.

I bolt down the stairs and out into the late afternoon. On the way home I have what, two years later, I will come to understand is a classic, stress-induced change of personalities.

One consciousness replaces another, and I find myself on a back road. I do not recognize it. I do not know where I am, never mind how I got there or where I am going. Abruptly, I realize: *I am driving a car.*

In horror, I snatch my hands from the steering wheel and my feet from the pedals. I do not drive. I am too young. Little girls do not drive automobiles.

The car swoops to the right. I take the wheel, and, elbows locked, guide it off to the side of the road as if steering a bumper car. I look down at the pedals, make a wild guess, and step down on the middle one. The car chokes, then shudders to a halt.

I am lost. Dead lost. I close my eyes and see my room with its fresh coat of butter-yellow paint, my stuffed dog Homer on the bed, and my little desk with its sloppy pile of workbooks, crayons, and drawing pads. I open my eyes, look around—and have no idea how to get from here to there.

When I find myself once more I am sitting, almost but not quite inexplicably, in my car on the shoulder of a shunpike. Over the gambrel roof of a nearby barn, the evening star appears. Then, in a jolt, as if jump-started, memory surges back: the student, the name-calling, the inadvertent cruelty, the ignorance, the mind-numbing fear of exposure.

I hustle out of the car and, extremely dizzy, vomit two, three times into the tall grass.

I have no idea how long I've been here, how much time I've lost. I am still not quite sure of the way home, but at each mysterious intersection I seem to know which way to turn. I drive the car like a sixteen-year-old, newly licensed, awkward, a little over-awed by what I am attempting.

Finally home, I go straight to bed and sleep in painful spurts. Days pass, and I cannot shake my anger and my hurt. What's more, I cannot shake an odd, queasy sense of guilt. For reasons I do not fully understand, I seem to think I should have told my fellow board members, quietly and simply, that I too am a dis-sociator. But each time I allow myself to hope that then they might have seen dissociation, and perhaps even mental illness, in some new light, I remember their reactions to the student—how horrified they were, how shocked, how angry, how quick to judge—and I fear that perhaps they would have seen only *me* in some new way. And that I am not willing to risk.

And so I evade the next two hearings—easy enough due to other commitments. But as time passes, I suspect I will never return. In the end, feeling cowardly, guilty, and not a little fright-ened, I resign my seat on the appeals board, and I never quite shake the feeling that I should have spoken up, should have said far more about dissociation.

Six years have passed since that last hearing. I now know that my dissociative disorder is not some mysteriously severe case of delayed post-traumatic stress, but full-blown Multiple Personality Disorder. I know, too, what led to the condition: the predisposing chemistry, the gaps in nurture and protection, the myriad episodes of violence. During therapy, I have come to understand the workings of MPD and its effects on my life, and I have come to be grateful that I have been blessed with a personality system that allowed me to do graduate work and to make a place for myself in a college community.

Still, my thoughts often return to the young woman at the far end of the table. And I find myself struggling still with the urge to tell about my life as a dissociator and a multiple—and with the equally powerful urge to remain silent.

The reasons for silence and secrecy are many and obvious. The first is pathology, plain and simple. A child creates multiple selves in order to keep her deadly secrets out of the way of her conscious mind so that she can continue to function and to survive. My secret selves protected me from the demands and expectations of a family focused in desperate ways on the sole, long-awaited magic daughter, the girl-child who would somehow bring happiness to a troubled family. My selves contained my fierce desire to live, a desire too dangerous to display in the face of a brother so tormented, so jealous, and so wounded he wanted to see me dead. My selves hid the secrets of incest and of other cruelties that, all these years later, still take my breath away. My selves wept and sorrowed; they plotted wild, improbable scenarios of revenge. But they also kept safe my dreams, formed a tight protective circle around my soul, and acquired talents and traits that I would later smuggle, unbeknownst to my family and indeed to myself, out of the family circle. I do not speak up because secrecy and silence have been my way of life since shortly after my third birthday. Secrecy equalled safety, and that is a hard equation to relinquish, even as I near forty.

Five years after I began therapy, my diagnosis as a multiple became official. A few months later, I sat in a campus coffee shop with a group of students. The conversation turned to term papers. One student was writing on MPD. Not only did she have her information completely wrong, but she and her classmates launched into a long discussion on the freakishness of multiples. They had all read *Sybil*, had all seen the films in Intro Psych, had all watched the morning talk shows. These students, thus informed on this vogue mental illness, drew the conclusion that multiples were weird, creepy, sick, and possibly very dangerous. One admitted that the thought of possibly having to deal with one after she became a nurse was almost enough to make her change her major—until she realized there would be other staff there to "protect" her. In such an atmosphere, one hardly feels inclined to say, "Well, perhaps it would be interesting for you to know . . ." What bothered me most was that none of them seemed to understand that a multiple is a person who, as a very young child, suffered abuse so frequent and so intense that it was literally mind-blowing.

The "freakishness" of the disorder, and the horrified fascination it evokes, prompts a kind of inverse reason, though, for maintaining my own dignity and quiet, and that is the fact that I am troubled that so many people, in these years of the "recovery" movement, seem to wear a diagnosis like a name tag. I am always distressed, although I seldom let on just how deeply, when students on the first day of class, by way of introduction, feel obliged to announce their status as recovering alcoholics, as former cocaine addicts, as adult children of alcoholics, or as "survivors." It is clear that these tags are, for the moment at least, a crucial element in their self-definitions, but how I wish that they would *also* say that they love to paint in oils, or rebuild old Jaguars, or build scenery down at the theater—or *some*thing.

Yet, in a way I understand the impulse. For the first year after I began to abreact episodes of sexual abuse, I wandered through my life saying over and over to myself, "I was sexually abused, I was sexually abused." It was a source of wonder and amazement to me as it did, indeed, explain rather a lot about me. Still, I think I always knew—or desperately wanted to believe, and perhaps there is a difference—that I did not want my diagnosis, first as an adult survivor of sexual abuse and later as a multiple who had suffered other and, in my case, worse forms of abuse, to become my identity.

The irony is that I became a multiple because it was not safe to be myself, because one self could not cope with all there was to be coped with. And so, I became my selves, playing a kind of instinctive, survivalist shell game of identity. But as an adult, during these long and grueling years of therapy, what I have sought to become is, indeed, myself. *My self:* pronoun, first person singular possessive; noun, singular. And so it is antithetical for me to become known as my disorder, when that disorder may still hide my so-called birth, or original, personality. Multiplicity clearly saved my life, and it can even be argued my sanity, but it robbed me of my identity in childhood and, in a different way if I chose to make my diagnosis public, could do so again now that I am an adult.

And yet, and yet . . . there is the other side: the urge to tell. And it is a powerful, mysterious, complex urge.

In its most obvious form, there seems to be the simple fact that human beings somehow feel better, their troubles eased, their burdens lighter, when someone else has sat and listened. The problem, though, with multiplicity is that what one has to tell is far too much, too horrifying for the ordinary, untrained listener. Listeners react in all too human ways: they minimize, they disbelieve, they laugh, they deny.

It needs to be said here that when I was first diagnosed, I told my family and three friends about my disorder. My parents' response was a carefully worded letter. My perceptions, they said, were "interesting." Tucked into the envelope, without comment, was a set of typed notes on my childhood medical history—information I had requested several years before. The same week, they wrote more angrily to my therapist that my general failure to live the life they had planned for me was the cause of whatever problems I might have—or might be pretending to have. The youngest of my three brothers, although he sometimes talked wistfully of entering therapy, was clearly frightened of what nasty family truths I might yet conjure up. My oldest brother, who had moved to Mexico and cut his ties with all of us, was silent. My middle brother wrote a letter so vicious and destructive that it served as a dramatic, if unintended, confirmation of his destructiveness during my early years.

I had had higher hopes for my friends. One, a woman I'd known since graduate school, responded by making sly but pointed jokes about me and my disorder to my face. Since I too make jokes when I am frightened, I knew what this meant—however much it hurt me. What I didn't expect was that she would in turn tell all the members of her family. Her older sister, with whom I had always gotten along rather well, let out a little gasp and took an involuntary step backward the next time she saw me.

Another friend was one of my health club buddies. Quite by accident we'd found out that we both came from violent backgrounds and occasionally we talked about how things were going and what we were talking about these days with our therapists and the ways in which the world seemed new to us after each small victory or discovery. When I told him my diagnosis, on a day I was feeling especially glum, he from that time forward began to compete with me about which of us was "sicker." It was an odd reaction, but I was glad to cede the title to him.

The most painful revelation was to my oldest, closest friend. We've known each other since second grade, and when she told me she was gay, or when she decided to move two thousand miles away, our friendship remained strong and deep. When I told her the charming man I married turned out to be a drunk, she helped me pick up the pieces. But when I told her I was a multiple, she reacted with a fury that wounded and astonished me. In time, she would calm down and we would talk—but warily. She read a book I recommended so that she could understand, but I will never forget her initial anger and her attack. Time has passed, and we still talk and still spend what time we can together. But now I am careful, in a way I never was before, about what I say about my life, my feelings, and my thoughts, because it is clear that my disorder distorts our equilibrium: what we need from, and what we offer to, one another no longer works out in the old, easy way.

Still, one sometimes aches to tell one's secret. There are times the weight of it as a secret becomes almost unendurable, and I think, Well, if I just blurt it out, then it will no longer be a secret. Life may be awful if everyone knows, but life is awful now, too. So let it be awful in some new and different way.

The urge to tell comes, too, from the urge to set up a wail that will scour the hearts of those around me. *Life is hard!* I want to shriek. My head aches, my mind roars with voices, I have no extra money, I'm exhausted, and I can barely think straight. I scream in the night, my body aches with remembered abuses, and therapy requires that I recall and then relive those old, horrifying traumas.

But I recoil at the thought of pity, which I do not want. All I *do* want, some days, is just a little breathing room, a little quiet, even a little boost or a break. If I were to have a leg in a cast and were making my way on crutches, I would be pleased if someone were to think to hold a door open for me or bring me a cup of coffee. There are days I would like the psychological equivalent: a break from students who want counseling for problems that are personal and not academic, a respite from the endless political machinations of the college, a chance to slide into a brief, restful trance after lunch instead of attending yet another meeting.

There are times, too, when I think telling would somehow make me just a little bit heroic. How often I listen to my colleagues being admired for the way they raise their children and teach and continue to do graduate work on the side. *No sweat!* I think to myself. I teach, I write, I go to conferences—and I have more internal kids than I can identify or count, and a major mental illness to boot. Of course, there is an irony here, too. One can only be heroic with MPD if one leads a life so successful that no one could possibly know. But if no one knows, one is heroic only to oneself and to one's therapist, and what good is that? And my therapist, it must be added, wishes always for a little less heroism and a lot more rest and common sense.

There are also times that I would like to tell because I would like to ask a lot of impertinent but genuine questions of people who are not multiples. How does it sound in your head? I would ask. What did you think about while you chose your clothes this morning? What sensations does your body have? Is it boring being just one person?

But I would also like to be able to tell because it would, if people knew and if they understood, put an end to my social lies and prevarications. I find myself repeatedly in awkward situations. I cannot, for instance, plan ahead with any amount of reliability. I can say that, yes, I would love to come for dinner or go away for a weekend. But, the truth is, that if I have been screaming night after night, I must stay home and rest. If I am coughing up long-buried traumas, I must also stay home and rest. If there is a dramatic revelation between two selves in the system, or a fusing of their memories and functions . . . I must stay home and rest. And so I often cancel long-made plans so I can slide into a prescribed, restorative trance. Otherwise, I run the risk of switching personalities without control—or of becoming ill because of the sheer willpower required to prevent the shifting from one mind-state to another. I also parry impromptu jaunts and last-minute invitations that threaten time my nonpublic selves have been promised and, indeed, require. I even discourage people from dropping in on me unexpectedly because my home has become the only place where I do not camouflage my disorder or seek to hide my selves.

I have become a master of the phony excuse. I say that I am reading, or prepping for a course. This is sometimes true and has earned me the reputation for having remarkable and sometimes selfish discipline. I say that I am not feeling well. This, too, is sometimes true, and I have deliberately allowed those around me to believe that my digestive problems are far worse than they are. And, when I cannot face the business of telling lies, when I am tired of the energy and fear that go into maintaining my facade, I simply let the phone ring and ring until it stops, establishing another popular myth among my friends: that I spend three-quarters of my free time out walking my dogs. How much easier it would be, I sometimes think, if I could simply tell the truth.

But all of these reasons, to tell or not to tell, are in some way self-centered. They have to do with *me,* with *my* life, with my own ease, comfort, and convenience. There still remains the question of the student at the opposite end of the table. And there still remains the larger question of whether telling, of making my diagnosis and my circumstances known, might in some way do some good.

I know that, for myself, whatever I had read and heard and thought, I did not truly understand what the war in Vietnam did to the men who fought there until I came to know and feel compassion for older students whose lives were forever changed by what they did and saw there. The same is true for alcoholism, autism, cancer, depression, suicide: what I have learned with my intellect is not remotely similar to what I have learned with my heart because I came to know people whose lives have been changed by these tragedies and troubles.

I have to wonder if my friend the psychology professor would change her lecture on MPD from a few remarks, a quick video, and an assurance that the disorder is fairly rare to . . . well, to something different if she knew she'd been lunching with a multiple for years. I wonder if the science professor, whose promotion committee I chaired two years ago, would rid his vocabulary of the word "loony" if he knew the author of the report that helped him up a step on the academic ladder was a multiple. And I wonder if my fellow members of the appeals board would have been somehow kinder to our student. Would they possibly have come even half a step closer to accepting the dark and hidden lives some of us are forced to lead? Or would they have seen me as a "psycho" too?

But, in the end, I will never know. I cannot do it: I cannot tell. I know that I require privacy, rest, and quiet. I know that I need to learn the world is not quite as violent or as cruel as it was when I was a child. I know I do not need or want to be a target, a victim, any longer. I have read that multiples who go public substantially decrease their own chances for full integration. And I know that I am already gambling, pushing myself to the limits of my strength, by undertaking a course of therapy that rocks the foundations of my own identity and demands ungodly grit and stamina—while trying at the same time to lead a somewhat demanding professional life.

And yet, when I think of what has been written so far about multiplicity, I sense a terrible gap. There are the chillingly cold-blooded studies of pathology, and the warmer, more kindly therapeutic texts (many of which are maddening, hilarious, or both to actual multiples). There are also accounts of actual cases written by professionals, which strike me as a combination of boasts and rip-offs. And then there is the writing already done by multiples: the autobiographies that focus on the horrors, and others that focus on the healing. And there are emotional outpourings, too, written by multiples for each other. Each serves its own purpose, but what's missing is the dailiness, the odd but telling textures of multiplicity.

There are few accounts of the struggle to feed, clothe, and provide for a host of secret selves. Little about the top-flight diplomatic skills required to get enough internal consensus in order to do something as simple as see a movie or do the laundry, never mind go to work and lecture to a class of fifty or apply for a promotion. I have not read about the heartbreak and relief of estrangement from family, or about the way friendships decay as alters shift and fuse, or about the delicious feeling of waking up rested after the first night of undisturbed sleep in three months, or about the ecstasy in the abrupt way the world seems utterly new after some internal revelation, or about the brief but precious moments of utter quiet. Or, of course, about the queer experience of listening to a group of colleagues and professionals say what they really think about someone with MPD.

So, in the end, I choose an old dodge, one laden with paradox and irony: One last time, deliberately now, I decide to adopt a new identity. The task of actually finding a new name, a pseudonym for my book, proves oddly difficult. My youngest selves are fascinated by the endless lists in a book for naming babies, and they seize on one wild possibility after another, switching merrily between names which are essentially feminine to ones that are more masculine. Each of their proposals—Erica? Micah? Claire? Piper? Alex?—gets shouted down by some other part.

As usual, I assume the role of arbiter. The Kids, I decree, can pick one name as long as it doesn't drive any other part in the system truly crazy.

In a little while, The Kids decide on Philip or Philippa. I've made the mistake of reading them the derivations, Philip is Greek for "lover of horses," and that's that. The Kids are absolutely, positively crazy about horses.

Interestingly, after a long pause, the adolescents in the system suggest using Phillips as a last name and then shyly offer up an old, old secret nickname of their own: JJ. I am a little surprised by this contribution, and wonder if they truly know what it means.

But, in time, it becomes clear that they do: the adolescents feared a life of madness, they secretly dreamed of writing, and, recently, they have become more active participants in daily life. Their offer of a favorite nickname strikes me as a brave gift.

I pause, feeling both pleased and bemused: pleased by the high level of internal cooperation, bemused by their actual choices. I ask The Teenagers for permission to formalize JJ into Jane. After some thought, they agree to compromise. Compromise is what keeps us functioning, and, besides, they are old enough to under-stand that it's not the name that matters: what matters is the decision to yield, deliberately but discreetly, to the urge to tell about what it's like to live as a multiple in a world of "ordinaries."

FACES IN THE MIRROR

 THE LIGHT IN TOWN was dingy, late October, and the old brick buildings seemed to hunker down beneath their ornate facades. Across the street, the bank's time and temperature sign counted the minutes toward the hour. I turned, stared through a steamy bakery window, and thought briefly of going in. There was almost time. I stared a moment longer, then walked slowly down the little side street, breathing hard and dragging out the minutes.

I was thirty, at the very start of therapy, and so far, for each of the last six weeks, I had come to my appointment, the last one in my psychologist's workday, and had sat in my chair, miserable, confused, and inarticulate. I had taken eight hours' worth of tests, and although we had cursorily discussed the results, each week he told me it was up to me to identify my issues and my goals. But I could not. I had ransacked my journals, made lists, and plain old sat staring out my study window late at night. With all I'd been through recently, it should have been quite easy. But I just didn't *know,* I thought, even though last week he'd told me that today would be the final deadline. If I didn't think of *some*thing, the implication seemed to be, this would be my last session.

Ever since junior high, I had been painfully conscious of the suspicion that something was profoundly wrong with me. I had no idea *what* was wrong, or even why I believed there was a problem. Mostly I just never seemed to be who I really was—although I had no idea who that was. It seemed to me that I was no one;

that when other people were around, I simply didn't exist—instead I assumed a role and then performed it, often badly. Perhaps it was true that I *was* the dumb kid in the family: the crybaby who never understood, and who was always ill, injured, or in tears.

As I grew older, I carefully studied the behavior of those around me, and did my best, on one hand, to force myself to be bright, cheerful, and outgoing, and on the other, to eradicate every suspect feeling, thought, and foible I detected in myself. It wasn't easy, because I couldn't think with any clarity in the presence of other people. And, when I was alone, it didn't matter quite so much.

When alone, I often steadied myself by spending long hours staring into my mirror. I was far from vain, actually believing myself to be quite ugly, but when I stared into my mirror, I somehow slipped out of myself. The faces that looked back at me were not really mine. They all seemed related to me but they were sometimes very young, sometimes very old, beautiful, wise, boyish, feminine, mischievous. . . . These faces were all very real to me, separate folks, it seemed to me, friends of a sort, and in the quiet of my bedroom I listened to them speak. My favorite, and the one I often sought, was beautiful, powerful, and wise. Was I crazy to believe she was there? Maybe. I was a little old for imaginary friends, but I could not live without her or the others, and I felt calmer, stronger, and safer after our visits in the glass.

Secretly, through my high school years, and later on in college, I promised myself that, once I had finally left home and had put some distance between my family and me, I would see a counselor. But, during my twenties, although I often thought about finding a psychologist, I never did. Each time I imagined a first meeting with a professional, and imagined being asked what I was doing there, all I could think of to say was, "I don't know what—but there's something wrong with me." The prospect was so ridiculous I never went.

But during the past four or five months, I had begun sliding into trouble. The entire year had been rather stressful. I had started a new teaching job, had written and published two journal articles, and had won an award for my teaching. But, at Thanksgiving, I had given my husband an ultimatum about his drinking, then had helped him get started in AA, an organization that unfortunately helped him to stop drinking but allowed him to turn into a wide-awake dry drunk instead. I got through the days by sheer force of will, but by April I was suffering terrible headaches and, when my vacation started, I spent twenty hours a day in bed staring at the wall, an activity I found somehow reassuring, as I could not think, function, or control my emotions. Sometimes I cried. At other times I was terrified. At still others, blindly furious. One afternoon, when I was up, I carried the gas can from the garage into the house with the full intention of burning the place down. Another afternoon, I pulled up every flower plant in my much-prized beds. In the kitchen, the knives seemed to call out to me to slit my wrists, and for long hours I would stand inside my closet weeping because none of the clothing there seemed to belong to me.

At midsummer, I dragged myself to a language conference. The paper I presented was highly praised and I tried to coax myself back to sanity on the regard that I enjoyed. But the truth was that I had made the alarming discovery that alcohol, a lot of alcohol, drunk alone in the privacy of my room, seemed to bring me a kind of peace and quiet I had not known for months. Then one afternoon, there were suddenly two of me: one Jane lay on the bed and watched the other Jane sitting at the desk and reading. One of us had the foresight to pause and write a note. It said: "Something is terribly wrong. See your doctor when you get home."

But all that was several months ago, and now that the fall semester had begun I seemed to be up and functioning. I was admittedly frightened, as if I had had some kind of close call, although I was not sure with what.

That afternoon, at the foot of the little side street, I stepped into the psychologist's outer office and checked in with his secretary. Then, as I was sitting in a corner chair and staring blankly into the pages of a magazine, it came to me that I could answer the looming question about my goals in one of two ways: I could ask, in a calm and intelligent way, for a more detailed discussion of my tests. Or I could simply break down and ask that old anguished question I had so often asked of the faces in my mirror: "What's *wrong* with me? Why is life so *hard?*"

Soon I was ushered into the inner office. I refused a cup of tea and sat in my usual chair, facing straight at the door and the little clock and flower print that hung next to it. He sat as he often did with his feet up on the edge of his desk and a pipe in one hand. The October light was fading quickly from the caverns between the dark brick buildings. A small light burned on his desk; another illuminated a far corner. I gradually sank into my chair.

The appointment began rather casually. We chatted about the weather and about school; about how my week had been and about how my husband was managing his new job. There was no mention of the dreaded goals or the deadline to come up with some.

And then, without my asking, he brought up the tests. There had been some indication on them, he told me, that I had perhaps been traumatized. I stiffened in my chair. He defined trauma in a general way as a time I may have been so threatened I feared for my life.

Good Lord, I thought, everybody's been through that. No big deal. Or had they? I put my feet up on the hassock in front of my chair. I had often been terrified as a child, and even later in my life. If everyone else had not been terrified as often as I, it was because everyone else was braver, smarter, or stronger and was therefore better able to control what went on around them. The problem with me was that I was just too sensitive and too stupid to get along.

He pulled his feet from his desk, reached for new tobacco and a match, and said, "I'd like to try a brief experiment. You might close your eyes if you feel comfortable."

I widened them and stared out the window.

He went on. "Imagine that off in the distance is a blackboard and that on it an age is written. Take your time," he said gently. "It will come into focus."

I recoiled in my chair, pulled my knees together, and folded my arms across my chest. "Nine," announced a voice, presumably my own.

"All right," he said. "Nine. Just sit and think for a little about being nine years old."

I didn't think. I didn't have the chance. Suddenly, weirdly, I *was* nine years old again. My heart was racing, my skin was clammy, my breathing was fast and shallow, and I wanted to throw up.

"Well," he said, in the quiet understatement that in later years I would come to joke about, "you're obviously experiencing something. Can you tell me about it?"

I twisted in my chair, jerked my legs off to the side, and clamped one knee over the other.

"We have to talk about my brother then," I said after a while.

"Tell me about him."

I fell silent. I could remember but I could not talk.

Hank, four years older than I and the second oldest of us four children, had been extremely violent. He wept. He raged. He smashed windows, lights, things others cared about, things he cared about, too. At times he threatened to kill himself; at other times he vowed to kill my mother, my father, my brothers, or me.

"Tell me one thing about him," said my therapist. "Anything at all."

"He sh . . . sh . . . shot . . . Kip," I finally stammered. My teeth had begun to chatter.

"And Kip was how old?" my therapist asked.

I stared at him, then saw myself hold up two fingers.

He frowned. "Two?" he said.

I shook my head.

I could see him struggling to decipher my meaning. "Two years older than you?"

I nodded, trembling, then managed to add: "And two . . . two . . . two years younger than Hank."

"That's right," said my therapist. "And Josh was a year or so older than Hank." He wheeled his chair a half-inch closer. "So how did Hank shoot Kip?"

"In the . . . the . . . the . . ." I couldn't say it. My hand went up to my mouth.

My therapist was watching fiercely. "He shot him in the mouth?"

I was gulping frantically for air. I shook my head. "Pellet gun," I managed to say. "Shot . . . shot off his fingertip."

My therapist winced. "Then what happened?"

I squinched my eyes shut. "We . . . we . . . we lied. Kip said it was a . . . an . . . accident. Told Mom he did it himself. But . . . but . . . but . . ."

"But you knew, didn't you? You knew Hank shot Kip? Did he shoot him on purpose?"

My eyes were wide with terror. My head went wildly up and down.

My therapist sat watching me for a while, a quiet, almost protective presence.

"Was there more?"

My limbs turned rigid with fear.

"Did he do more than that one bad thing?"

Hank had also forced Kip to hold an apple on the palm of his hand and had thrown a knife at it; Kip's arm took a direct hit. Another time he frayed the brake cables on Kip's new ten-speed; Kip cut his hands so badly in the fall he had required stitches. Once he had even managed to trick Josh, tying him to a tree out in the woods and leaving him there for an entire afternoon. Afterwards, Josh was punished for it: because he had blacked Hank's eye and had refused to say why. Hank had gloated for days.

I looked at my therapist, unable to speak, unable even to nod.

"All right," he said, "I can see there was more."

I forced myself to nod. Then a small voice added, "A lot."

"A lot more?"

I nodded again.

"So," my therapist murmured, "what did he do to you?"

I froze. My brain produced nothing but a kind of static, as if I had some kind of built-in scrambling device.

"Tell me the worst thing," he said gently.

I sat for a very long time. In my mind, the appointment was beginning to resemble a Cubist painting come to life. The facets, the voices, the details all seemed to have to do with the same thing, but I could not get them to fit together in any kind of usual way. I slumped, barely breathing in my chair. I stared at my old gray Saucony running shoes. I thought about buying new ones. I found that if I pushed my feet down hard on the edge of the hassock that I could tip it toward me and make the wheels rattle. My left hand discovered, on a nearby stand, a heavy glass ashtray, and I watched my hand twirl the thing as if at some great distance. I wondered if it were even really my hand, this odd, flesh-colored mechanism so intent on its endeavor. The rest of my body seemed so large and dead and unfamiliar that I was pretty certain I would never be able to get it on its feet and walk it out the door.

Occasionally I glanced up at my therapist. He was sitting forward in his chair. His hands were folded and he had no pipe. He looked infinitely quiet and infinitely patient. Suddenly I hated him. I had no idea why. Time passed, and I realized that he had somehow moved his chair so close to mine that our knees were almost touching, and all at once I was deeply grateful for the sense of shelter and protection.

Inside me weird and terrible things were happening. I felt as if I were swelling up, then as if I couldn't breathe. My mind either chattered wildly or seized up into a kind of paralytic silence. My head ached. Pain flashed in my chest. My face and neck went numb. I felt an old childhood fear that my heart would just forget how to beat, or my lungs forget how to breathe, and that I would die. Then a rebellious rage surged through me and I offered up a private challenge to my therapist: I could outwait him, make him lose his patience, force him to give up on me. In a way, I wanted him to give up on me, because I wanted to give up, too, and I began to wish my heart *would* stop so I could just die and get it over with.

At five o'clock, the phone rang on his desk. It was his secretary saying whatever she said when his appointments were up. "We'll be a few more minutes," he told her.

I looked at the clock and raised my eyebrows.

"I should have asked you this earlier," he said. "Is there anywhere you have to be tonight?"

I laughed sharply. All those nights came back to me when I had had to sit alone at the dinner table staring all the way until bedtime at the plate of congealing vegetables that I refused to eat for supper.

"You mean you're prepared to sit here all night?" I said. "Until I cough this up?"

He smiled and shrugged. "It's more that you might find it difficult to be around people this evening."

"I have nowhere to go," I said. My hand went back to spinning the glass ashtray.

At one point he reached over and took it from its stand and emptied it. I had quit smoking long ago but the leftover butts in the ashtray were interesting. Had I really been a smoker? Had that been me? He put the ashtray back.

"Are you trying to tell me to stop this?"

"It doesn't matter," he said.

"Good," I said and my hand spun the ashtray the other way.

———

And then the memory of this session shifts. I remember the low, tempting murmur of his voice. I remember that I both fought it and responded to it. I remember that I wanted to talk and did not want to talk. I remember that I had to talk but could not seem to do it. I seemed to have something to say but I didn't know what and the minute I tried to put it into words it all seemed to disappear.

In time, I heard a voice begin to speak. It could only say a word, a phrase, a half-sentence at a time. Inside I heard other voices. One twittered with horror. Another muttered that it was all an utter lie. I was furious that some secret was being divulged—and strangely terrified and indifferent, too.

The flat, quiet voice went on. It halted frequently. It had to stop and search for words. It had to wait for a clear channel among all the interference. It was a voice that wasn't mine, that seemed to put my chest to sleep, but it was also a voice that seemed to me to have been there maybe since forever and that, to my horror, had finally found someone to listen to it.

The voice said that it was summertime.

"Can you tell me your age?" the murmur prompted.

"Nine," the little voice said shyly.

"Can you tell me what you're wearing?"

"Jeans," said the little voice. "And my blue checked shirt. Also my blue barrette." The voice paused. "You know. My best one. And a ponytail."

The voice also said that she was barefoot, and that she was going into the laundry room to take some clothing from the dryer.

"Is anyone there with you?" the murmur wanted to know.

"My mom is at the grocery store," said the voice.

Then I am there, too, walking into the laundry room. My brother Hank comes in behind me. In his hand is a battered copy of *Gray's Anatomy*. I have recently reached puberty. My breasts are developing. My parents have supposedly talked to my brothers about what is happening to me, and on this day Hank, fiercely curious, has been reading about female anatomy. And what he wants now is experience firsthand.

He offers me fifty dollars to do what he has planned.

The money scares me. In our family it is traditional for grandparents, aunts, and uncles to give us money for holidays and birthdays. I am saving all my money to buy a horse, but Hank is saving all of his to buy a motorcycle. He even hoards stray coins he finds, so his willingness to part with such a sum spells danger.

I stand quietly, my hands clinging to one another at my waist. My bare foot plays across the cool linoleum like the foot of a runner seeking its mark before a race.

Fifty dollars, he says again.

I say no.

He offers me more.

I say no again.

He lets the heavy book fall to arm's length. *"Ja-a-a-ane,"* he whines. "It's not fair. You have to let me."

I say no again.

The encyclopedia hits the floor. He lunges.

And the rest is only a series of stills in my memory, like the remnants of some old, badly damaged film.

My foot slips. My arm is wrenched. My head hits the corner of the clothes dryer. Hank reaches up under my shirt and wrenches my bra out of place. He yanks at my jeans and gropes between my legs. He reaches to open his own pants. Then a car sweeps up the driveway. Its tires make a familiar whooshing sound. It is our mother, coming home.

That was all I remembered. And I couldn't tell if I had remembered it or had made it up. It seemed dangerously real and dangerously false all at once.

My psychologist remained sitting quietly forward in his chair. He asked how I had felt during the assault.

"Petrified," I said.

"I know this may sound a little odd," he said, cocking his head. "But can you tell me where you were during the attack? What I mean is—"

I cut him off. If he was willing to ask such an illogical question, I was willing to answer without explanation.

"In the middle of the room," I said. "I watched the whole thing from the middle of the room."

"You dissociated, then," he said. And he went on to explain that dissociation is an ancient function of self-defense, still found in the so-called lizard brain. That after an attempt at flight or fight, if there is no escape and no chance to win, the conscious mind simply abandons the body. It might "watch" from some other vantage point, but later whatever happens will be sealed off somewhere out of reach of ordinary memory.

"You saved yourself," he said.

I harrumpfed. It seemed to me I had done nothing except make up some dangerous, lying tale.

He told me that he thought I had paid a big price, that he was surprised at how normal my tests had been considering what had happened to me and at what age. He congratulated me on how well I had done with my life and against what odds. He told me that what I had just done had taken guts.

I shrugged grumpily and twisted my fingers in my bangs and stared out the window. The city was dark by now.

He told me that I might be reeling all week and that I should call him if things got too bad or too confusing.

I nodded, but knew perfectly well I wouldn't.

Still, I felt relieved because it seemed to me that perhaps I had found someone patient enough and tough enough to really help. I was still worried, though, about the six-session limit, and I worked up my nerve and asked if I could come back next week.

He said he thought that would be a good idea.

I remember getting up and walking with great effort toward

the door. He opened it for me and stood well back to give me room—a gesture I still remember well for its thoughtfulness. I stopped at the front desk to make a new appointment. We had gone over by nearly an hour.

And so we began to work, and what we talked about followed an agenda no doubt familiar to many who were abused as children. It was a terrific struggle for me to even begin to express what I thought and what I felt. It was a struggle, too, to trust my therapist. I made painfully slow progress in this department, and even the smallest of untoward events—an incorrect bill, an appointment canceled or started late—would set me back for months. Still, we gradually began to discuss my family and my upbringing: my parents who had longed for the magic daughter to bring joy and balm into their lives; the dynamics of their marriage; Hank's behavior; the role each of us children had played in the family drama; and what had become of us as adults. We talked about my friends, many of whom were really more like dependents, or, on rare occasions, about my husband. In time, and without much discussion, I filed for divorce. With effort, I came to see myself in new ways, and my role at the college changed. It took a while to get used to the very startling idea that I was bright, not the dumb kid I'd grown up believing myself to be, and I worked hard to rewrite the other destructive scripting I'd received in childhood. We also talked about depression, nightmares, anxiety, my perpetual exhaustion, and my health.

We never again went trolling in my subconscious for hidden traumas. Instead, it seemed that whenever I'd begun to make a certain amount of headway on some problem centered in the here and now, I'd run smack into another submerged memory. Then the details would come surging back, flooding me with flashbacks, body memory, nightmares, and attacks of anxiety and panic. Because of the sheer number of old traumas, and the radical changes I was experiencing, we were soon meeting two hours every week.

And yet, as much as all our work was clearly helping me become a more capable and confident adult, I still had that old, sick feeling that something was terribly wrong with me and that we had yet to get to it. I never mentioned this secret fear because our office time was crammed with profitable work that was making substantial improvements in my life and health. In retrospect, I can see there were several indicators that, had we read them differently at the time, would have told us sooner exactly where we were *really* headed.

One indicator was the fact that every once in a while my psychologist would discuss the end of therapy—and I would panic. I feared becoming dependent on him, I feared becoming one of those people whose therapist is the very pulse of life—but I feared abandonment, too. Often he would say that, if we were still meeting two hours a week in six months' time, it would tell us there was some problem with our process.

Another indicator was that I couldn't seem to stop coughing up traumas. Sexual abuse, it turned out, had been just the starting point. But each time some new memory came up, always in response to a more current issue under discussion, the same thing happened: I doubted the memory and myself. I was far more willing to believe that I was crazy, that I was a pathological liar, that I had a sick and twisted imagination than I was willing to believe that my own brother had tried to rape me on a summer morning in the laundry room. I was even willing to believe that I was making all this up in order to be kept on as a client. Were I entering therapy now, when some writers have begun to challenge the accuracy of childhood memories, I can only imagine that I would have latched onto their arguments with terrific, if dangerous, relief.

Over time, there was more than enough corroboration. Kip was sometimes willing to talk to me, not only about Hank, but about the the general atmosphere and certain other hazards of our upbringing. My mother, too, confirmed, or silently accepted, at least parts of my history. Granted, I have memories which neither of them can or will corroborate, but each of them, in turn, offered me parts of my own history I admit I do not recall.

For his part, my therapist developed a typical response to each new remembered trauma. "So *that* was it," he'd say. "I had the feeling we were running up against something neither of us knew about." And then he would reassure me and tell me he was pretty certain that we had "got it all," and I would laugh and sniffle and make brave jokes about just how much, anyway, could one child endure and still become a functional, even if somewhat miserable, adult? I would feel a surge of hope that the dark days of recall might soon be over, but soon that old mysterious undercurrent would again be dragging at my heels.

Another telling event was mere happenstance. As an avid reader, I have acquired a kind of foraging habit that I indulge in libraries. I simply wander in the stacks, preferably in some unfamiliar section, and I pull interesting books at random from the shelves to see if I might like to read them. Foraging has led to some delightful books I never would have known to search out. One day, I happened upon Chris Costner Sizemore's first memoir of her life as multiple, *I'm Eve.* I stood there idly in the stacks, flipped it open to a page in the middle, and began read. All at once the afternoon seemed to stop. Here on the page was a mind that worked just like mine. After a while, it occurred to me to glance around and see if anyone was looking. Then, selecting a few more books to act as camouflage, I headed home.

As it turned out, I was unable to read the book from start to finish. It was simply too much for me, and it seemed to activate more turmoil than I could endure. I had enough of my own traumas; reading about someone else's was simply unendurable. I did, however, continue to open the book at random and read a few pages here and there until I felt the first stirrings of too much anxiety or excitement. That week the book was something of a compulsion, a kind of secret habit.

I felt somehow enormously enlightened and relieved to read Sizemore's realization that the only path to health lay in accepting all of her parts and selves. I remember that I wept for hours, and that I finally abandoned my adolescent strategy to create myself by trying to eradicate whatever it was about myself that I didn't like.

At my next appointment, I mentioned the book to my psychologist and, just as I was beginning to tell him how very much of myself and my own mind I sensed in what I had read, he cut me off. "You are *not* a multiple," he said. "I will not allow you to believe things are worse than they really are."

I shut up, and, in a way, I was glad to do so. After all, who on earth would want to be a multiple? I didn't. I felt embarrassed to have spoken up, surprised and puzzled by his vehemence, but admittedly relieved.

A third major indicator, so easily seen in retrospect, is that again and again I refused to do any of my work under hypnosis. I also refused all medication—waiting a good four years to agree even to the occasional light dose of Xanax to help with the aftermath of nightmares. His reason for advocating both hypnosis and medication was that the process of recalling and synthesizing trauma seemed to be causing me too much pain and to be far too taxing. He argued that I didn't have to suffer nearly as much as I was because of my insistence on full, drug-free consciousness at all times. We discussed drugs and hypnosis often, and my one joke was that if there was a hard way to do anything I would probably find it. Instinctively I believed I had to proceed as I was, and, once I am convinced of something, I can be inordinately stubborn and inflexible.

It was the hypnosis, however, that held special terrors for me. He repeatedly explained and reassured. He went over method, purpose, effect, depth of trance, what he would do, what he would not do, what it would be like. I can't remember whether I ever told him my specific objection until far later, but it was simple and I was adamant. I was absolutely certain he had no idea how things worked "in there" in my mind, and I was therefore terrified to allow him any latitude to do or say things that might destroy what I believed was my mind's very fragile balance. I had gradually learned to trust him in other ways, but I absolutely would not allow him anywhere near the delicate gearing of my sanity.

And then came the signpost he did not miss. We had often talked about the rigid and absolute external control I wielded over my emotions. It took four or more years, but I had gradually learned to laugh, to cry, to grieve, and to hope. More than once, however, he told me that sooner or later, in order to "get well," I would also have to get angry. We talked about rage as the result of terror. We discussed the function of anger in human beings. We analyzed my childhood experiences of anger in others as life-threatening, and we decided that, in my family, anger was a kind of license for harming others. Despite all that, he insisted that anger was a foreign territory that I would have to enter, explore, and endure. He suggested, in an effort to be helpful, that I might try getting angry at him once in a while if I needed someone safe to practice on.

But I, in turn, insisted that I would *never* get angry at him.

"Tell me why, Jane," he said more than once.

Each time, I folded my arms across my chest, tucked my chin, and said, "You won't know me. I swear, I'm someone else when I get mad. You'll hate me."

One day he laughed.

I refused to look at him.

"I'm a *shrink,*" he said, half chuckling. "I deal with intense emotion all day long. I'm sure I can handle whatever you dish out."

I held onto myself even tighter. "You don't know what you're saying," I muttered.

"Try me," he said, holding his hands up and out as if to make himself vulnerable. "You won't know until you try."

"You don't know what you're saying," I muttered again.

"Jane," he said, "it'll be okay. I'll know what you're doing. I'll understand."

I shook my head; the subject was closed.

During the following months, there was a variety of changes in his practice. His fee scale changed, my access to him between appointments changed, the terms of our no-suicide contract changed. Then we went through a stretch when, because of the conferences, court appearances, and other conflicts in his schedule, we met at erratic times. Multiples crave stability and routine, and I found these changes frightening, chaotic, and infuriating. He told me he felt he was bending over backward to see me every week no matter what cropped up on his schedule; I told him that, if he didn't want me as a patient, he should just say so. At one point he tried to explain, as gently as he could, that I had to bear in mind that I was paying only a token fee; I was taking up a lot of time and bringing practically no money into the practice. "I have a family to support," he told me. I sat and scowled out the window and cursed myself for ever trying to trust this person or the therapeutic process. At another point during this siege, he took a deep breath, studied my face for a long time, then spoke what was probably the underlying truth: "I need some distance, Jane. I care too much about you."

I've read that multiples have a way of conjuring intense emotion in the people around them, and that therapists are more likely to get tangled up when treating multiples than when treating any other kind of client. Strangely, his admission that I truly mattered to him, although touching, was also maddening and scary.

I had spent a good deal of time over the years keeping straight in my own mind what my relationship to him was all about. A secretary of his once told me that she had never seen him get along with anyone so easily and so well as he did with me, and it was true that a fluid and natural affinity between us had deepened over the four years of our work together into a genuine regard. But every time I thought about the ties I had forged with him, it didn't take long to reach, what was for me, the bottom line: Working with a compatible, skilled, and understanding therapist was probably a chance in a lifetime. I had no desire to jeopardize the opportunity.

One night, after yet another session that my therapist wanted to spend discussing the "rules," I got mad: ripping, raging, ready-to-kill, I-don't-care-what-happens mad. I pulled out my typewriter, loaded it with paper as if I were loading a gun, and began to write him a letter.

Over the years, I'd written him scores of letters. Abuses I could not recount face to face I could pound out at the typewriter, and I was often more willing to break new ground in writing than in speech. Flashbacks, revelations, questions, nightmares: nearly all were written down and many were sent along by mail. He read them when he had the time, and from there we would begin to talk.

That night my fingers flew over the keyboard. I filled page after page. One thought ignited another; each remembered slight, each past misunderstanding triggered the recollection of another. He'd said it would be okay to get angry at him, I *was* angry at him, and I was determined to get every last scrap of all my pent-up rage onto the paper. I wrote in a kind of white, blinding blaze. The typewriter hummed and clattered, the dogs dove for cover in another room, and all the while I felt nauseated, terrified, furious, and somehow relieved.

I was so furious that I got up twice during the night to add postscripts, and the next morning, feeling numb and stupefied, I took the letter from my desk, and, as I had with so many other letters in the past, stuffed it into an envelope and mailed it on the way to school. He wanted me to get mad, I thought exhaustedly. I had finally gotten mad. I had no idea what I had written, and I found the experience rather frightening. Based on past experience, I assumed I would arrive at my next appointment feeling anxious and humiliated, but that he would be perfectly calm about it, glad to have read my letter, and that he would help me accept or understand myself a little better.

Wrong.

Forty-eight hours later I had a letter back from him—sent Federal Express. The envelope was addressed to "Ms. Jane Phillips," but the letter itself began: "To The Terrified Child Who Wrote to Me on Wednesday Night." My therapist explained that, while he knew I was scared out of my mind, it was unacceptable to attack or vilify him. I read the letter several times, feeling baffled and badly shaken. All I could conjure up was a vague recollection of a night at the typewriter. It was a good guess I'd spent that night writing him an angry letter, but I had absolutely no idea what I had said.

At my next appointment, he stalked into the room after me, shut the door with exaggerated control, waited until I was sitting down, then thrust my letter toward me. His face was dark, and he himself seemed furious.

"Did you write that?" he said.

I recoiled, then took the letter and unfolded it. But when I tried to read it, my eyes simply would not focus, and, before I knew it, something deep inside me was wrenching out of place.

"Did you write that?" he said again.

I thrust the letter back at him, leaned forward, and put my head between my knees. "I don't know," I mumbled. "I guess I must have." I thought for sure I would either vomit or black out. I could see my hands on the arms of the chair, my feet on the carpet, but I had no sense of touch and my vision seemed to be doing something very odd.

"I'm sorry," I heard him say.

I glanced up. He seemed troubled, still somewhat angry but shaken, too.

"Maybe I shouldn't have done that," he said after a moment. His voice softened, although he still looked grim. "But I had to know," he added.

I put my head back down and closed my eyes. It still seemed to me that I would pass out. I heard him open, then close, a desk drawer. A few minutes later, when I looked up again, the letter was out of sight.

What *I* learned from this episode initially was that anger was every bit as dangerous as I'd always assumed it to be. Clearly it had rocked a working relationship carefully built over the last four and a half years, and I doubted anything between us would ever be remotely the same. Later I would find out that what I had learned to call "anger" was closer to a kind of paranoiac homicidal rage. That was what I'd grown up with. Plain old garden-variety anger was something I would have to learn just as one learns any foreign skill.

What my therapist learned from this fiasco was that, in some way, I hadn't been exaggerating: his client *was* a different person when she was angry. The tone, the logic, and the language of the letter were completely outside his rather extensive experience with how I thought and wrote. Showing a multiple concrete evidence of another self is one way a therapist can bring the workings of the disorder out into the light of day. My violent reaction to the letter itself was a pretty clear confirmation of a tentative but as-yet-unspoken diagnosis.

We found ourselves in very foreign territory. While in some ways we seemed to know each other, in other ways we were strangers once again. The old familiar trust issue came up once more, but this time with a new wrinkle: now it was his turn to take a chance on trusting me or we'd never get much further.

More than half a year passed between the time he read my

letter and the day he finally told me his conclusion. Sometime that spring he attended a conference on dissociative disorders, and when he returned we discussed some of what he'd heard there. Since I had already known I was a dissociator, all that was really revealing to me was that he had come back with some new techniques to try and some new avenues to explore. Two of them I found almost entertaining.

The first had to do with my sense of safety in his office. In the past year, he had moved to a new office, which I had never particularly liked. His old office had been on the first floor in the back of a rambling commercial building. Granted the place was dark and somewhat run down, but it had a kind of honesty about it and a familiarity, too, since I had grown up near an old industrial city where some of the buildings had looked much the same. His new office, however, was on the fourth floor of an enormous old house that had been gentrified into offices. The acoustics were lousy, the walls were thin, and without a radio playing full blast, conversations in his waiting room could be overheard in his consulting room and vice versa. If you were at all quiet, you could hear doors opening and closing on the floor below and along the particular corridor where his office was. As a dissociator, my hair-trigger startle reflex got a thorough workout every time I saw him and, depending on what was going on in his outer office, there were things I refused to talk about at all until a time I felt it would be safer. By appearances, it was a pleasant office; for me, however, the move had been a nightmare. We had, of course, talked about all of this again and again, and his basic response had been to say he was sorry but that I would just have to get used to it as best I could.

After the conference, his attitude changed and he was at least willing to acknowledge that it was probably unreasonable to ask a client who'd been through what I had to sit with her back toward a door. What mattered, he saw now, was my perception of safety. We were never able, of course, to do anything about the acoustics, except turn up the radio in the waiting room, but we moved the chairs around, barricaded the door, and I stopped feeling apologetic and exposed every time I flinched at some noise somewhere in the building.

More importantly, he'd learned that since dissociators are going to dissociate wherever and whenever they please—no matter what the therapist's goals are—it was now suggested that dissociation become open and accepted during an appointment. Before this time, in my everyday life, when I lost track of myself, or slipped out of my body, or could not quite remember where I was or who I was talking to, I had somehow failed. It had been made clear to me that the goal was to give up dissociation, forgetfulness, and spaciness altogether.

In my view, though, it had begun to seem to me that there were two kinds of dissociation. One, I agreed, would have to go, and that was the dissociative state brought on by stress and fear. And I agreed that I probably dissociated as an adult not so much because my life was in grave danger but because it was a habit and because there were a lot of situations I didn't know how to handle.

But, for me, there was another kind of dissociation, when I would let go of the tight grip I had on the workings of my mind. I would generally lie down, stare fixedly at a wall or some simple object, and soon the barriers of my mind would dissolve. In these states, I was able to fully relax, and I often would slide into what I later learned was a self-induced hypnotic trance as a way to relax, plan my day, solve a problem, find out what I was really thinking or how I felt. It was in this state that, to me, I seemed my wisest, my most honest, and my most perceptive, and I had often thought that he and I would make more progress if we could talk to one another while I was "lying down"—my personal euphemism for these trances.

I have seldom been so grateful for an opportunity in my life as I was for the chance to openly dissociate. I remember piling some cushions on the floor near the wall, settling down into them, letting the barriers in my mind dissolve. He sat on the floor near me that afternoon and, while I felt, finally, enormously relieved, I could sense that he was startled and perhaps a little anxious. If there was anything I'd ever hoped for, it was the chance to talk with someone, to be with someone as I really was. I let my mind slip and slide, talking a little as I went. It was the most relaxing, effortless session we'd ever had—at least as far as I was concerned. All I remember with utter clarity was reaching out my hand toward him and saying, "So now you've seen the real me. Finally, Jane in her natural state."

After that day, the direction of our work changed. He suggested I draw a map of the various aspects of my mind and character, and that I write descriptive pieces about whatever aspects of myself I could identify. We would also continue the dissociative work during appointments as I chose. The new work was a relief to me. Every word I put on paper and every minute I spent sketching out my map seemed to ease some of the pressure in my head. It had taken five years, but finally, whatever the mystery was, it seemed we were getting to it.

That summer I spent a stretch at an arts foundation. It was a wild month. By day, I worked on a translation and tried my hand at writing short stories. By night, at my therapist's request, I sketched some episodes from my past which I had never before acknowledged.

There had been the time I unaccountably found myself in a car parked along an interstate. A nearby sign said I was 43 miles from Cleveland. I was alone, I was in my early twenties, and I had no idea what I was doing in Ohio. After some rummaging in the glove compartment, I found directions to a friend's house in Indiana. I made the wild guess that I was headed there, although I was hundreds of miles off any reasonable route from my home to hers. I drove to a telephone and called her. She was frantic when she heard my voice: I was two days late. Where had I been? I had no idea.

I remembered that, as a student at a large university, I supposedly had a double. All my apartment mates had seen her and, assuming it was me, had spoken to her, but my supposed double had no idea who *they* were. According to my roommates, she wore the exact same hiking boots, carried the exact same book bag, and owned the exact same watch as I did. "It's so *weird,*" they would say, and I would shrug and nod.

I remembered people in the French department at the same school commenting on what a terrific dancer I was at our annual end-of-the-year fling. Although I vaguely recalled setting out for those parties, whoever my compatriots had seen could not have been me: I never danced; I was too shy.

Then there was the grad school picnic at which, by all accounts, I climbed to the top of a tall, ancient pine. This story, I was certain, could not be true: I was afraid of heights. Once in a while, though, I still ran into someone who recalled this feat and reminded me of it with some awe.

It began to dawn on me that I had peculiar habits: Whenever I traveled to a new city, I always tucked a hotel matchbook in my pocket, so I could find my way back to where I was staying —and so I could remember the name of the city. It abruptly occurred to me that I faithfully filled out the emergency information card one finds in a new wallet in case *I* might need it as a memory prompt. Inside the back cover of each year's new pocket calendar, I wrote my own phone number because, although I could rattle off every phone number I'd ever had, I often had no idea which was current. At home, when I answered my phone, I jotted the name of the caller on a pad so that, part way into the conversation, I would not forget who was on the other end of the line.

In my free time, I also read Sizemore's second book, *A Mind*

of My Own, and Robert Mayer's *Through Divided Minds.* I found
both fascinating, enlightening, and hilarious. I lay on my bed at
two A.M., sometimes giggling and stuffing my pillow into my
mouth to avoid waking the arts fellows in the adjoining rooms.
Then I would read some more. I caught echoes of my own mind-
voices in these pages, saw some of my own mental posturings and
habits, and even once or twice experienced an odd sense of yearning toward the wild and startling loneliness of being just-one. But
then I would draw up short: I was not a multiple. I remembered
the harshness in my psychologist's voice some years back when
he'd told me not to be a martyr. I thought with care about the
differences between myself and the cases recounted in these books.
I had only one name. I was an utterly functional, mortgage-
paying, drug-free college professor. How could I feel so closely
tied, so intuitive about Multiple Personality Disorder and yet be
lacking so many symptoms? And why hadn't my therapist said
anything?

The more I thought about this last question, the more I wondered. For starters, I reasoned, how *could* he have said anything?
At what point had there been an opportunity for him to say, "Oh,
by the way, I'm pretty sure you're a multiple"? And besides, he
and I had often talked about the dangers and limitations of labels
and diagnosis. He knew that, while I was dedicated to and worked
hard at therapy, my real goals in life were to right the skewed
learnings of a violent childhood, to put the hobgoblins of the past
to rest as much as possible, and to live a little more quietly and
calmly. And I knew he was an utterly pragmatic fellow. What
difference would it make whether or not I knew that he thought
I was a multiple? All that would probably matter to him was that
the pace of work had suddenly become so rapid and so rewarding.

For the next few months, I accepted my own reasons for his
reticence on a new diagnosis. Privately, I found the idea of multiplicity both terrifying and appealing. Terrifying because evidence seemed to be mounting on a daily basis: journal entries I

didn't quite recall making, mysterious items on grocery lists, people on the street who knew me well whom I only vaguely recognized. But multiplicity was appealing, too. It seemed to *fit*. It explained a hundred inexplicable episodes from the past; it offered to order the chaos of my mind and to shed light on all my dark urges and my mysteries.

During these months I often paced the house at night, debating: I'm a multiple, I'm not a multiple. I feared just how dangerous a step it would be to ask: would he agree? would he be angry? I wondered just how much one should risk so that one's life made sense. Was the heavy diagnosis of multiplicity a fair trade for the end to all this anxiety and fear?

Unfortunately, during this time, we were once again at loggerheads over issues of management. For instance, although my appointments sometimes started late, he was strict about their always, without fail, ending on time. He had also changed his booking method and would only give me appointments four weeks at a time. This wouldn't have been a problem, except his calendar was always solid two weeks in advance, which meant that every other week I had to ask for new appointments. If I asked too soon, it seemed to annoy him. If I forgot, I was out a week's appointment.

The problems with the schedule upset me all the more because I had begun to realize that I actually couldn't recall my entire sessions. One week all I knew for certain was that I had lost the afternoon. I was frightened and called him that evening to check in. When I told him I seemed to be suffering from some kind of memory loss, he told me not to worry. "You've been through a lot," he said. "You're under too much stress."

"But I can't even remember *seeing* you," I said.

There was a pause. Then he said, "Try to think of it this way. I spent the session talking directly to your subconscious."

I said nothing.

"How did you feel when you got home?" he asked. "Better? Or worse?"

I thought. "Better," I admitted grudgingly.

"For now," he said, "let's leave it at that."

Losing an afternoon is a very hard thing to leave alone. The following week I was rigid with vigilance at my appointment. My head ached terribly, but I remembered every last word that was said. I was exhausted when I left, but forced myself to make a quick stop at the drugstore after the appointment.

While waiting for my turn, I glanced around. There were the usual pharmacy items as well as a rack of children's games and books.

A young piping voice announced: "I want a coloring book!"

I looked at the rest of the people in the store. There was not a single child in the place.

"I want a coloring book!"

This time, the voice was almost a wail. Once more I glanced around. No one else seemed to hear it.

"I'm *not* buying a coloring book," I hissed back at it.

I was watching my fellow customers. No one seemed to hear me, either.

"You didn't let me go today," accused my little internal voice.

"You've been seeing my therapist," I said, angry and astonished.

"He's *nice* to us," the voice grumped. "We go and talk about stuff. *You* won't even get us a coloring book."

"Fine," I snapped and stepped out of line. "Get a coloring book."

I was furious as I stood in front of the rack. To this day, I can't quite explain how this works, but book after book was taken from the rack, examined, then replaced. Then the debate began. Did they want the collection of fish and sea flowers? Or the book of castles, knights, and maidens?

"You can have *one,*" I said. "Make up your mind."

They couldn't. One little voice wanted "the fish book"; the other little voice thought the fish book was "stupid."

Later, when I was calmer, it would strike me that one book was for very young children. The pictures were large, simple, and easy to color. The other was finely detailed. It would also strike me that there was actually a whole chorus of young voices.

In the end, I snatched both books and stepped back toward the counter.

"But we don't have *crayons*," someone begged inside my head.

"Jesus Christ," I said.

I stalked back to the rack, grabbed a box of crayons, and heard an instant protest: "But we want colored *pencils*."

I grabbed a box of pencils too. At that point, I would have bought the whole damn store just to be able to get out of there.

When I finally got to the counter to pick up my prescription and to pay for my unexpected loot, Kevin, a pharmacist I'd known for years, took a second look at me.

"Are you okay?" he said.

"I'm fine," I said. I was frightened and I was angry.

"You look as if you're about to pass out."

"I think I'm getting the flu."

He nodded. "Well, it's sure going around," he said, and rang up my purchases. He handed me the bag. "Go home and get some rest," he said.

"I will," I said.

I didn't. Or rather, *we* didn't. That entire night vanished from my memory. My students' homework went unread, but in the morning, on the kitchen table, I found the two coloring books: one marked up by someone who couldn't quite color within the lines; the other more carefully worked on by someone who preferred colored pencils. I shuddered, swept the whole mess into a drawer, screwed up my courage, and went to the college to teach my classes.

The following week, I fortified myself for my appointment. I wore my wool blazer, a garment that is a kind of psychic armor when I have to go someplace or do something unpleasant or unnerving. Then I did something I'd never done before. I left the college early, went to a bar, and had a drink. By this time I drank very seldom, but I believed I needed alcohol's quieting and oddly clarifying effect on my mind. And I took along a list of questions. Question One read: "Am I a multiple?"

I only recall fragments of the session. I went in, sat down, pulled my blazer tight around me, and, skipping the whole routine of how I had been the last week or how I felt that day, I simply announced that we had things to talk about.

My therapist has a wide and sometimes amusing range of intonations of the word "mm-hmm." The one he used on this occasion was wary but cool.

But then I couldn't speak, and feeling both angry and embarrassed, I handed over my list. "I have some questions," I finally said.

He took the list. He held it in both hands and looked down at it. I swiveled in his chair, scowled out the window, and shot him occasional fearful but, I hoped, determined glances.

Late afternoon light was filtering through the blinds. In the distance, the river glittered, and the hillsides beyond the town were brilliant with fall foliage.

Neither one of us spoke.

Finally, he said, "Do you mind if I step out for a minute?"

I nodded. What choice did I have? But it seemed just like the old days. I was miserable, frightened, and despairing. He couldn't even stand my presence, I thought. No one would be able to help me. I felt so ill and so tormented, I thought I should just give up. I would never be well, would never be myself, and I had been a fool to try. I stood up and stared out the window. I memorized the view. I looked straight down at the street and wondered what would happen if I jumped. Five years and all that time and pain and grief and hope and money. And for what? For nothing. I seemed crazier than I'd been five years ago. There seemed to be no point in going on.

The door opened and he came back with some papers in his

hand. He looked—I don't know: sheepish, cocky, nervous. Certainly not at this very moment his quiet, reassuring self.

"I'd like to give you this," he said.

He handed me a photocopy of an article. I read the title.

He nodded at the materials in my hand. "Does that answer your first question?" he said quietly.

I stared at the article a long while. Then I rolled it into a tube and tapped it on my leg. I got up, stared again out the window. I let the article unroll. Reread the title. It hadn't changed. Finally I turned. His eyes seemed somehow too alert, yet infinitely sad. I looked straight at him.

"Yes," I said. "It does answer my question."

There was another pause.

I looked down and read the title again: "Understanding Multiple Personality Disorder."

"So," I said, and let out a long, painful breath. "I really am a multiple."

I knew he'd taken care to let me be the first to say the word aloud.

"Yes," he said, "you really are a multiple."

I looked around the office, then picked my way over to the chair where I usually sat. I stared into space a good long while, and he just sat, his old familiar self again, patient and quiet.

I told him about the voices at the drugstore and about the fact that I'd lost nearly every evening that week to some presences who were desperate to color in the books.

He nodded. "Those are The Kids," he told me.

"They've been coming to see you," I said.

"Yes," he said gently. "They have."

"For how long?" I wanted to know.

"A while," he told me.

"So that's how you knew," I said.

"That and other ways."

I fell silent. I felt defeated and betrayed.

"Well," I finally said, "I guess we have a lot of work to do."

"Yes," he said, "we do."

I paused. "We've already done a lot though, haven't we?" My voice was tight with hope and desperation.

"Yes," he said. "We have."

There was another long silence. My head was roaring, my chest and abdomen were rigid, the vision in one eye was all but gone.

"Promise me you'll stick it out?" I said. My eyes were wide with terror. I could feel the whites briefly drying from too much air and too little blinking.

"Yes," he said. "I'll stick it out. Will you?"

For a long while, all I did was nod and stare and study the view out the window as if I'd never before seen leaves turn gold and red in October.

"So I'm a multiple," I had said.

"Yes," he'd said. "You're a multiple."

So that was it—the thing that had tripped me up, the mysterious presence that had been lurking in the far, dark corners all these years. It meant there *had* been faces in my mirror back home in my old bedroom—faces and voices, too. *I'm a multiple,* I thought. The idea was startling and terrifying, yet somehow a comfort and a relief. And I found myself thinking, not so much about The Kids as about the older, wiser self I had consulted all those years ago. I wondered if she was still there, waiting somewhere, wondered if she would still be wise and strong and beautiful, wondered if she would help me now that I so desperately needed her again.

"Where do we start?" I asked after a while. My voice was small and shy.

"At the beginning?" he said, trying to get me to smile.

I felt a surge of panic. Where on earth *was* the beginning?

As if reading my thoughts, or glimpsing the struggles of the future, my therapist deftly added: "Of course, first we have to *find* the beginning."

I stared at him and wrung my hands.

"I'll help," he said. "I promise I will help."

THE MAGIC DAUGHTER

THE SPRING AFTER I was born, my mother and my
grandmother took us four children to the park. They
spread a blanket, unpacked a picnic basket, and prepared
to enjoy the afternoon. My brothers played with their various balls
and toys. I wriggled on the blanket.

Finally Josh asked to be taken to the swings. My mother
agreed. Soon Kip was begging to be taken, too. Hank, when asked,
refused to accompany them.

My mother hesitated. Would Nanna keep an eye on him?

Of course, she said.

Kip and Josh led my mother toward the swings.

When they came back, my grandmother had taken me onto
her lap. She was rocking me back and forth and singing me a
long lullaby. I was a rarity within the family—a baby girl—and
my grandmother's attention was riveted.

My mother took one look at us, then panicked. Where was
Hank?

My grandmother looked up. Right there somewhere, she
thought.

He wasn't.

Frantically my mother called for him. Soon other picnickers
joined the search, and within minutes the park police arrived and
headed straight for the shores of the park's lake.

But Hank wasn't anywhere near the water. He was found
crouching under the seesaws. When asked what he was doing

there, his answer was full of chill prediction: he had run away because he wasn't a girl and no one loved him.

My grandmother's focus on me that afternoon was not unusual: I was born into a family desperate for baby girls. My mother was an only child, but her father had a gang of brothers, her mother more brothers than sisters. My father had four brothers and a sister. His father had come from a family of brothers and sisters both, but his mother, who died when my father was five years old, had had mostly brothers. My parents' generation produced children not in the same numbers, but in the same ratios. I have more male than female cousins, three brothers but no sisters. Both sides of the family longed for baby girls; that longing was the first direct contribution to the disorder that lay ahead.

Girls were rare, and they were special. Girls were bright, strong, sweet, uncomplaining, and devoted. They did well in school, played instruments, worked hard, and did not give their parents trouble. They were pretty, quiet, and domestic. Life was better for all concerned when there was a daughter in the house.

My parents' hopes for me were even more specific. I would be bright and sweet, never sad or angry. I would help my mother, comfort my father, befriend my brothers. I would be so thoughtful, so intuitive, and so obedient that I would see what needed to be done and do it without having to be asked. When I grew up, I would go to college, then marry, raise children of my own, and later, as they aged, tend my parents' needs.

It is easy to see why my brother Hank so quickly came to hate this intruder, this magic daughter. Who would want to grow up with such a perfect creature for a sibling? Who could ever compete for attention or win parental favors against such odds?

Sometimes I hated the magic daughter, too. My parents' expectations were impossible to meet, and naturally I often strayed from them. Sometimes I was merely reprimanded, but at other times I was spanked, had my mouth washed out with soap, or, on

at least one occasion, was sent outside so that I could learn a lesson
from my brothers in "how to get along." In time, however, I
would find the perfect way to play the role of ideal daughter.

In private moments, my mother often hugged me close and held
me a long while. She would whisper how much she loved me,
how no one would ever know what I meant to her. "You're my
daughter," she would whisper, fiercely but with wonder and astonishment. "You're the best gift I ever had."

Being my mother's best gift had powerful implications: She
loved me more than she loved my brothers. She saw me as an ally
when she was angry with my father. She loved me in a way that
was more piercing and more encompassing than the way my father
loved me. As a child, these clandestine moments behind closed
doors made me feel special but uneasy. As an adult, when I look
back, I do not doubt my mother's love for me, and I can see that
I derived some strength from the doggedness of her belief in her
daughter. But these memories also rankle, because a child is not
a gift, for gift implies possession. My mother's love was not only
powerful and fierce; it was also blind and in some ways selfish.

One Christmas morning, I found a larger than usual pile of
gifts with my name on them under the tree. I had been begging
for a Barbie doll; my friends all had them and I wanted to be able
to play with them, exchanging clothes, handbags, and shoes.

"Open this first," my mother said, handing me a large boxy
package.

I shredded the paper. Inside was a large pale pink box. Maybe
a doll case?

Something made me hesitate. The color was wrong. Instinct
told me it was the wrong shape and size. My friends' Barbie cases
were brighter, sleeker.

"Go ahead," my mother said.

Gingerly, I opened the case.

Inside, swathed in tissue paper, lay a porcelain doll with a handpainted face. It had blue eyes and blond curling hair, and was dressed in a cascade of lace petticoats and a pair of delicate embroidered slippers. I wanted to burst into tears. I lifted the doll from the case and held it out to inspect it.

"Isn't it wonderful?" my mother said, with a small contented sigh. "I had to look everywhere for it. I wanted one exactly like it when I was just your age. But *my* parents," she added, "couldn't afford to buy me one."

"Oh, thank you," I said obediently, and laid it back inside its case. I wanted to hurl it across the room and stamp up the stairs toward my room.

"I never believed you wanted a Barbie," my mother said. "It's only because your friends already have them."

I sat blinking hard and saying thank you and wishing the next person would open a gift so the attention would turn from me.

Half the rest of the gifts in my extra-large pile that morning had to do with that stupid doll. There were costumes: a shepherdess dress, a colonial ball gown, and a ruffled nightgown. There was a whole catalog of other costumes with a little note that I could pick out three more dresses of my own choosing. One package contained a stand to hold the doll upright when I was not playing with it and another held a glass dome so dust would not collect in her hair and clothes when she was standing on my shelf. Clearly my mother had thought of everything, preparing the surprise she had wanted as a child. Sometimes I thought that I had only been born so that my childhood could make up for her own. I played with that doll off and on, always grimly and always because I knew I'd better, for the next year or so. Whenever I eased up on it, leaving it for longer and longer periods without touching it, my mother would say, "You haven't played with your doll recently. You have no idea what a lucky little girl you are."

It wasn't just the doll, either. There were clothes she had wanted as a girl, other toys, even special foods. To be fair, I often received things I wanted, but gifts, for me, were fraught with hazard: no matter what they were, I knew I would be required to like them. One small but potent contribution to multiplicity was that I had to form a personality who would reenact a happier version of my mother's childhood.

At other times, however, it seemed to me I was a scapegoat for the poverty in which my parents had grown up. By the time I was nine, my mother sometimes required that I do the family laundry: washing nearly all day one day, ironing the next. On summer days and on the weekends, I often woke to long lists of chores that might consume half the day or more. Early on, I was made to cook and clean up after some family meals—as my mother pointed out, just as she had done when she was my age because her own mother was so often ill. I worked daily in the garden, which I loathed, weeding and hoeing vegetables I despised because gardens had been crucial to the survival of my father's family. And at summer's end, long hot days went by in the kitchen, parboiling vegetables for the freezer and putting up preserves. I hated all of it—and still do—because it often seemed to me I had been born a girl so I could be a slave, or because my parents wanted someone to punish for their childhoods.

I also became a surrogate for my father's older sister, who died of a sudden virus around the time of my birth. My aunt was, from all I have heard, a warm, generous, self-sacrificing woman who did all she could for those around her. Legend has it that she was never angry, that in addition to the hard work of raising her younger brothers, she had hired herself out as a secretary in order to help support them. What's more, she was capable of countless thoughtful gestures, she did not complain about her life, and she did not mention, ever, the fact that she had forgone a good marriage in order to hold the family together. My father had relied heavily on his sister for many reasons, and because I was born at the time of my aunt's death, the need for these traits was somehow passed on to me. I, too, would be warm, generous, self-sacrificing, thoughtful, and, when necessary, silent and uncomplaining.

In my darker moments I wonder if my life would have been better or worse had I turned out to be a boy. How would the extended family have welcomed me? How would my mother and my father have accepted my gender? How would Hank have treated me? The irony of my position is that, because I was much wanted especially because of my gender, I was placed at enormous risk for what would later happen to me. What's more, studies in recent years suggest that my family position is the one in which a child is most likely to be abused: the youngest child who is the only girl in a family of boys.

Illnesses in a family of six are quickly passed from one child to another. My brothers and I seemed to get sick often, sharing nearly every sore throat, cold, and stomach virus that came along. To my parents then, my sudden nausea and vomiting must have seemed at first like the start of just another childhood illness. Fairly soon, though, it became evident that something was amiss. My temperature climbed, I vomited repeatedly, and I screamed when my mother touched my abdomen. The doctor was called in, and after a quick look, he called the hospital to arrange an immediate appendectomy.

Before we left for the hospital, Hank came into my room. He explained that I was being taken to the hospital to be put to death. That made sense to me. I knew that babies came from the hospital in the first place, so I easily believed they could be returned there for disposal. After all, it was clear that I was defective: I could not stop throwing up. Further, my parents, who I now understand were frightened, expressed their fear by being angry—specifically at the thing which caused their fear: me.

When the time came, I was bundled into my coat. My father carried me out to the car and, in his own clumsy way, tried to make me comfortable on the scratchy back seat of our station wagon. My mother was in the house, taking care of some last detail. My father turned and left me, perhaps to get my mother. I remember the little velvet cap that tied under my chin. I remember my mother's train case propped at my feet. It was dark red and had a zipper that I had loved to work back and forth because it made a wonderful crunching sound. I also remember that the basin for throwing up in kept slipping off my lap, that I was crying, but most of all that I was terrified because I had been left alone and because I was never coming home again.

I don't recall the trip to the hospital, but by the time we arrived there I was crying uncontrollably. My parents, who could not calm me down, seemed even angrier and, to me, more determined to be rid of me. I was handed over to a nurse who was cold, stern, and enormously displeased to have such a wild patient.

I was soon stripped and standing naked and shivering on a wide expanse of cold dark linoleum. Then I was forced to lie facedown on a bed to have my temperature taken. I fought so fiercely I had to be pinned down by several nurses so that a thermometer could be inserted in my rectum.

I screamed the entire time. I screamed again on the gurney when I realized my parents had completely vanished. I was still screaming on the way into surgery. Two nurses stood over me. One fretted that I might die if the ether mask was applied to my face while I was so hysterical; the other was sure I wouldn't.

When the surgeon came in and found a thrashing, screaming, and probably hyperventilating patient, he was furious. The mask was abruptly put over my face, and, years later, I would relive those moments of sheer terror: the anger, the voices going back and forth over me, my terrible helplessness, the world going suddenly black, and the terrifying sensation of being sucked up and up into darkness and nothingness.

Then, possibly because I was hysterical and the dose was therefore slightly inadequate, I briefly regained consciousness during the surgery. Again, years later, I would startle awake in the night, gasping for breath. Shadowy figures huddled over me. A light drove itself down into my brain. Then the black thing would swoop down again and cover my face—and I would be sucked up once more into the darkness and the void.

When I came out of surgery, I was a different kid. Literally a different kid. I was starving when I should have been nauseated from the anesthesia and the infection. I was wild with energy when I should have been drained and limp. I was overjoyed to see my parents. I would do anything, be anything, sever any part of my self, annihilate any sensation just so they would take me home again.

It would take more than thirty years for these memories to make sense. The medical history sent by my parents to my therapist included the interesting note that my parents had been so alarmed by my behavior that they had asked the surgeon about me. After all, they had seen Josh and Kip weather surgery in a far more usual way. Not to worry, the surgeon had said: young children often don't feel pain. In fact, I had dissociated, probably for the first time.

Six months after my appendectomy, my mother was spending a day shopping in the city. It was a Saturday and my father was keeping an eye on us. My brothers had spent most of the morning tormenting me, and finally my father had grown so tired of both their taunting and my crying that he ordered us outdoors to play. He fled to the garage and took the tires off the car to rotate them.

Within minutes, I was screaming again, this time for my mother. I had forgotten she was gone and was struggling to climb the three steps of our back porch. Blood was streaming from my mouth and cheek.

Hank had rigged up a "game" for me to play. With a piece of rope he tied a swing to its upper bar with some kind of slip knot. Then he handed the end of the rope to me. This was a new game, he told me. If I pulled the rope, the swing would come down for me and I should catch it. He waved for Josh and Kip to stand to one side, counted down from three with great and deliberate drama, then yelled for me to pull.

I pulled.

The swing shot down from the bar, caught me neatly under the jaw and sent me flying up through the air. My teeth were broken, my cheek torn, and the inside of my mouth badly lacerated. I can still hear the graveliness of broken teeth in my mouth.

I was stunned and breathless. The first thing I remember was Hank lying on the ground and laughing. Josh and Kip cried and whimpered. In time, I picked myself up and staggered toward the back door.

My father panicked. He yelled at me. He yelled at my brothers. The tires were off the car, and he couldn't think how to get me to the hospital. Finally, he called Helen next door. She stayed with my brothers, and my father drove me in her car to the hospital.

He was so angry and so flustered that the doctor banished him from the treatment room. I screamed for him to come back, and I fought so hard that the emergency staff had to pin me down. Swabs and needles swooped at my face, glinting in the light. When someone finally thought to cover my eyes, I dissociated up into the pale green cloth. Another self had been created.

As a multiple, I can be said to have been born more than once. The first time I was a standard-issue but much-wanted baby girl. Each trauma that followed was another birth. Terror cut the strings of my identity; over time, I blossomed into a full-blown multiple the same way a handful of escaped balloons rise and scatter in the air.

In terms of pathology, multiplicity has three main causes, and each must be present for the disorder to begin. The first, as I understand it, is that a predisposing brain chemistry must exist for the process identified as dissociation to take place.

The second cause of multiplicity, stated bluntly, is sheer terror, usually repeated, always occurring before certain developmental stages. Estimates range from the age of five to the ages of eight or nine as the upper limits for the onset of the disorder.

The third requirement for the onset of MPD is that the child's environment does not "compensate." That is, the child is not held, consoled, or debriefed in any way, and often the terror itself is not acknowledged by anyone whom the child believes to wield power.

My mother and father are good people. They are not, and were not, ill-intentioned or deliberately destructive. They are, however, emotionally immature. My psychologist, after hearing yet another tale from my childhood, has sometimes muttered that, as far as he can tell, neither of my parents ever made it past the emotional age of five. There were times, like all faithful, abused children, that I leapt to their defense, but the sad thing is that the evidence supports him. Neither parent has much sense of anyone else's needs or emotions, and usually neither has much awareness of their own emotions, never mind the impact their actions have on others. They also dealt with problems in a simple, childlike way: If I can't see it, it's not there. Often my mother snapped at me: "If it has to do with your brothers, I simply refuse to listen."

The way my parents handled both my appendectomy and my later "accident" with the swing are classic illustrations of the lack of so-called compensation. The pattern we would follow in all the years to come was quickly and firmly established. First, my parents' emotions were paramount: their fears, expressed as irritation and even anger, took precedence over my own panic. Second, they were generally unable to sense what I was experiencing nor were they able to comfort or console me. Third, they seldom knew what went on in the far corners, or behind the closed doors, of our house. Hank's promise to me that I was being taken to my death was the first of his major cruelties. The accident was next, and over the years, more violence would follow: molestations, guns fired in my presence, my pets threatened with death. My parents acknowledged few of these actions. They punished him for even fewer. Hank and I quickly learned a lesson that would prove dangerous: he could do pretty much what he wanted to me, as long as no one found out.

And so I became a multiple. The ensuing years saw a blossoming of selves, and, in retrospect, it is clear that my disorder was my salvation. My system had a simple start, but as I grew older, and as my world grew more complex, and as the number of physical and sexual encounters grew, my system grew more complicated. There were, of course, the original children who pleased my parents, and there were the parts who endured what there was to be endured. But there were more secret selves who plotted revenge, or who wept in their room or in outdoor hideaways. There were tough tomboys. There were the consultants who appeared in my bedroom mirror. And there were selves who whispered promises about the future.

Multiplicity abounds with ironies.

Irony: My parents were so desperate for a daughter, for their magic girl-child, that they set her up as a little doll or statue and then failed utterly to protect her.

Irony: Their fixation on me as a girl caused a remarkable level of sexual intensity, and set me up as a target of sexual abuse.

Irony: Because my mother was intent on using my childhood to rectify her own, she couldn't afford to acknowledge what was actually happening to me. She broke her silence on these matters only once when I was young: after I reached a certain age, she cautioned me against being alone with a certain relative. Ironically (again), when he did molest me, groping abstractedly underneath my skirt when I was a teenager, I said nothing. I thought it would hurt my mother if I told her. Besides, I had been warned. In a way, I felt I had gotten what I deserved.

Irony: I was able to be the good daughter my parents wished for and projected into existence only because I had developed a major mental illness. I was the magic daughter, all right, the child who met most needs and fulfilled many wishes—but I had to create an army of selves to pull it off. I was able to be the magic daughter only because I was a multiple.

I have felt everything from hilarity to despair over the origins of my disorder. At times, I believe I should stop whining and play the cards I've been dealt. I don't like whining, and can't stand the plaint and timbre of my own voice when I do it. Besides, multiplicity doesn't seem at all like a hand of cards one has been dealt. Nothing so small as *cards* contains the power of the forces that backed me into the deep corner of multiplicity.

I have tried to accept my disorder as an accident of birth—but that idea suggests that babies, or their souls at any rate, are somehow pre-formed, drifting in some ethereal holding pattern, waiting for assignment to a family. The substantial contributions made by both brain chemistry and family behavior cancel out this possibility.

At times, multiplicity seems like a cosmic conspiracy. One imagines the old gods tormenting some human for their own entertainment. I think too of the Book of Job; I feel as if I am being sorely tested and I sure wish I knew why. A religious friend of mine groans every time I bring this up and suggests I'd best reread Job: Hope for a better end, he tells me. Hope for a better end.

And then, of course, there is reincarnation. If my current life is just one in a consequential series, I must have really blown it last time around. What is it, I wonder, that I so failed to learn or to accomplish that multiplicity is now my lesson or my penance?

As someone who teaches literature courses, however, I cannot help but see the impossibility of the circumstances of MPD. The sheer complexity of family dynamics, and their unrelenting nature, is almost absurd. A character in a play or in a novel gets one smidgen of these external forces and then struggles mightily for two to three hours on the stage or for several hundred pages in a book. And those characters generally have what I suppose I never had completely: a choice. My psychologist and I go back and forth on the concept of choice in MPD. Did I or did I not "choose" multiplicity as a three-year-old? It seems to me that I did not, that it was my only option if I was to survive, and that, overwhelmed by circumstances, I fell into it as the only way to cope.

For many years, there was no escape from my role as the magic daughter. When I came home from school with straight A's on my report card, my mother would smile and say, "That's because you're my daughter." When I baked a particularly fine pie, sang a concert solo, won a ribbon in a horse show, or was recognized or rewarded in any way, I became "My Daughter." This nickname stuck with me for years; at times of success or of achievement, I was never Jane, never JJ, but always my mother's daughter. As I grew older, I sometimes wondered if anything I ever accomplished would be my own, but I wondered, too, what would happen if I blatantly failed to measure up.

Throughout my school years, though, I could never quite bring myself to act in any way that might displease my parents. I never rebelled or gave them trouble although, during my last years of high school, I did have a secret stash of shoes and even clothing in my gym locker which I wore at school, but would never have dreamed of wearing in front of my parents because they might have been upset.

My college years offered at least some respite from family pressures, and while away I took up habits and made a few friends who would have shocked my parents. But, when home for vacations, I behaved exactly as expected.

Then one May I arranged to come home from college on the bus. My mother would meet me at the bus station. At the last minute I was able to catch an express instead of one that stopped in every town along the way, and I arrived almost two hours ahead of schedule. There was no answer when I called my mother on the phone, so I settled down to wait. I made my way into the snack bar, ordered coffee, then debated about smoking a cigarette. My mother hated cigarettes. I looked at my watch, tried to guess when she would arrive, then, a little irritated, decided I was too tired from the semester to really care. Let her be angry, I thought. Let me strike a blow for freedom. And so I sat at the counter in full view of the wide glass front doors, drinking coffee and smoking cigarettes. Soon I pulled a book from my bag, began to read, and generally lost track of my surroundings and of the time. When I finally looked up, there was a little pile of butts in the ashtray and my mother was extremely late. I thought it odd she wasn't there yet, but just to stretch my legs, I packed up my things and walked out to the street.

There my mother sat, waiting in her car.

I waved and hurried over.

"How long have you been here?" I said. I told her I'd been inside for a good two hours.

"Well, I've been out *here*," she said, then added that she had come in to look for me, not once but twice. "But," she said, "I didn't see anyone who resembled my daughter."

I have often wondered whether she did know I was there, and had forced me to come out and look for her as a way of punishing me for my bad behavior, or whether she simply could not acknowledge this chain-smoking stranger as "my daughter."

After college and throughout my twenties, I struggled with my role as daughter. Usually I made a point of living at some distance from my parents, but I visited often, wrote letters, and kept in touch by phone. I cajoled my brothers into visiting and calling home, reminded them of birthdays and anniversaries, argued with them for hours about why our parents deserved more of their attention and understanding. I was still the magic daughter, smoothing over differences and listening for hours to everyone else's problems. Throughout these years, I had a few more clashes with my parents than I'd once had, mostly involving my choice to live several hundred miles from home. Although he was still in his fifties and strong and healthy, my father sometimes asked, "Who will take care of me when I'm old?"

My former husband used to remark sometimes that my parents were a little strange, and on the day I had sat for testing at the very start of therapy it became evident to me, perhaps for the first time, just how swift and dangerous were the currents within my family. I had listened with both care and horror to my answers to life script questions and to my responses to the thematic apperception tests, those shadowy enigmatic images into which one reads one's own history, but, despite all that I was revealing, I had still believed that I could pursue a course of therapy, keep my changes personal and private, and have no impact on my family or those around me. In the early years of our work, my psychologist and I discussed my family at length, but whenever possible I evaded confrontation, accusation, even the mildest of articulation that things had been something less than wonderful as I was growing up.

But, as the years passed, and it became evident I was a multiple, it also became clear that being the good daughter and being a multiple were so closely linked that I would have to make a choice. If I wanted to remain the daughter who pleased her parents, I would have to remain a multiple. If I wanted to give up multiplicity, I found out the hard way, I would also have to relinquish my role in the family.

What I feel for my mother and my father swings back and forth between rage and heartbreak. It infuriates me to have had such a childhood and it infuriates me that they have never directly acknowledged my disorder.

But then I remember good things, and, after years of self-examination and of trying to recognize and capitalize on my strengths and skills, I find there are aspects of my childhood for which I am truly grateful. I am grateful that my parents fostered reading and that I was taken almost without fail to the city library every week. I was encouraged to play the flute, I rode horses, I had the freedom of nearby woods and fields, I attended church and Sunday school. I had good manners and was therefore liked —and often looked out for—by adults outside the family. I sang in a choir, and was, with my parents' blessing, active in everything from orchestra to tennis and field hockey in high school. All of these activities, whether social or solitary, figured heavily in helping me build character, in releasing pent-up pressures, and in learning about the promises and possibilities of the outer world, and I am often grateful to my parents for these opportunities.

Rage and gratitude, however, make for an uneasy mix, and my parents, while more than open to my gratitude, will hear nothing of my rage or about the shambles wreaked by my disorder. And so I segue into heartbreak: perhaps my parents have no way to acknowledge my multiplicity. I don't expect my dogs to read Latin or do calculus, and expecting any kind of a healthy emotional response from my parents seems sadly in the same category.

Much bad press has been given to adult children who have cut ties with their parents after starting therapy to deal with issues of childhood abuse. All I can say is that I had to make a choice, and I have made it as gently as I know how. My parents reacted with such remarkable hostility when they heard I had begun to see a psychologist that, had I not been in such a state of crisis, I might have realized what their reaction boded. "You're asking for trouble," my mother told me once, and for a long time, my parents' attacks did not let up. One week they would insist that I change therapists to someone of their choosing because they felt my psychologist had cut them out of the process, but then, when asked yet again for their version of my history, they reacted first with fury, then with silence. For a while, they seemed to be positioning themselves to file a suit against my therapist. Their anger and manipulation served repeatedly as evidence of family problems that I was, at that point, still eager to deny.

In the end, I made what was, I thought, a final break: my parents were not to contact me any longer. In cases of emergency, they were to call my therapist, who would relay whatever messages he deemed necessary. They responded with a flurry of outraged letters, some addressed to him, some addressed to me. I read none of them. My therapist relayed news and information. The letters remain in my file in his office; someday I will collect them.

Often I felt guilty about this arrangement. Later I was surprised to find that some inpatient treatment programs and well-known clinicians also severely monitor and limit a multiple's contact with what is known as the "family of origin." I also was surprised, and yet comforted, to read that my family's behavior fit a common pattern: they veered back and forth between apparently genuine concern and vicious attack.

In time, the situation gradually eased. I got to the point where I could read the mail from them myself and pretty much sort out what I needed to know—the health of relatives and so forth—from the insinuations about my life and the endless manipulations and attacks. I still find letters from my parents wearing, and wait to read them until I am feeling sharp and clear-headed, but I am able to read what they have to say and, again when I am feeling strong and well, I am able to write back.

I have also, through these years of decreased ties, forbidden them to come and see me, although every once in a while I make the long drive and visit them at their home. Afterwards, I check into a good hotel, have a good drink, a good meal, and a long hot bath—and head home early the next morning.

The first of these visits terrified me for weeks in advance. By the time I coasted my car to a halt in front of their house, my mouth was dry and my feet were numb. I hesitated before going in. Was I supposed to knock? Ring the doorbell? Did I use the front door as proper guests did? Or the back door as did family and friends?

I compromised, standing at the front door calling through the screen door.

My mother appeared first. She stood looking at me for a moment, angry but close to tears. My father brushed past her and gave me a hug.

I thrust the little gift I'd brought at my father. He smiled and thanked me. My mother frowned.

"Let's go into the living room," she said.

As a family we had always sat in the den together, never in the living room. My father and I followed my mother.

I sat in the chair nearest the door, then glanced around. All my pictures had disappeared from the mantel. I took a quick sharp breath. Photos of my brothers' children had taken their places. I tried to pretend it didn't bother me. My mother was watching me closely. Did she know how much I was hurt by the missing photographs? Had she brought me in here on purpose?

"So, ah, how are you?" my father asked.

My mother snorted.

"Long drive," I said.

My father asked about the car I owned now. For a good ten minutes, we discussed gas mileage and tire wear.

I wanted to burst into tears. I wanted to hear them say they loved me. I was desperate to hear them say they were sorry about my illness. I wished they would ask if there was something they could do.

I cleared my throat. "So how are things here?" I managed to ask.

My parents looked at one another.

"You know Helen died finally," my father said. Helen was the next-door neighbor, a widow who'd been very kind to me while I was growing up.

"No, I guess I didn't," I said.

"How would she know that?" my mother said.

Gamely, my father labored on. He told me how quickly Helen's house had sold. He told me what had been paid for it. He told me how much their own house was now estimated to be worth.

My mother relaxed. She chimed in with the current rate on school taxes.

They argued briefly over the exact percentage, then launched into a discussion about how incompetent the school board was and what all the new outsiders were doing to the area.

I said nothing. I sat, dumbfounded, blinking back tears, feeling as if my heart would break. I wanted to say I hadn't seen them in two years. I wanted to hear them talk about other things—me, for instance; themselves. I would even have gladly heard the news of Josh and Hank and Kip. I wished I had the strength to say I loved them.

I tried not to look too often at my watch. "Ninety minutes," my therapist had said again and again. "You're to stay no more than ninety minutes."

I stayed fifteen minutes beyond that. My parents had moved on to the controversy over the new sewer lines.

Finally I stood up and made my way to the door. My father gave me a long hug, and whispered that he missed me. My mother hugged me, too. "Come again," she said pointedly.

"I will," I said.

"Take care of yourself," my father said, sounding as if he feared he would never see me again.

"You too," I said.

"Oh, we will," said my mother.

I cried myself to sleep that night, and the next day I cried for eight straight hours on the interstate. I can see now that tire wear and taxes were the only topics they safely could discuss. I had, after all, behaved in ways that were outrageous and that utterly violated every last rule that had been laid down for the magic daughter. It was the first time we were seeing each other face to face, and my parents had to confront a stranger. For me, however, the disappearance of my pictures and the discussion of real estate carried a powerful message: they wouldn't, or couldn't, tell me they loved me. I had disrupted the family and I would pay the penalty.

There have now been several of these annual visits, and they have gradually shifted over time. I have grown stronger and have acquired so-called psychological size. There is less anger in the air, but I still feel a terrible sense of loss whenever I see them; the grief, however, no longer is for me, but rather for them. What might their lives have been like if they had ever learned to face their own fears and problems? What would they have been like if they had ever had the chance to grow up? When I see them, I struggle always for a fair balance: I cannot allow myself to create new selves nor allow myself to say anything I do not feel or believe. On the other hand, I do not want to hurt them. I find that I speak in a weirdly truncated manner, sounding like a person speaking a new language or reading from a clumsily censored script. I tell them about the good parts of my life, but, in respect for honesty, I try to mention briefly, and as tactfully as possible, the bad parts too.

I find these encounters exhausting, but I am glad they are possible now. The limitations placed on my parents' right to contact me have been the equivalent of a cast on a broken limb. My psyche, my central self, needed protection from the blows and pressures long enough for me to gain at least enough integrity and strength so that I could end my pathological response to their demands. I have gradually grown stronger, and the rules between us have slipped just a little, but I will never be able to return to my old position in the family: I will never have the strength.

The last time I saw them, it struck me how exhausting it must be for them to see me, too—even for half a day. They smile and try their best to be congenial, save up things to tell and show me, and probably choke back all kinds of things they'd like to say. But the truly hard part, I believe, is having to come face to face with what I have become.

For in a way, in my long absences, I have once again become the magic daughter. They have accepted my physical absence from their lives and they have accepted the lack of communication beyond newsy correspondence. What they have done, I think, is re-create me in my absence, imagining and reimagining me, using what truths from my life they can (she's a professor, she speaks French, she just won a grant) and simply eradicating the rest. My actual presence in their home must be horrifyingly disconcerting: as if an imaginary friend assumed a corporeal, and highly contradictory, presence one afternoon a year.

The last time I saw them, I held them a long time when I said good-bye. I cried all the way down the street from the house where I grew up: cried because I would never have the parents that I needed; cried because they were growing old and would probably die without ever really understanding; cried because they seemed to have relinquished me, and, in fact, seemed to find me and some of what I had to say not especially interesting.

It came to me that I am not magic after all, and I grieved this loss of special powers, grieving also for my younger selves at ages twelve and ten and five and three—especially at three, when I let go of my identity, and when what lay ahead were a few joys but much loneliness, more expectations, hurts, and terrors, and certainly more traumas and more illnesses.

WHAT HURTS

 WHEN I WAS SIX, and in the first grade, I was seriously ill again. My digestive tract was severely inflamed, and I was in bed for weeks. I was so ill and so weak that, for diversion, an uncle gave me two marmalade-colored kittens who clambered for hours across the mountain ranges of my bed quilt. Our family doctor came to the house every day, sometimes making visits morning and evening. I can remember lying quietly in my bed, staring myself up into the patterns on my tile ceiling and hearing Dr. Wagner's old black Cadillac swoosh to a stop in front of the house. Day after day, he came down the hallway with a certain measured pace, paused in my doorway, and asked how I was feeling. Day after day, although I was too ill to eat and too weak to walk or sit up, I did the exact same thing: I gave a little smile, plucked at my quilt, and did not speak.

I left it to my mother to tell the doctor how I was; I had vacated my body entirely, surrendering it to my mother's care. Throughout that long siege, and throughout my childhood, I seldom told her I was sick. Often, she would look at me with a sudden watchfulness, then touch my forehead and ask me questions. If it seemed to her I was ill, and often I was, she was in complete charge: making doctor's appointments, doling out medications, applying compresses and hot packs, and telling me when to sleep and when I might get out of bed for a while. If my mother believed I was sick, then I was. And if I was sick, she took care of me. I had as little to do with the whole thing as possible, drifting for hours and days, and sometimes weeks, in and out of hazy trances when I was confined to bed.

Even at the age of eighteen, when I was teaching riding at a summer camp five hundred miles from home, I relied solely on those around me for information about my health. At the beginning of July, I stopped in at the infirmary because I thought I might have a sore throat. The nurse asked me a few questions, and, since I wasn't especially happy at the camp, she told me that as far as she was concerned I wasn't ill; I was homesick.

Well, I thought, maybe she was right. There certainly was something about the rah-rah atmosphere of the place that I disliked. Her diagnosis embarrassed me, and I was a little angry that she hadn't even bothered to check my temperature or look at my throat. But, as was my habit, I simply took her word for it; if she said I wasn't sick, I wasn't sick.

I went back to work, standing all day out under the hot sun teaching my classes. Two nights later, some other counselors and I went into town to see a movie. A few minutes after the opening credits, I apparently blacked out. What I remember next is standing outside the theater with a policeman on one side of me and my friends on the other. The policeman was extracting from my friends the promise that they would take me straight to the hospital.

They did. And what I had wasn't homesickness; it was pneumonia. My temperature was 105.

Over the years, I had a ridiculous number of similar episodes. Suddenly I would be so desperately ill that I would find myself in an emergency room. I thought little of these sudden and severe illnesses, and simply believed what I had been told as a child: that I was somewhat frail and that I tended to become very ill very quickly.

Then I began therapy. At my very first meeting with my

psychologist, I described recurring and relentless headaches that had been troubling me for a while. He asked me a few questions, which I answered vaguely, and then, telling me that not everything was psychological, he sent me to a TMJ specialist.

As it turned out, because I clenched my teeth almost constantly, the tissues of my face and mouth were severely inflamed. During the specialist's exam, he palpated various ligaments and muscles and asked me to rate the pain: mild, moderate, severe. Gingerly at first, then more firmly, he poked and pinched and prodded. My answer, each time he asked, was the same: "It doesn't really hurt." Finally he stopped and told me that I had either severely damaged the nerves in my face or that I had an extremely high pain threshold. Did I know? I didn't.

He asked some astute questions. Could I tell when I had been hurt? Say, when I cut a finger? When I went to a doctor with an illness, was the doctor likely to say, "That's the worst sore throat I've seen in a long while"?

"Doctors always say that," I told him. I thought back over my history. "I've never heard one say anything else."

The specialist examining my face suggested I try a small experiment: the next time I had so much as a twinge, I should see a doctor and find out if there was a problem. Then I would have some way to gauge the level of my pain threshold. He added that I might want to discuss this problem with my psychologist. "I think something's really wrong here," he told me. "I certainly hope it's not the nerve structure in your face."

It wasn't.

A few months after my TMJ appointment, I had a mild pain in one ear. Not even a pain, really—just an awareness of mild discomfort. I felt idiotic, but I made an appointment with my physician. He looked in my ear. "Yep," he said. "That's quite a good infection." He looked in the other ear, which didn't even hurt. "Yep," he said. "That one's infected, too." I walked out of there that day totally stunned, looking again and again at the prescription for antibiotics as if it could somehow explain to me how something I could barely feel could actually be an infection.

Long before I knew I was a multiple, I knew I was a dissociator, and one of the first revelations I had about dissociation had to do with my health: It wasn't true that I got sick suddenly. What was true was that I didn't *know* when I was sick because I separated myself from all physical sensation. As a six-year-old, when I lay in my bed and let my mother speak for me, it's possible that I had nothing to say. It's possible that I felt nothing at all. When the camp nurse told me I wasn't sick, I believed her: I had little evidence to the contrary until I blacked out from the fever.

For a long time I marvelled over this discovery, and I began to deal with all health problems in a simple way: if I was aware of any untoward sensation, I went to see a doctor, and each time it turned out that I was ill. It was an odd system, and I wasn't terribly articulate in reporting my symptoms, but overall I managed to get care before I was falling down from fevers. I passed off my high pain threshold as just another quirk.

But, as therapy progressed and it occasionally occurred to me that I might actually *have* a body, my pain threshold began to rise and fall, setting and resetting itself at levels impossible for me to identify. In time, I had a new problem: I could feel pain, but I couldn't sort it out and thus decide whether I required medical attention. I thought I hurt, but did I really? And was I sick? Or was I now overly sensitive?

During this time, I was getting ready to leave town for a month. I felt ill; my ears and throat ached. A worried friend, pointing out that I had a four-hour flight ahead of me, urged me to see my doctor. I did, and after a quick exam, he muttered that he was "unimpressed" by my symptoms. He seemed baffled and perhaps annoyed, and even wondered aloud what had *really* brought me in to see him. I left there furious and humiliated, and

I vowed that never again would I see a doctor unless I was violently ill or blatantly injured. I felt betrayed by physical sensation and by my therapist and my friends, all of whom had been encouraging me to take better care of my health.

My dealings with the medical profession grew quite haphazard. Once or twice more I made appointments when I thought I was ill but my doctor, growing ever more frustrated, could find nothing wrong. Each time I vowed I would never humiliate myself in such a way again.

Then one night I woke up from a sound sleep and began vomiting. I vomited repeatedly, and as the night wore on, I wasn't able to walk back to my bed. But I didn't call for help. I was living alone, it was well after midnight, and I didn't want to get any of my friends out of bed. I knew I was sick, but figured I wasn't *that* sick. My brother Kip and I have sometimes joked that we would probably apologize like mad even if we were bleeding from an artery; we grew up knowing that however carefully we were tended our illnesses were an imposition. So I waited for a reasonable hour, then called a friend for a ride and made an appointment with my doctor.

My appointment was scheduled for the early afternoon, and as soon as the doctor saw me, he began to lecture me on the dangers of having waited so long to contact him. After a quick exam, he was inclined to have me hospitalized for observation. The repeated vomiting, a high white blood cell count, and pain centered in my abdomen were cause for concern. The only catch was that the first time he palpated my abdomen I nearly screamed from the pain. But the second time I had no response. And none the third time or the fourth. Baffled, the doctor put me on a pre-surgical diet and sent me to stay with friends as I wasn't well enough to be alone. I was to check in at least once a day until my symptoms improved or worsened. He was worried, he told me, but, on second thought, my pain lacked the consistency that would warrant a hospital admission.

It took a week, but I gradually improved without surgery. Probably just a nasty virus, my doctor told me; still, he offered dire warnings about being so cavalier about such symptoms in the future.

But when my psychologist heard this story, he was somewhat shaken. Few dissociators would *allow* pain to register the second, third, or fourth time. For safety's sake, he insisted, I needed a doctor who understood and could treat a patient with a dissociative disorder. At the very least, he felt, he should be allowed to call my current doctor and explain to him that dissociators can't be counted on to respond to or report pain in any normal way. They require, he insisted, close scrutiny and a thorough, conservative approach.

After some discussion, we decided that I would change doctors altogether. My therapist recommended a physician he often worked with. "Tim doesn't fully understand dissociation," my therapist told me. "But he'll at least listen to me and he'll do his best." I gave permission for my therapist to call and briefly discuss my case, and in a few months I headed off to my first appointment.

It was far from perfect. Tim was clearly an excellent physician, and in some ways I felt sorry for him. He approached me with some trepidation, and in time I would realize he was less focused on the problems caused by dissociation and more on the fact that I had been molested as a child. At times, his wariness made me even more nervous than I might have been, but Tim had many traits any dissociator needed in a doctor.

For starters, he was personable and focused on his patients as human beings. Nearly all of our appointments began with his walking in, sitting down, and simply talking for a few minutes. For me, this approach was critical. When a doctor walks into an examining room, remains standing, and focuses instantly on the problem, I panic and my mind goes blank. Several minutes of chat about teaching or the news or the coming weekend reinforces in my own scattered mind that I am an adult and that my doctor is a human being—not another angry surgeon.

He was also willing to listen, even to my recounting of symptoms that did not necessarily make sense. He moved slowly and quietly, explaining every move before he made it, warning of possible discomfort and cold stethoscopes, and apologizing when things somehow went wrong. On more than one occasion he scouted through the whole facility to find me a gown of substantial cloth rather than the flimsy disposable paper ones stocked in every examining room in the practice. He quickly learned that I was a compliant patient if I understood what I was being asked to do and why I was being asked to do it. He gave me things to read, realizing I was often too tense in his office to remember much, and, like my therapist, he often recommended that I read further on my own, depending on the problem.

Still, as much as I knew Tim was concerned about my well-being, I often left his office feeling angry and frustrated. Why *couldn't* I answer his questions when he asked them? Why *did* my mind go blank in his office? Why *hadn't* my psychologist been able to explain dissociation in a way my doctor could actually understand?

I was Tim's patient for several years before my multiplicity was diagnosed. It didn't take long, because of the stress of learning the diagnosis, for me to get sick again. And it didn't take too much longer after that for my therapist and me to realize that dissociation, and the inability to feel and report pain, was almost a simple problem compared to the messy tangle of multiplicity.

One model of dissociation suggests that a multiple can excise four cross-sections of experience from the working memory: physical sensation, behavior, knowledge, and emotion. All four aspects can be excised at once, effectively sealing off an entire memory for many years, but the four will not necessarily be stored together nor will they necessarily return in any way that immediately makes sense. Dissociative barriers cannot be breached at will, nor is it possible to predict when barriers might decay or fail.

Three or four years ago, I hurt my shoulder. At the clinic, when asked, I assured the attending physician that I had never before injured my neck or shoulders. Good, he said; that makes a difference in how we treat this. I was questioned some more, examined, and sent home with a sling and directions for self-care. Two days later, however, it suddenly dawned on me that I had, in fact, once sprained the exact same shoulder. I had been in high school at the time and the sprain had been severe enough to warrant a good six weeks in a sling. I had missed months of tennis and had been quite depressed because the injury had rendered my newly acquired driver's license useless. But, when asked as an adult, I had no memory of the old injury because the information had been consigned to a separate self.

Because different selves recall different chapters of my history, I do not have immediate access to medical information. The real answer to a doctor's question can take days to surface from some far-flung corner of my system. Worse, because I shift reflexively from part to part, I can't sequence the fragments of my history I actually do recall. Did the rash start before or after the fever? Hard to say if one self has kept track of the rash and another of the fever. Is the pain worse in the morning or the evening? Is it severe enough to disrupt sleep? Unfortunately, my parts track symptoms the same way incompatible and surly members of a committee might carry out their work: in secret and with an air of martyrdom. I never get their clear, unified report.

An especially spooky problem occurs when dissociative barriers decay and long-buried symptoms or sensations come rushing back. Flashbacks are intrusions of recollection so violent and so vivid that the past nearly obliterates the present. My body pulls this same trick. My chest, my abdomen, a leg, a hand suddenly register physical sensations that are utterly real, utterly terrifying, and utterly breathtaking. Often I must decide whether the pain in my chest or leg or abdomen is happening now—or is it a phantom from the past? Do I see my doctor? Or talk to my psychologist? Two years ago, my shoulder injury flared up again, and Tim asked if I had pain anywhere else—specifically, say, in my back or neck? I took a gamble and said no, when in actuality my lower back flashed with intermittent pain. But I decided privately it was a phantom from the past and that it would be better not to confuse the issue. How much safer life would be, I sometimes think, if I could be honest about this. Yes, I could say, but I don't know if the pain is past or present.

What I dislike most is the return of old mysterious behaviors. I have woken in the night gagging on "blood," have found myself cupping a protective hand over an eye, or have realized I am cradling my ribs and breathing shallow careful breaths. I once lectured for nearly an hour, pausing every few moments to touch my fingertips to my lips to explore phantom cuts and bruises. All of these gestures were responses in the present to some sensation I had once felt in the past, and in nearly every instance someone nearby asked me what was wrong and suggested that, since I seemed in such distress, I see a doctor. I fell for this advice only once, and after being reprimanded because there was, after all, nothing wrong with my eye, I've learned as a multiple that pure behavior, without other corroboration, is more likely some reminder from the past than a symptom in the present.

To this day, I have a fear of nurses, doctors, and examining rooms that at times is nearly paralyzing, and for many years I was accompanied to appointments by vigilant and suspicious children. After all, one member of my system is the screaming, writhing three-year-old who was twice pinned down at the hospital.

Some writers describe the moment of dissociation as a kind of psychic death, and each time I step across the threshold of a medical facility I feel a wave of chill terror and find that I must tell myself yet again that I will be coming out alive. If I don't flat-out panic, I assume a tough, cool exterior and behave as if my only task in these circumstances is to appear so invincible that I will not be pinned down again. But my cool tough selves feel no pain and stoutly deny any hint or evidence of ill health. At the same time, my interpersonal radar gets turned up to a supersensitive level. When I don't know the answer to a question, even sometimes when I *do* know the answer to a question, I simply read the doctor's face and say whatever I believe will get me out alive: appropriate treatment isn't half as important as getting out of the office in one piece—and as soon as possible.

After I learned that I was a multiple, the question soon arose as to whether or not we should tell Tim about my disorder. When I was feeling optimistic, it seemed to me that if he knew I was a multiple he would be better able to understand the hodgepodge of symptoms I presented and the vague and sometimes contradictory answers I offered to his questions. My therapist said the decision was up to me. Tim, he was pretty certain, would accept the diagnosis, but, he warned, revealing the exact nature of my problem wouldn't guarantee Tim's immediate understanding. For years, I went back and forth on this decision.

One reason not to tell him was confidentiality. Tim is conscientious, and I feared he would automatically note multiplicity in my file. If he did, then I would have had to cope with the reactions—curiosity, wariness, fear, skepticism, disbelief—of every person who handled that file. I also feared the inevitable loss of privacy. My college has programs in nursing and pre-med, and I knew full well that confidentiality in odd or interesting cases is more an ideal than a reality. The chance of jeopardizing my integrative process was too great.

A second reason was that it often seemed to me that Tim had some difficulty adding together what he knew of me from experience and what he knew of me from talking with my therapist. At times, I was pretty certain, I seemed only like a bright, clear-eyed adult. I got his jokes, I had intelligent things to say about American education, he was interested in foreign languages. Although he'd also seen me grow anxious and inarticulate, it seemed to me that if my therapist told him about the multiplicity Tim might see me as a malingerer or as a lonely, mixed-up person in search of special attention. It won't be like that, my therapist assured me, and he often reminded me how much time he spent explaining dissociators to doctors and doctors to dissociators. But, given the choice, what I wanted most was to be the bright, normal, articulate person Tim halfway thought I was. I wanted to be able to go and see my doctor like an ordinary person—without a lot of fuss.

So what I had to do was manage as many of the medical variables as I could. I coax my parts to write things down. Whenever anything untoward occurs—symptom, sensation, oddity—it gets noted on the calendar in the kitchen. When a doctor's appointment looms, I post a list somewhere, and over time, write down everything that might have some bearing on the problem.

Before I actually set out for the doctor's office, I track down every kid I can find in the system and do my best to convince them that this doctor's appointment is mine, not theirs. You don't have to come, I tell them. This is an appointment for The Grown-ups. Sometimes I offer a small reward if, as promised, they do not show up in the midst of the appointment.

To stack the odds a little more in my favor, just before the appointment I take half a Xanax—just enough to knock the edge off my pending anxiety. Then I sit and wait, reading and rereading my notes, rehearsing my history and my symptoms.

Once in the examining room, I take ridiculous comfort in reminding myself how much I hate nurses. I feel some guilt about this as I know the fierce pride nurses take in the way their professional roles have changed in recent decades. But nurses were among the villains in my childhood history, and while I can choose and gradually get to know a doctor, nurses remain a random factor. The ones who are quiet, relaxed, and confident don't especially bother me, but the ones who are tough, brusque, or impatient, or the more recently trained ones who offer their own commentary and advice, or even their own preliminary diagnosis, frankly scare me to death. Perversely, if I allow myself to hate them, even while being cooperative and polite, I feel safer.

Once the doctor shows up, I take a deep breath and remind myself yet again: I can get up and walk out of here any time I choose.

I was Tim's patient for a full six years. I grew to rely on his prescriptions for Xanax, as well as on the way he kept close watch on just how much of it I was taking, and, at the request of my psychologist, he signed the paperwork for my medical leaves. However frustrated I was at times, with him, with the medical process, and with myself, I grew to trust him and to rely on his compassion, good sense, and expertise.

A year ago, my college faculty signed a new contract, which included changes in health benefits. Before we voted, we were assured that the only real difference was that each of us would be required to have a primary care physician who would coordinate our care and monitor our access to specialists. There was a low level of panic among the faculty, but we were reassured that we would be able to keep our current doctors; the only real change was that there would be penalties if we didn't have a primary care physician to oversee our access to specialists. These requirements didn't seem unreasonable, and we voted for and signed the contract. Within weeks we were handed a large book that contained a list of doctors who had been "approved" by the insurance company. Despite the promises made before signing the contract, we discovered that we had been lied to: some of us would lose doctors we'd had for many years.

I felt sick with betrayal, but also sick with fear. Tim's name was not on the list. I couldn't imagine what it would be like to start over with a new physician, and at the time these changes were taking place, so much other turmoil was under way in my system that I couldn't bear to think about it. For a year or so I continued to see Tim whenever I needed a doctor, and simply paid the insurance penalties.

But over time, I sensed that the choice was too much of a gamble. Office penalties I could afford; hospitalization penalties would wipe me out financially. I spent a year praying I would stay out of car wrecks, that I would not do something stupid like fall down a flight of stairs, and that my digestive tract would remain cool and dormant. Throughout, I wondered how it saved money to force patients to relinquish doctors they knew and trusted.

In the end, I knew I would have to find a new doctor. I talked over the decision with my therapist and came away with a list of local doctors who are especially poor physicians for dissociators. "The best I can do," he said, "is tell you who to avoid." I talked to friends in the medical field, and to several friends who are demanding patients. Then, with my list of options narrowed to four, I started calling doctors' offices. One practice was closed to new patients. Another, because of these insurance changes, was taking on so many new patients that the first free appointment was in six months' time. The response I got at the third office seems promising and, when necessary, I will venture out to see her, the woman who might become my new doctor.

Recently my therapist was talking to The Kids, and he asked them how they felt about having a new doctor.

"Oh," they said airily, "*we're* not going."

"You're not?" he said.

"Grown-ups go see doctors," they informed him. "Kids don't."

"That's smart," said my therapist with a laugh. "Let The Grown-ups do it."

"Yep," The Kids said, brightening. "Let The Grown-ups go."

I sure wish we grown-ups felt less daunted.

On days when I am feeling brave, I think about what I would like to tell this new doctor. If I could tell her anything, I would tell her that I need kindness, especially when I am ignorant or unaware. I would ask her to accept my lists and my notes, and to accept my falterings too, my blank looks, and my occasional waves of anxiety and panic. Be patient, I would tell her. *Seem* patient. Explain every procedure, every diagnosis, every treatment. Hide your surprise, I would say, especially when I pose a question any eight-year-old could answer. Finally, I would ask her to accept the fact that I might appear in her office for reasons that seem mysterious or unfounded. As a multiple I sometimes need to find out not what is wrong but *if* something is wrong.

One thing I will never tell her is that I am a multiple. If my disorder remains hidden, The Kids remain hidden, too: hidden and, with luck, protected.

"You've seen doctors before," my therapist reminded them that day he talked with them about my having to find a new physician.

"Yes," The Kids said grumpily. They wriggled and squirmed, scuffed their feet together and flung themselves back into the cushions. Then they grew very still. "Yes, we did," they said softly, then added with heartbreaking understatement: "And we didn't like it."

GIRL STUFF

I WAS A SOLITARY CHILD. Not only was I often sick, but usually, because I was so frightened of my brothers, I was happy to be left to myself. At times, however, I was desperately lonely and desperately jealous of the closeness among my brothers. It was true that Hank sometimes did horrible things to Josh and Kip, but it was also true that they had fun together, riding away on their bikes with their fishing poles, playing catch, building forts, even sharing a paper route. At times I wanted nothing more than to be included. "Get away from us," they always told me, and even when our mother insisted that they include me in a game, I would soon be sobbing because of some trick or slight of Hank's. So, the afternoon that Hank and Kip came to me and invited me to hike to a certain wooded stream to hunt for crayfish, I was ecstatic. I was seven, and I rejoiced that maybe I was finally old enough to be included.

My parents were not quite so enthusiastic. My father wanted us to wait until the next day so that either he or Josh could come with us. I pleaded. We wanted to go *now*. To my amazement, my brothers pleaded, too. We would be good. We would hike to the stream, stay for one hour, and hike straight back. We would take a watch, a canteen, even a whistle for emergencies. Grudgingly, my parents gave their permission. But, they warned us, if anything went wrong, if there was *one* problem, we would never be allowed to hike out there again.

We promised. I pulled on my jeans and my old sneakers for

scrambling in the stream. I even wore a sun hat without grumbling and stood obediently while my father sprayed me with bug dope. Kip got a milk carton for the crayfish, and Hank went to the garage for nets. We set off in a line. Quivering with joy, but a little nervous that I would do something wrong and get sent back to the house before we even reached the woods, I walked quietly behind my brothers.

We hit the margin of the woods and, instead of bearing west toward the stream, Hank took an abrupt turn the other way.

"But," I said, unable to keep quiet, "the stream is *that* way." I stood and pointed.

My brothers snickered. I shut my mouth and we continued walking in the wrong direction.

Soon we came to an abandoned barn.

I followed them inside. They dropped the nets and milk carton at the door, then rushed for the ladder to the loft and climbed it. I stood at the bottom.

I heard some rustling and giggling above my head. Soon Hank looked down over the edge. "Come on up, Jane," he called. "We have a surprise for you."

Kip leaned over, too. "It's really neat up here," he said. "We come here all the time."

I climbed the ladder.

The surprise was that both my brothers had taken off their jeans. They had been hearing a lot about sex at school, it turned out, and now they wanted to see how the whole thing worked.

"You're so stupid," Hank said. "You didn't think we'd really take you *fishing*." I was given a vulgar and rather skewed explanation of intercourse, then ordered to pull down my jeans, hold my legs apart, and wait. If I didn't, Hank said, they'd take my clothes from me and lock me in the barn.

For what seemed like forever, my brothers masturbated and rolled on top of me. Because I still desperately wanted them to like me, and because I didn't want to be stupid, I remained lying there—obedient, queasy, horrified, and frightened. Fortunately neither achieved penetration before Kip, who was in charge of keeping an eye on the time, said we had to be getting back.

On the way home, we stopped at a little brook. They wetted the nets, smeared mud on the milk carton, and announced that we had caught only two crayfish and had decided to let them go. Each boy put his feet in the mud, and when I refused to wet my sneakers, Hank gave me a shove. I fell, picked myself up, and walked the rest of the way back, filthy and numb.

My sexual education continued solely at their hands, and the elements were often the same. I was sometimes sweet-talked into situations, and, grateful for the attention and optimistic that *this* time it would be different, I would give in. It was never different. There were games of strip poker that always ended in some form of sexual humiliation for the loser, usually me. There were times I was forced to choose between having Hank overpower me in the swimming pool and hold me under or allowing myself to be stripped and touched. There were episodes with pornographic magazines in which I had my first view of a developed female body and from which I drew the same conclusions about mature women that my adolescent brothers had already drawn: I would grow up to be nothing more than a vessel for lust and denigration. The very shape I would someday assume would advertise my true worth and therefore determine my fate. Whatever happened to me I would thus deserve.

For three full years, everything I learned about sex and about myself as a girl I learned from my brothers. My only hope was that perhaps what they told me wasn't true or that, in the end, I could somehow avoid it.

One afternoon when I was in the fifth grade, I was in the den practicing my flute. My father and my brothers were away from home, and I was enjoying the luxury of more or less having the house to myself. But then my mother came into the room, reached over my shoulder, and closed my music book. She settled herself on the couch and patted the cushion next to her.

"Come here," she said.

I sat some distance from her, and began plucking at the elbows of my sweater. She reached around my shoulders and pulled me closer.

"Not so far away," she said, and kissed my forehead.

Then she held out a book and, with no other preamble, announced: "You're going to start menstruating. Soon, Dr. Wagner thinks."

I recoiled. My mother and the doctor had been talking about me behind my back? And about disgusting girl stuff?

My mother was beaming. "You'll be a woman soon," she whispered. It was, she added, the most wonderful thing she could wish for.

Numbly, I opened the book.

There were the same naked breasts and flaring hips that sprawled in my brothers' magazines, along with illustrations of what my mother claimed were *my* insides done in garish pink and hospital green.

My mother pulled me closer, then leaned excitedly over the book, eager to point out certain pictures.

I yanked away from her in horror: my own mother wanted me to be everything my brothers had already told me about. I snatched the book, slammed it shut, and shoved it back at her.

"I don't want to be a woman," I managed to whisper.

My mother looked at me and laughed. Sounding just like Hank, she laughed again, this time harshly. "You have no choice. What did you *think* you were going to be when you grew up?"

She leaned toward me again and tried to kiss my forehead. I turned my face away. Hurt and angry, my mother stood up.

"I'll put the book in your bureau drawer," she told me, then added sharply: "I've always wanted you to be a woman. It's the best thing that can happen to you."

I could think of nothing worse. Didn't my mother care what I wanted? Didn't *anybody* care what I wanted?

For the next six months or so, I seemed safe enough. Nothing happened. But then one day my mother and I were standing in front of the bathroom mirror. It was our morning ritual that my mother brushed my hair for me, then either curled it or combed it back into a ponytail. It was a summer morning, and I was wearing an old T-shirt.

"Stand up straight," my mother told me. Part of the morning ritual was that she would nag me about my poor posture.

I straightened.

"Not just taller," she said. "Put your shoulders back."

I sighed, shifted uneasily, then squared my shoulders.

"That T-shirt's getting snug," she said and smiled to herself.

"Well, I'm *growing*," I said flippantly. "It's last summer's shirt."

"No," she said. "You're not growing. You're *maturing*."

The word was downright horrible. I rounded my shoulders and tried to cave in my chest.

"Stand up straight," she ordered and gave an extra hard pull with the hairbrush.

I stared into the mirror and, feeling as if I would faint, squared my shoulders.

"That's right," my mother said, smiling again. She brushed and brushed my hair that day, and, in the mirror, her eyes never left my breasts.

My menstrual cycles began soon thereafter, and I was miserable. My body was betraying me. Not only was it doing exactly what my brothers and my mother had so gleefully predicted, it was bleeding so profusely and discharging such huge black chunks of tissue that I felt as if I were dying.

One afternoon I was lying on my bed, curled into as tight a ball as I could manage. I clenched my teeth, trying unsuccessfully not to cry.

Suddenly, my bedroom door flew open. My mother burst into the room and slammed the door behind her.

"Get *up,*" she said.

"But I—"

"Get *up,*" she said again. "Just get up and *do* something."

I closed my eyes. I thought I might throw up.

My mother came closer to the bed.

"*My* daughter," she hissed, "is not going to be one of those . . . those . . . those *fe*males who sulks every month. Is that clear?"

I held very still.

"Is that *clear?*" she said again.

I took a deep breath.

She gave me five minutes, repeat *five minutes,* to get myself sorted out.

I waited until she left the room, then dragged myself off my bed. Publicly, I never again acknowledged to anyone when I was menstruating.

One bleak day, however, when I was bleeding heavily and breaking out into cold sweats—all the while struggling to appear cheerful and free of pain—I took the book my mother had given me from the back of my bureau drawer. After some searching, I found what I was looking for: the number of years I would have to endure menstruation. The answer shocked me. Bitterly, I sat at my desk and calculated the number of periods I was likely to suffer before menopause.

That night, I stayed awake long after the rest of the family was asleep. Once the house was silent, I slipped down to the kitchen. Maybe my mother thought I had no choice about being a woman, but I'd spent the entire day planning my escape.

Carefully, I took everything from the sink. Then I lay my left arm on the cool stainless steel, and with a knife point traced the pathways of my veins. I didn't break the skin that night, and felt much relieved when I finally crept back to bed: not because I hadn't hurt myself, but because I now knew how to evade womanhood. When the time came, I would lay my left arm in the kitchen sink and open all the veins that I could find.

My brother Kip sometimes jokes about our family home being "the house without sex," and there is some weird truth to this, because despite the florid activity carried on behind closed doors, there was no public acknowledgement of sex in any way. Even after we had all grown and married, my parents assigned visiting children and their spouses to separate bedrooms. The first time this happened to my brother Josh, he supposedly picked up his suitcase and moved in with his wife—much to my parents' embarrassment. While I was a teenager, sex was so unspeakable and so revolting that I simply could not imagine having any kind of physical intimacy with any of the boys I knew. I was actually grateful to avoid dating and thus avoid the possibility of becoming just another set of breasts and hips begging to get laid.

I was lucky in that I went to high school during the late sixties. My high school's dress code was abolished during my sophomore year, and from then on, like my classmates, I pretty much lived in jeans and trousers, turtlenecks and army shirts. My only obvious feminine traits were my rings and my auburn hair that billowed everywhere in waves. When I was required to wear a skirt, I opted for the incredibly short skirts of the times, worn with tights, as if to say, "You want female? I'll give you more female than you can stand." Even my choir director, who was determined that girls should wear skirts for concerts, blanched when she saw my attire for the first performance of the season— and promptly decided that, yes, perhaps trousers would be quite as appropriate after all.

It was also during high school that, almost by default, I began a trend that has continued throughout my life. I had two close friends as a teenager. One, predictably, was a girl. But the other was the boy who sat behind me in algebra and next to me in French. In retrospect, I can say he was good-looking, but all that mattered to me back then was that he was bright and kind, a little clumsy, and a terrific companion. If I refused to see myself in terms of gender, I seem to have overlooked this same aspect in those around me. I ignored the fact that he was a boy and that I was not, and we happily spent hours and hours together, talking, sailing, swimming, driving around, and studying. He was my pal, my buddy, my confidant—but certainly not a boy.

"How on earth," my psychologist asked one day during the first year of therapy, "did you survive?" It is a question he has asked again and again. One answer is that, because I suffered at the hands of both males and females, I do not, as some victims do, see one gender as safe and attractive and the other as dangerous or repulsive. I seem to have made a habit of seeing the world in other terms. I have friends who assume that all women health care providers will automatically be gentle and understanding—only to be nailed from time to time by cold incompetents who—surprise!—are women. I make my judgments differently, looking only at demeanor, expertise, and compassion. I do not assume women are kinder or more giving, or that all men should be viewed in terms of their potential as mates or rapists.

There are distinct differences between what was done to me by males and what was done to me by females. Somehow it has always been easier to come to terms with the actions of my brothers. I can tell myself they were young and ignorant. I can understand why they hated me and my position in the family. I can also see my brothers' treatment of me in terms of overt, discrete episodes: this attack, that molestation, and so on.

What has been far more insidious, and in the end far more destructive, was the way my mother treated me. Granted, her actions and her words took place in a context she was unaware of. That she should have *been* aware is another matter, but everything she said, everything she did, underscored the sickening "truths" I had gleaned from my brothers. What I cannot forgive, somehow, is that her own glee about my developing body made her so blind to my emotions. What I cannot forget is what it was like to have to stand in the bathroom—"Shoulders *back!*" she would command—while she measured and remeasured my bust and waist and hips. It was no coincidence, I think, that she could never quite get the "exact" measure of my bust, measuring and remeasuring it in every session.

What my brothers did I at least could guess was wrong. But my mother's rights to my body, and her power over me, I took for granted. I equally feared what she sought to turn me into and assumed it was her right to make me become anything she wished. What she taught me about being a woman or a girl, directly or by implication, I still struggle to articulate and understand.

It isn't easy.

One day, during a session, The Kids announced that they were going to stop growing if they had to "turn into" either a boy or a girl.

At the time, we guessed they were roughly age six or seven.

My psychologist quizzed them for a while. "What makes you think you have to do that?"

The Kids squirmed and then said, resentfully, "Because you and The Grown-ups keep talking about girl stuff."

"And you don't like that?"

"We *hate* girl stuff," they told him.

"Do you want to be a boy?" he asked.

"*No!*" they said.

"No? Why not?"

The Kids scowled and fidgeted. "Don't wanna be like Hank," they said finally.

"Well, that makes sense," said my therapist. "Who'd want to be like Hank?"

"*Nobody,*" said The Kids.

"But what's wrong with being a girl?" he asked after a while.

"Bad stuff happens to girls," they insisted.

"Bad stuff happens to boys, too," he said. "That's not right, either."

They squirmed some more. "But girls get told what to do," they grumped. "And nobody's telling *us* what to do."

"It's really not like that anymore," my therapist told them. "It was while you were growing up, but it's not anymore."

"We're only growing up if we can stay just the same," they insisted. The Kids are nothing if not incredibly stubborn.

"And what's that?"

They sighed dramatically, and explained as if he were being deliberately stupid: "We're not a girl and we're not a boy." And, in case he hadn't gotten the message, they added: "And we're not *going* to be one, either."

In time, he let it drop. After the session, he and I talked about The Kids' fear and resentment, and we decided to turn them loose. The next time he saw The Kids, he assured them that no one would ever try to make them be either a boy or a girl, that they could grow up in whatever way they chose, but that, if they ever changed their mind and wanted to talk about it again, they were certainly welcome to do so. There was a period of quiet brooding, then The Kids once again began to age and to develop.

My psychologist and I guessed that they would raise the issue again—when they were really ready. We would turn out to be wrong about that. Very, very wrong, because in the end The Kids outwitted us, finding a way, once and for all, to avoid all that disgusting girl stuff.

HORSES, HORSES, HORSES

ONE DAY WHEN I WAS ELEVEN, our neighbor Helen took me for a drive out into the country. She was going to visit an old school friend who was staying at an inn known for its riding program, and she thought I might like to spend the hour or two of her visit wandering around the barns and looking at the horses. That afternoon I studied every single horse standing in its stall in the inn's immaculate stable. I leaned on the rail of the ring and watched someone take a riding lesson. I stood in the afternoon hush of the indoor arena and tried to imagine what it would be like to be able to ride every single day of the year, no matter what the weather. Helen finally found me out near a pasture, watching three horses alternately graze and groom one another's necks.

That was on a Saturday. For the next few nights I read and reread the brochure on the inn's riding program that Helen had thought to bring me. I kept turning back to the announcement that, by arrangement, the inn offered lessons "to serious local riders." I had never ridden before, and I didn't know if I qualified as "serious," but I worked up the courage to ask if I might spend my savings on riding lessons.

I confided in my grandmother first. When I was three or four, she had made me a cowgirl outfit with hat, boots, fringed skirt, cap gun, and holster. On family drives, she pointed out horses standing in fields along the roads, and she knew that half the books I lugged home from the city library were by Marguerite

Henry, Sam Savitt, or Walter Farley—my favorite horse writers. Although I didn't ask her to, my grandmother spoke to my parents on my behalf. My father said yes, then my mother agreed. Riding would be good for me, my grandmother assured them, and no one could have told, back then, the many ways her argument would prove true.

The very first horse I ever rode was a gangly gray gelding. He was sweet and quiet around the barn, willing and indeed glad to stand for hours while I curried the itchy spots on his back, whispered in his ears, and brushed his face and tail. He was quiet under saddle, too: he didn't buck, spin, bolt, or shy. What he did, however, was exactly what he pleased. One day, it took me half an hour to get him to leave the barn. I had tacked him up, but then he planted his feet and point-blank refused to walk one step up the little lane toward the riding ring. In the arena, he was full of these same tricks. He would decide, for instance, not to trot, or not to make a full circle, or he would veer to the center for a little schmooze with my instructor. Anyone who has ever taken riding lessons has probably ridden a similar horse: the tractable creature who insists that you convince it to do your bidding.

I can still hear my instructor, Mrs. White, saying, "Jane! *Make* that horse trot! Jane! *You* are in charge! Jane! *Make* that horse obey you!" Riding is not a matter of the rider dominating the horse but it is certainly supposed to be a matter of the rider deciding the horse's pace and path. That I was to make these decisions, and that I was to insist the horse do as I wished, was utterly intoxicating. It was also extremely difficult, because for a long time I kept waiting for "something to happen"—my euphemism for pain or danger. But all that happened was that the horse performed, my instructor praised me, I felt rushes of utterly alien sensations, and I moved on to other skills and other mounts.

Soon all my Saturdays were spent at the barn. My lesson consumed only an hour, but Mrs. White believed that riding students should do more than climb on a horse and ride it. The rest of the day I spent cheerfully mucking stalls, cleaning tack, grooming horses, throwing hay down from the loft, and watching the guests' lessons. I lived for Saturdays, and during the week faithfully studied the books loaned to me by Mrs. White on anatomy, equipment, etiquette, and equitation.

That spring, I rode in my first horse show. Over the years, I have come to see that how one views competition says much about oneself, and it makes me smile to think that, for me, my first horse show had much to do with clothes.

What a painful subject beauty is. Recently, I sat in my therapist's office looking at old pictures of myself—and was speechless to discover some photographs of me that were quite lovely. Of course, I refused to tell him what so amazed me about the pictures, and, having aged some ten years since they were taken, I rushed to tell myself I didn't look that way anymore. I have become comfortable with the idea of my own homeliness, but in my early teens the idea was excruciating.

My sense of my hideousness came from my older brother, who cultivated it deliberately, and from my mother, who fostered it by accident. For years, Hank's house name for me was "Her Ugliness," which my parents allowed without reprimand or comment. If he had to give me a lift somewhere when a friend of his was nearby, he would apologize for his disgusting sister. And, on more than one occasion, I was kept home from after-school events because Hank convinced my parents it would be too humiliating for him to have me in attendance, too.

My mother's contribution was more direct; she never allowed me to wear clothing that remotely resembled what my classmates wore. Her stance on this was so extreme that once, for a little concert when all the girls were asked to wear navy blue skirts, I wore a brown one. She bought all of my clothing without consulting me, and often I felt I stood out like the proverbial painted bird. Sooner or later, teacher after teacher in elementary school stood up in front of the class and gave a little homily on how *lucky* some girls were because their clothes were so unique. No one was fooled; certainly not I.

Mrs. White, however, managed to impress upon my mother the absolute need for correctness of attire. I had a proper velvet hunt cap, and I was taken to a saddler where we shopped for the best fit in boots, breeches, and hacking jacket. Few memories compare to the thrill of riding in my first show in proper turnout: boots gleaming, shirt blinding white, pretty printed tie pinned in place with my very first stock pin.

I was not a star that day, and did not even win a ribbon. The weather was cold, I was shy and nervous, and, under pressure, I couldn't sort out my diagonals at the trot. My instructor was reassuring; she rattled off all the things I had done well. And, a few days later, she called my parents and suggested that I lease a horse for the summer. Since I was so eager and hardworking around the barn, they would charge me only the cost of bedding, grain, and shoeing. My parents said yes, and for the first summer of my life I was able to make myself scarce nearly all day every day.

My favorite time to arrive at the inn was just before morning feeds. The horses were field-kept in the summers, so it was my task to walk through the barn, clean and fill the water buckets, toss a little hay into each stall, then step out the back of the barn. By this time, someone from the family had come out, often Drew, a girl near my age, and together we would stand on the little plateau of the barnyard, cup our hands to our mouths, and holler gaily: "Ho-o-orses! Bre-e-akfast!" And soon the little band of mares would barge over the top of the ridge or appear from the cool grove on the stream bank, and come cantering down the long gentle slope toward the barn for their morning grain.

At home, I was likely to be yelled at for things I hadn't known I was supposed to do in the first place. "Ja-a-ane!" my mother would yell with a shattering tremolo that suggested I'd better get there double-quick. Then she would order me to wash the dishes, or clean the bathroom *now!*— when I hadn't known I was supposed to have done it in the first place. During the testing at the start of therapy, I was asked to list the most important rules of my upbringing. "There weren't any," I said. "You just waited to get yelled at and then you knew you'd done something wrong."

Sometimes my mother made a joke of the way she summoned me. "Ja-a-ane!" would come the yell. I would obediently rush to present myself—and she would laugh at my quick appearance and, no doubt, at the expression on my face. Then she would smile sweetly, give me a hug, and tell me how much she loved me. Even when very young, I hated her for this prank.

The randomness of my brother's violence and my mother's moods left me with the habit of perpetual vigilance. Any noise, any change, any nuance—and I was on guard. I tried to know exactly where Hank might be at any given moment, and for whole days I braced against the sound of my mother's summons. But I could not seem to outwit my brother nor could I predict the next change in my mother's mood. Despite my best efforts, I could not get the teaching I heard at church each week to line up with what went on in my own family, so I concocted my own "rules" to explain human behavior, and, sadly, after years of therapy, I can see I left home with some unfortunate and long-abiding misconceptions on human nature.

One of the few consistent aspects of our childhood days was that my mother hated to see a child "doing nothing." I learned early never to say that I was bored and never to appear idle. Reading books was an acceptable occupation; reading certain magazines was okay too, but other magazines were deemed a waste of time. Playing the flute was approved; listening to music was allowed only if you were doing something else at the same time. Sleeping was okay up to a point; lying on the bed staring at the ceiling was not. Swimming was fine; basking in the sun afterwards for more than a few minutes dangerously approached slothfulness.

Oddly, despite my mother's penchant for activity and industry, our house was often a complete shambles. The dust and the grime grew very deep; mail, towels, dishes, newspapers, toys, and paperwork piled up for weeks. The desk, the couch, chairs, counters, end tables seemed to overflow. Each night we emptied the kitchen table, spread a tablecloth, and sat down to eat together, sometimes like shipwrecked castaways clinging to one last shred of civilization.

My father was a generally quiet man. He had grown up in orderly and immaculate surroundings, but he made only two specific demands on my mother: he expected dinner to be served more or less on time, and he wanted to have clean shirts in his closet. For weeks, he would endure the growing mess around him in utter but increasingly ominous silence.

My mother learned to read his moods, and when things began to slide too far she would enlist my aid, summoning me to help with a whirlwind cleaning job. "Hurry up! Your father will be home soon," she would say. More than once, she sent me to his closet with an armload of quickly laundered clothes, telling me to hurry back, presumably so that I would not be caught in the act of supplying clean clothing at the last minute.

But she knew how to cross him, too, and sometimes she deliberately started trouble. Often she worked very hard, and when she felt unappreciated, she had a favorite trick: she would greet my father at the door with the news that she would not be cooking dinner. Inevitably he would offer to take the family out somewhere. "I'm not going," my mother would say. And, when my father would suggest that we send out for pizza, my mother would veto that idea, too. "There's plenty of food here," she would say. "But one of *you* is going to have to cook it. And by cook, I mean cook for the whole family. A real dinner. No snacks."

Then she would stretch out on the couch, turn on the television, and—vigilant, angry, satisfied—she would keep an eye on the kitchen door. Everyone else would slink off to some corner of the house to hide.

Eventually my father would come tapping on my door. "Jane," he would wheedle, "can't you do something?"

"Like what?"

"Like, oh, ah, um, say, get dinner?"

My father had never learned how to cook.

"What am I supposed to make?"

"Think of something," he would say. "I'm getting faint."

And I would go out to the kitchen and prepare a meal, my mother barking orders and making nasty remarks all the while. Then we would sit down to eat in angry silence. My brothers would make faces at the food, I would get stuck cleaning up, and then, enraged, I would cry myself to sleep.

The farm, by contrast, was blessedly serene. The entire care of the horses centered on routine. They were fed at regular times, and, so that they wouldn't colic, they were always given water first, then hay and grain. They were turned out to pasture, brought back to the barn, had their stalls mucked, their feet trimmed, their shots administered, all according to a schedule. Even riding had safety and tradition as its foundation: we tacked up, mounted, entered the ring, even spoke to one another while we rode in ways that had been handed down for generations.

There were few surprises. Even when I fell off or managed to get kicked or stepped on, or when a new horse collapsed coming off the van, these were not frightening mysteries; these were events that, like the barn routine and riding etiquette, could be explained in logical, concrete terms. The resulting knowledge was expected to help prevent at least some accidents and disasters in the future.

The first month of the summer, I leased a fat bay mare named Abigail. She was nearly twenty and her muzzle had begun to turn white. Her back was broad and, despite her age, she never hesitated to kick up her heels in a little warning buck if I allowed my saddle to slip too far back. That whole month, I rode her six days out of seven. Even without supervision, I was faithful about doing my exercises in the saddle. I rode without my stirrups, I rode with my arms crossed; I vaulted on; I vaulted off; I worked hard on my transitions. At the end of the month, I was called into the family wing of the inn. I was a little surprised to see my mother had arrived early and had been in conference with Mrs. White.

I was asked to sit down. I wrung my hands, swallowed hard, wished I'd pulled my boots off before I'd come into the living room. Mrs. White announced that she'd already told my mother the news: the inn would be selling off some horses. Abigail had a new owner as of the end of the week. Mrs. White smiled at me, then at my mother. As far as she was concerned, the little boy who would be getting Abigail was a little better suited to her; he wouldn't ask her to work *quite* so hard as I had in the last month.

I looked down at my boots and held my breath. I bit back my habitual remark that I was sorry, as Mrs. White had pointed out more than once that I had little to be sorry for.

There was a new plan for me. My mother had agreed to it, and now it was my turn to think about it. We would skip the money for the lease altogether. If I would help with the guest lessons, and if I would continue to pitch in with the chores, Mrs. White would see that I had at least one horse to ride every day.

"It won't be the same horse each time," she warned me. "A good rider can ride anything."

Her words came to me like little shocks. I looked up at her.

"You *can* be a good rider if you keep at it."

My throat closed. I was glad Drew was off somewhere else.

"You have no idea how hard your daughter works," she told my mother.

My eyes widened.

"I have a secret," she said, hesitating, as if making a decision.

"There's an old office in the top of the barn. From up there, I can see both rings and most of the fields." She gave me a knowing smile. "I've been keeping something of an eye on you. You're ready for a challenge. New horses—" she paused again, "and, if you'd like, a little showing. What do you think?"

I looked at my mother.

She smiled. "It's up to you."

"I'll keep her working," Mrs. White said.

I felt a little sad, actually; I'd miss Abigail. I said good-bye to my old mare with a fistful of carrots and an extra-long grooming session.

"Jesus, I didn't bring my sunglasses," said the father of Abigail's new owner. He made a show of squinting at my precious mare as if blinded by her coat. "See this?" he said to his son. "This is how clean this horse has to be kept."

"An hour a day will do it," I told the little boy quite seriously, surprised when everyone around me began to laugh.

I felt a little lost once she was gone, but every morning I was assigned a horse or two to ride, and soon Drew and I had picked out a few shows and were schooling hard in the rings and fields. She and I became closer friends, and by midsummer I was at the farm for days on end.

Life at the inn mystified me: there were few arguments. Mr. White managed the inn itself, greeting the guests, supervising the small staff, and presiding over the somewhat formal evening meal. There were just ten guest rooms and if the inn was not full, he generally also took charge of cooking breakfast. He was a funny, cheerful man who, although not a horseman, quizzed me about my riding. Mrs. White ran the stables, not only overseeing the daily chores and the buying and selling of horses, but she did most of the teaching, too, and sometimes coordinated week-long clinics run by various high-profile instructors. Everyone seemed to laugh a lot. Each family member had some daily chores, but we girls had an incredible amount of freedom, too. Drew and I loafed in the afternoons, swam in the pond after dark, and slipped out to the fields and tore around bareback on our favorite horses. I always chipped in with the work, asking what else needed to be done, which made Drew roll her eyes, and I faithfully made my bed every morning and spent as little time in the family bathroom as possible.

"We hardly know she's here," Mrs. White would tell my mother, although there was much joking that I was the only person in the place who would willingly sit down with Mrs. White and eat a long leisurely breakfast. She was a diabetic and required a substantial morning meal, but although Mr. White cooked for her, he could not spare the time to keep her company. Drew and her sisters tended to snatch milk and toast, then bolt for the door. I, however, loved the long chats with Mrs. White and with the more interesting guests in the quiet of the inn's morning room. Besides, I'd never before eaten breakfast on good china.

Toward the end of July, we began showing. Drew was just enough older than I to be riding in a different and more difficult division. She was also riding a younger and more difficult horse. She did well, but at times I picked up more ribbons. Mrs. White once told my mother that she worried that I was winning far too much too soon; she feared that it would ruin me.

One day at a horse show, I came trotting back to the van with a second-place ribbon streaming from my horse's bridle. It had been a big class, and I was jubilant and grinning. Mrs. White frowned, then told me to stop smiling. As far as she was concerned, I had not earned that ribbon and my possession of it was not a cause for celebration.

I was stunned.

Yes, she explained, I had been the second-best rider in the class. *But* I had not ridden nearly as well as I knew how. I had been a little lax and sloppy, and the riders I had beaten had not been riding as long as I had. Or if they had, they did not have the talent. She knew I was capable of a better, cleaner performance. "Do *you* think you rode at the top of your form?" she said.

The concept that what *I* thought mattered, that my opinion counted, was stunning. I had all the self-esteem problems any abused child does, and I had always looked not to myself but to the people around me for reward or rebuke. Period. But Mrs. White worked hard with me, teaching me to evaluate my performance. It would be a long time—possibly not until graduate school—before I would realize the value of my own efforts in any field and feel pleased with myself when I believed I had done well.

I had two glorious summers at the inn. At the beginning of the second summer, Drew was given her first thoroughbred as a birthday gift. I was thrilled for her, but jealous, too. But then one day a new horse arrived on the farm, and Mrs. White assigned him to me to groom, ride, and, if he was ready, show by summer's end. In many ways this summer was much the same as the one before; the big difference was that I fell in love with Gabriel, the little, beguiling chestnut gelding.

I use the word "love" deliberately. I had learned early on— and it is a trait that I still have to some extent—to be careful of expressing my feelings about anything that mattered to me. An elderly relative, for instance, had established the tradition at each holiday of giving each of us children an old silver spoon from her collection. It was impressed on us how valuable they were, but it was left to us to decide what to do with them. I was not so much interested in their value, but in their beauty and their age. I openly treasured my silver spoons: the elegant engravings, the very heft of them, the remarkable fact that I was holding something at least a hundred years old in my hand, even the tradition of being given them by my oldest relative. But I made my interest in my small hoard too obvious; my antique spoons began to disappear. Each time one did, my brother Hank made a point of coming to me. He had found a pawn shop in the city that gladly took my spoons, and he would wave the money in my face. Once or twice, he threw a dollar bill on my bed: that was to be my "share" of the silver spoon he had stolen. I loved those spoons, and his stealing and then pawning them was the perfect way to hurt me. Our parents refused to step into our quarrels, so I finally carved a hole in the bottom of my mattress, hid my last two silver spoons there, and thus managed to smuggle them out of my childhood.

Other things were destroyed, too: the legs on my china horses, books, even friendships. Like many abusers, Hank threatened to kill the family dog, which often slept on my bed, and he laughed outright when my kittens were torn to shreds by a stray dog in our backyard.

Gabriel, however, was safe from Hank, who never went near the inn. As the summer progressed, I taught him to come when I called him by name. I struggled to tame his unruly mane, I worked faithfully with him in the ring, and more and more felt as if he were somehow mine. One day our blacksmith came, and walked up to the ring to watch me ride. I was glad to have him there: he was a sharp but jovial man, and had been a good friend of Mrs. White's for many years. He stood leaning on the rail, one hand loosely holding his file, leather apron still tied around his waist, and as I trotted and cantered various figures for his inspection, he was surprisingly quiet. After a little while, he called me over to him. He leaned over the fence, patted Gabriel's neck, and hesitated to speak. "Jane," he finally said, "I have to tell you I've seldom seen anyone so . . . so . . . close to her horse."

I grinned at him, and began to praise Gabriel—his willingness and his intelligence.

The blacksmith's eyes grew abruptly bright and wet. "You've done a beautiful job," he said roughly, then turned back toward the barn.

I rode Gabriel nearly every day until the start of school, but then I learned what had brought tears to the blacksmith's eyes. I had known that Drew would be heading off to boarding school, and I couldn't imagine the inn without her, but what I hadn't known was that Mrs. White's diabetes had worsened and that the entire management of the riding program would be handed over to an outside instructor-trainer. Drew's new thoroughbred would remain as a family horse but, to streamline the operation, some other horses would be sold. Gabriel was up for sale.

I had no money to buy him, and knew better than to ask my parents. I made it a point not to be at the inn the day he was shipped out; I had already spent too many afternoons crying into his neck. Mrs. White made it clear that she was sorry he was going. She explained the logic behind his sale, and reassured me that I was still welcome to come and ride, even without Drew and Gabriel. But I went back only once, feeling clumsy and heart-broken.

In time, I packed away my ribbons and my riding clothes, and I took up other things: I learned to play tennis, I joined a trio and the orchestra, I had the lead in a one-act play. More than once, my parents remarked that it was good to have me back.

I believed my riding days were over, but when I found myself looking for my first summer job, I naturally turned back to horses. Every summer after that, and even on a few Christmas breaks, I found a day camp or a stable and took up riding once again, giving lessons or helping out with chores. Even during graduate school, I found jobs at breeding farms or training stables, mucking stalls, handling young horses, or starting the occasional colt or filly under saddle. I needed the money; I also needed the change of pace, the chance to be outdoors, the chance to ride.

But, after I married, I had no time to ride and I gave it up with little thought. I took up less time-consuming sports: I ran, I played more tennis, I tried my hand at racquetball. Riding was something I had once done in the remote and hazy past. If I ever thought about it, it was only to notice the amount of space my equipment took up in my closet.

Eight years passed. And then, two years ago, near the end of an academic term, a colleague called me at home one night. He seemed a bit abashed. His wife and daughter, he explained, were crazy about horses, and he had heard that I put myself through graduate school training horses. I laughed and told him that that was not exactly accurate, but he bravely went on with his speech. His daughter had had quite a fall; her nerve was shaken. And, in addition to their usual crowd of horses—he paused and sighed—his wife had somehow managed to acquire two new ones that were, well, not quite as well-behaved as she had thought they would be. What they were wondering was whether I could be induced to come down to their farm and give some private lessons.

At first I said no. They lived too far away. They probably couldn't afford what I would have to charge them to make it worth my while. What's more, the kinds of problems he was describing would take a lot of time and patience to sort out. I couldn't commit myself to that.

He put his wife on the phone, and as I began to listen to her describe her horses and her concern for their correct training, and her worries about her daughter, something began to tug at me. I heard both fear and dedication in her voice. Against all good judgment, I agreed to set up a date and see what quick advice I could offer.

I made the drive the first day, with my helmet and my freshly cleaned saddle in the back of the car. I had pulled on my old riding breeches and a pair of boots. Just having those clothes on again made me feel somehow different. I was headed out as a semi-pro again to teach and school.

The first day was wonderful. I gave mother and daughter a lesson, coaching both on their position and helping the mother with the way her horse was traveling. I joked with the daughter, then set her to work on exercises to build confidence and balance. Afterwards, I did a little schooling with each of the younger horses.

There was something about the little private arena, the quick perceptions of the mother's questions, and, despite her fears, the daughter's eagerness. Tall pines sighed around the ring, and I could hear the old *flick-flick* of sand against the horses' hooves. I tired more easily than I had at twenty-two when I rode three to five horses every day in the summer, but I remembered more than I thought possible and my body seemed to remember things on its own.

At the end of the ride, with all of us talking a mile a minute because we'd had such a good time, we made arrangements to carry us through the rest of the summer. Since then and over the past few years, the progress in the horses and our riding has been dramatic. I suppose, given the fact that they are willing students and that the horses are well suited to their work, none of this should be too surprising. But it *is* surprising—mind-blowing, breathtaking, shocking.

It was on horseback that I entered a new and critical phase of the treatment of my disorder: I began to experience a kind of orderly co-consciousness. In the earliest stages of my process, I had been unaware of my multiplicity. Later, my selves—especially The Kids—butted in as they chose, making demands, sulking, struggling for what is known as executive control. But in the saddle, quietly and without threat, I was first aware I could share consciousness with my selves, that I could sense, and learn about, and perhaps accept their varying identities, needs, and whims. And they, perhaps, learned that I could offer them something they so desperately wished for.

My selves who are still caught in their early twenties, and who have yet to sort through their dark days, are marvelously calm and competent around the barn. They are sticklers for correctness—in the adjustment of equipment, in the way the aisle is raked after a ride, in the polishing of boots and bridle bits. They are so pleased with themselves they scuff their boot heels in an old familiar way, and they very naturally resumed their old role of coach and teacher.

The young teenager who once rode is entirely astonished. When I quit riding at the age of thirteen, I had done a little jumping, but certainly no lateral work or dressage. In fact, I had a copy of Alois Podhasky's classic *The Complete Training of Horse and Rider*, which I often tried to read but genuinely couldn't understand. So twenty-five years later, this teenager eager and delighted to be on horseback finds that if she listens closely to her older selves, somehow she can understand the principles of dressage and do a dozen exercises well that she has never heard of. She can get her horse to bend, to balance, to mouth its bit, to leg yield. The effect is startling; it is almost any teenager's dream: to simply wake up one morning and be a more competent and more educated rider than she could have imagined.

Then a long-hidden eight-year-old joined the ranks of my selves. She was locked for an afternoon in a tool shed, where black widows sometimes nested, and hers were the tales of the repeated torments and small tortures inflicted on her by her older brother. She was the one who first began to try to figure out how to dodge Hank and his cruelties, and unfortunately she was the one who first believed that because she could not outwit him she was stupid and therefore doomed to be everyone's dupe, doomed to live with near-daily terror.

In an effort to orient her, since she did not know she was a multiple, my psychologist and I had her look at pictures taken of me over the years. Several fascinated her: mostly those of my dogs and those of horses. Although she still did not understand where she was or that she was not alone, she became furious about the passage of time: she looked and looked at the pictures taken of me at horse shows or riding an old favorite horse over a jump, and she muttered to herself about having missed everything. All those years, she had been figuratively locked in that tool shed,

locked in her terror and her desperate attempts to outwit her
brother.

Intellectually, I knew that as the barriers dissolved, she would
have less the sense of having missed the good parts of her life but,
in a way, she was right: that particular part of me never got to
ride as a kid. My therapist, however, told her every week that she
could go riding, any Saturday she chose, if she was brave enough
to peek. Sometimes when I am riding I sense her brief, sudden
consciousness. What she feels is a mix of awe and glee.

During these years of riding, I find myself slowing down at
certain points while driving familiar routes, looking in a particular
pasture for the pinto ponies, or scouting a sheltered barnyard for
the "baby horses." My Saturdays are clearly, blackly marked—
Ride!—and I notice that by Wednesday some part of me is listening with dread and worry to the long-range forecast. Will it
rain? Will it be too hot? Or will it be clear and fine? Meanwhile,
I brush my boots, clean my saddle, make sure my breeches are
washed and ready.

And so each week, as I first did at age eleven, I step across
the simple threshold of a barn and into a world of quiet order. I
listen once again to the swish of tails and to the heavy grinding
of the horses' jaws as they pull hay down from their racks. I stroke
a horse's warm, well-groomed neck, and an old familiar peace
settles around my soul. I am grateful that certain of my selves can
share this love among them, but, as my therapy progresses, I sense
the utter absence of certain selves: my fourteen-, fifteen-, and
sixteen-year-olds, who did not ride, and who, shut away from the
world of horses, for a while found quiet in more destructive ways.

JJ AT 15

 JJ HURTLED BACK into my consciousness the exact same way she had done everything: in a rush and with great drama. I knew it was she because of the fierce twitch in my left eyelid, because of her profound restlessness, and because her old wire-rimmed glasses, which I hadn't seen for years, appeared abruptly on my bureau. I knew she would also like to find a few other things: her flute, her Peter Max scarf, even her long rambunctious auburn hair. But these were nothing to what she craved most. On her second night back, she nearly tore my house apart, tossing the contents of drawers, ransacking every nook and cupboard, desperate for that small bottle of green-and-yellow capsules.

I admired her single-mindedness, her relentlessness, but it also struck me as ironic that she looked so hard for something she had sworn off. In a way I understood: seeing those capsules, holding them in her hand, would prove she was so far keeping her promise—to Evelyn, to Paul, and, although she would discount it, to herself. I admired her fierceness, and admired the way she turned me down flat on the offer of a little Xanax.

In the years after Gabriel was sold, I hung on to one basic precept: whenever possible, I made myself scarce during the summertime. I spent a month visiting a school friend who had moved halfway across the country, I went to music camp, I played a lot of tennis. The summer I was fifteen, through a project at school, I won a place at a conference for young people. I went because I was wildly restless and unhappy, and because I'd do anything to get away from home; I had no idea that that week would change my life.

The conference schedule was quite hectic. We had been divided into small groups, and after meeting twice a day to listen to a speaker on some current hot topic, we headed off to a secluded spot and spent the next few hours in a kind of free-for-all discussion.

Perhaps it only seemed like a free-for-all because of the incredible variety of participants. In my group, I was the middle-class white Protestant girl. There were also two teenagers from the ghetto—one a gang member (missing an eye from a knife fight) and one not—the son of a radical professor being harassed by the FBI, a Boston prep school boy who could discourse on his starter investment portfolio, a Catholic girl determined to join a convent, and so on. We were led by a college dean and a child psychologist, who asked questions, challenged our opinions, and kept our discussions humane and fair. We talked about homosexuality, the war in Vietnam, class structure, education, religion—the works. One day we talked about drugs. As usual, each group member was asked for his or her initial view. When it was my turn, I said I didn't do drugs. (The year was 1969: one did or did not "do" drugs.) Nearly every young person in the group sneered at me, and so I hastily amended: I didn't do drugs recreationally because I *had* to take them because I had a bad nervous system. The other kids were instantly sympathetic: what a drag. But Paul, the college dean, and Evelyn, the psychologist, were instantly on the alert.

To my astonishment, it seemed to be my turn on the hot seat. Instead of challenging the street kid who liked to smoke dope and imagine he heard zebras on the roof, instead of confronting the status-symbol drug ethic of the prep school kid, Paul and Evelyn questioned me relentlessly. Who said I had a bad nervous system? What kind of drug was I taking? What did I do before taking the drugs? How long had I gone without medication? Had I gotten a second opinion on my problem? Had I ever seen a counselor? Was anyone else in the family on medication?

At first I was resentful. Why me, after all? I didn't use drugs for *fun*. I used drugs because I had to. For heaven's sake, they were given to me by my parents. By my *doctor*. I had been taking them all my *life*.

My first medication was a thick, sticky liquid that had a slightly pinkish cast. It burned as it went down; it was so powerful that it seemed to tingle in my toes and fingertips and felt as though it made my teeth sparkle. "Mint soup" I began to call it, and in time, my parents used that name for it, too. I never knew exactly what the medication was, probably a sedative of some sort. When I was in college, I learned during an anatomy course that essence of peppermint was an old remedy for digestive disorders, and since I had had so much trouble with my digestive tract, even when very young, I wondered if that was what I had been given. My therapist has a more prosaic guess; he's pretty sure it contained a lot of alcohol.

Mint soup was administered in a variety of ways. There were times it was given to me regularly, by the clock. I can see my mother cocking her wrist to read her watch, pouring out the liquid, and carefully lifting the spoon to my mouth. There were times it was given to me in the context of worry: a cool hand on my forehead, the spoonful of medicine, my mother rocking me and whispering that she did not want her little girl to be so ill.

Sometimes it was given to me because no one knew what else to do. My multiplicity began when I was three, but from my parents' perspective, my problem was that I was too "unruly" and too often ill. Not only did I suffer inflammations of the digestive tract, but I often fainted, broke out in strange rashes, or began vomiting for no apparent reason. I also was too "wild," I cried too easily, and, occasionally, I threw tantrums so severe I began to hyperventilate.

And then there were times I was given mint soup as a kind of punishment. On afternoons when I cried too much, when I simply could withstand no more of my brothers' torment, my mother would barge into my room, slam the door behind her, and say, "That's *enough!*" The spoon would click against my teeth, once, twice, three times as she dosed me. She would point to the bed, tell me to lie down, then close my curtains and tell me to get some *sleep.* Medication was a way to get rid of me.

Medicating children for emotional disturbances must be fraught with hazards, and certainly I carry some bitter memories and conclusions from those years when my mother would approach me with the sticky, familiar bottle with the doctor's handwritten label. Medication meant that I was bad. It meant that I was unable to control myself. It meant that I was unacceptable and needed to be corrected or remodeled through the addition of chemicals to my system.

Medication did mask what was going on in the house. After all, a kid who's on drugs can take a whole lot more than one who's not. I vividly remember one afternoon at the grocery store when I suddenly became restless, frantic, and irritable. If I remember the feeling at all correctly, it was similar to what I feel when I am about to switch personalities under duress. My mother gave me a little shake and hissed that she would never again take me anywhere without giving me mint soup first. I don't believe she held to that threat, but I do know that that bottle of medication went nearly everywhere I did during all my early years. And often I was grateful for it: after the sweet glisten of the burn as the medication went down came a thick and muffled calm, which I rather liked because then I would no longer be in trouble.

As I grew older, my circumstances and my medication changed. Grade six was the best year of my upbringing. I was president of my class, I was the pitcher of my playground softball team, I got straight A's. Best of all, my brothers were no longer attending the same school. I missed the fewest days of school, and seem to have had the fewest traumas. I also took the last of mint soup.

The following year, however, I moved on to the large junior-senior high school. Instead of being president of my class, I was one of a crowd of frightened seventh graders. Instead of being the pitcher of my team, I was in a gym class of sixty older, tougher girls. On Saturdays I had begun to ride, but five days a week, I was back within the scope of my brother Hank's vicious attentions. Problems quickly began, and soon my mother took me to see our new family doctor.

Dr. Wagner, who had been our physician for so many years, had died in a car accident. He had often gently probed into my life, and, although I had steadfastly refused to speak, he had tried, I later learned, to get my parents to take Hank to a psychiatrist. But the new doctor seemed to take it at my mother's word that I was a nervous wreck, and he had me do a little test: he gave me ten days' worth of Valium and ten days' worth of Librium. I was to take first one and then the other, and then come back for a follow-up. At my second appointment I was given a choice: Which did I prefer? The Valium or the Librium? Without a second thought, I chose the Librium. It was a kinder drug: I did not wake up in the morning with the nearly incapacitating headaches that resulted from the Valium.

In retrospect, this whole experiment strikes me as bizarre. The idea of asking a twelve-year-old to choose her drug, the idea of prescribing it so easily, without the least effort at some other kind of intervention, seems irresponsible and absurd. At the time, however, it did not seem strange in the least. All my life I had heard that there was something wrong with me, and by the time I was in junior high I had come to accept the explanation that my nervous system was much too delicate and that there was too fine an interaction between my mind and my body. Had I been born a hundred years earlier, I suppose I would have suffered from "the vapors."

I began to take medication by the clock, and continued to do so for several years. Breakfast was a bowl of cereal and a tranquilizer. Lunch at school was a bottle of milk, a piece of fruit, and a tranquilizer taken on the sly. Dinner was whatever my mother served and, of course, the little green and yellow capsule. I took another one before I went to bed, and I carried an extra supply with me everywhere I went, so that I could take an additional one as needed. The doctor preferred not to notify the school that I was on medication, and he had coached me carefully that I was to bring no more than I would need during the day, and he even suggested what I was to do if I was caught with the medication in my possession: I was to pretend I had just picked it up off the floor and say, "Look what I just found!" Two teachers did take me aside and gently ask if I was doing drugs: my pupils were nearly the size of dimes. At home, however, my use of medication was completely open. Whenever I seemed irritable, tired, out of sorts, or restless, my mother would always ask, no matter who was there to hear: "Have you remembered all your pills today?"

Several months after I began therapy, my psychologist first brought up the possibility that I should be taking medication. He made his case clearly: I was exhausted, I was hardly sleeping, I was depressed and wildly anxious all at once. He recommended that I take something for a while to help me cope, to knock the edge off the worst of the symptoms, and to help me get some rest. I remember his exact words: "You'll still be able to function, although perhaps not so well as you do now. But it's only for a little while."

And I remember my response: I thrust myself backward in my chair, shook my head, and did little but glower at him for the rest of the session. Every instinct I had lined up against medication.

He sighed, and looked sad and disappointed. "Okay," he said. "What you are doing is making a choice."

Which, translated into ordinary speech, is the clinical equivalent of "Don't blame me for what happens to you next."

Over the next years, he often brought up the subject of medication, and my answer was always the same. At times, he seemed quite concerned about my decision: "Any professional reviewing your case would question why you're not on medication."

When Prozac was first available, he handed me all the brochures and said, "I know what you're going to say, but it's my *job,* Jane, to keep you informed."

I glanced at the brochures, handed them back, and said, "Okay, thanks, I'm informed. You know my answer."

One day, four years into my therapy, I did finally say that, yes, I wouldn't mind a prescription of Xanax to calm me down after the bouts of screaming during the night. My psychologist moved so fast to dial my doctor's phone number I nearly laughed. It was a comfort to have the medication available, but it perhaps meant as much or even more to me that I took it very, very rarely.

Then, during March of the seventh year of my therapeutic process, my old self—wild, unhappy JJ, at precisely age fifteen— came hurtling back into my consciousness. It seemed exactly right that she should reemerge against the restless backdrop of changing seasons.

After the conference session during which Paul and Evelyn quizzed me relentlessly about my use of medication, I could not seem to shake their questions and their very obvious misgivings. I had developed far too much respect for them, since they led our group with such integrity, vigor, and fairness. And, for that matter, I could not shake them either. One or the other was often with me, delving into my life, asking about problems, helping me to see as many things as possible in a new light.

One evening Paul walked me around the conference grounds. I was feeling helpless and despairing. "Fine," he said in playful frustration. "Tell me your biggest problem."

I refused to speak. I had no idea what it was, except that I knew I couldn't talk about it. I shook my head.

"Okay," he said, still half-teasing. "Any problem, how's that?"

"College," I said promptly.

"What's the deal on college? You're a bright kid."

I made a face. "No, I'm not."

"Oh, god," he said. "So, you're not bright. Tell me what the problem is."

I scuffled moodily along next to him.

"You have to learn to talk," he said. "It's not going to hurt to tell me."

Suddenly the story came pouring out. I didn't want to attend the nearby college my parents had selected for me. Hank was already a student there, and Kip would soon be joining the freshman class. It was bad enough that next winter my tennis team would be practicing in the college's new field house. I desperately wanted to do what Josh had done: I wanted to break free and go away to school—as far away as possible.

I was wiping my eyes on my sleeves. Paul walked steadily in silence.

"So where do you want to go?" he said.

"I don't know," I muttered under my breath, then quickly added: "Away. Away is all that matters."

He nodded. "Sometimes that's important," he said. "What's the problem?"

"I can't."

"Tell me how you know."

"I just can't," I said. My hands had begun to shake.

"Have you *told* your parents you want to go away to school?"

I walked more and more slowly. It was too big a thing to tell anyone, I thought.

"I can't," I said finally.

"Why not?"

"You don't understand," I said. "You don't understand what

my family is like. They get what they want and what they want is for me to go to their school."

"Okay," he said. "That's what you *think.* Here's what I think. I think we need to dream up as many solutions to this as we can."

We spent hours sitting under a tree. Paul smoked one cigarette after another. I shredded blades of grass; it seemed dangerous even to be plotting the means to get my own way.

The list of ideas, all his, as he was trying to demonstrate there were more options than learned helplessness, was exciting and terrifying. His first suggestion was that I sit down with my parents and tell them why I wanted to go somewhere else to school. "I'm sure they love you," he said. "They'll probably understand." The ideas went on to include making such a hash out of the application to my parents' college that I couldn't possibly be accepted, to my enlisting the aid of a teacher or two, to his driving the hundred miles to sit down with my parents. "I'd come," he said. "This matters." His zaniest idea was that, since he happened to know the academic dean at this particular college, he would simply "see to it" that my application was rejected.

"You have to learn to *try* things," he kept saying. "You can't just keep giving yourself more reasons to take drugs. I'd be on tranquilizers too if I thought about the world the way you do."

I shredded more blades of grass, alternately sniffling and giggling.

Most of the free time I had at the conference, and some time that had originally been scheduled for other things, I spent with either Paul or Evelyn. While Paul tended to challenge me and put me on the spot, Evelyn tended to listen to me and draw me out.

By the end of the week, I had made a promise to each of them: not that I would give up Librium entirely, but that I would take as little of it as possible and only as a last resort. I was to brainstorm other ways of coping. I was not to assume everything was impossible or that I was weak and stupid. I was, especially, to keep in touch with them, by letter and by phone. Paul vowed that if things got too bad he would drive the hundred miles and have a meeting with my parents, and Evelyn gave me a list of every phone number where she could be reached.

Over the next few years, they kept their word. They talked to me on the phone, they read and answered my despairing letters. They gave me advice, they cheered me on, they answered questions, they read between the lines of my letters and listened hard for what I could not bring myself to say on the phone. Neither knew the full extent of my problems, but I didn't either, and I certainly felt better knowing that if my life really got unbearable I could call outside the family for help.

They so demonstrably kept their promises to remain a part of my life that the least I could do was keep mine. I would give up Librium. And, although that was not exactly what they had asked me to do, that's what I decided. It was probably easiest to go cold turkey and to be absolutist in my thinking; I was suffering enough without having to differentiate between when it would be okay to take medication and when it would not. All that seemed to matter to me was that if I slipped back into the old pattern, then I would let down two people who meant more to me than I could say.

It was tough going. Adolescence is bad enough: a time of such pain, intensity, and confusion. The prospect of being an adolescent multiple and giving up a prescription drug habit is almost more than I can comprehend. When fifteen-year-old JJ suddenly re-emerged, she was reliving parts of the experience: trembling hands, nervous tics, painful skin, and a nearly unbearable craving for medication. Mostly, I suspect I made it through by overeating and by creating still more selves and fragments. What I could not cope with, and there was plenty, I delegated to newly formed alters. Every time I contemplate meeting the personalities of my mid-to-late teenage years, I think it will be like attending a very large costume party to which everyone has come dressed as me.

Within a week after JJ's return into my adult consciousness, I decided to sit and read her journals. They were sketchy, and the gaps were notable, but I found myself deeply moved that she had wrestled so many words onto the page, notebook after notebook. It amazed me that she wrote at all, and amazed me too that such a sense of struggle as well as some accurate references to MPD were evident in those pages.

> *November 14:* There were seven trios in the competition to see who would go on and play at the regionals. The others were fantastic. Especially the one from Central High. They were so poised. . . . We congratulated them on winning —and they accepted the congratulations. When it was announced, none of us could believe it. . . . So on to regionals. We'll never win *that* one.
>
> *November 26:* Wrote a rather crude poem the other day. There is symbolism in it I didn't fabricate & it puzzles me. . . . I'm in pretty bad shape if I can't understand my own writing.
>
> *December 1:* I talked to Mr. Drummond . . . about a sentence in Latin. I was holding the paper & my hand was shaking. He asked was I nervous just then or was I always nervous.
>
> "I'm always nervous."
>
> "Once you're 21, we'll call it a nervous condition and give you a pill for it."
>
> "I have a pill for it."
>
> "What is it? Downey?"
>
> "It's Librium."
>
> "You can get hooked on that."
>
> "Yeah, well," I said.

December 3: Yesterday was my 15th birthday. P*** came and we played our flutes. . . . I was hoping to get \$ from the Phillipses but they didn't give me anything. . . . I wanted to buy a pair of blue jeans.

December 21: On Xmas Eve, we'll have the traditional argument, whether or not to exchange a few presents. Mother will go to bed at 7:30 and Father will mope. Kip and I will watch television, Josh will read in his room, and Hank will go out. I hate Christmas. . . . Maybe I can get a lot of homework done.

December 26: Christmas was all right. No major fights. . . . We have 15 inches of snow.

January 4: The new year and decade are four days old & it's no different. . . . I'm still frustrated, worried, and restless. School starts tomorrow & none of my presents have come. . . . J*** & I went skating last night.

January 14: Mr. Drummond's "social recluse" has turned out to be better at the [tennis] drills than even the senior girls. I was the only girl who could do every one. . . . On the way home, [he said] "You & Kip aren't much for talking."

Me: "Runs in the family."

Him: "Do you & Kip talk to each other often?"

Me: "Sometimes."

Him: "He & Josh & Hank are really close, huh?"

Me: "Yeah."

Him: "Where does that leave you?"

Me: "Lost."

Him: "Do all of you know your IQs?"

Me: "I don't want to. They're all smarter. . . ."

Him: "I wouldn't say that."

Me: "Ummm."

(I don't know what good it even does to write this.)

January 16: . . . lost the regional trio competition.

January 21: Tennis last night was really great. I wonder if it will ever be the same as riding.

January 24: I might as well put this into my diary too. F*** died of leukemia. It was merely waiting for death after Thursday. . . . She was a fairly good friend of mine. It's hard to believe she's dead, but I never cried for her. She'll never suffer like the rest of us.

January 25: I housecleaned my room. I had trouble throwing my childhood out. I kept two china horses & 2 carved ones. . . . I threw out 8 big shopping bags full of stuff. Somehow my room feels empty. . . .

February 26: My nerves are all uptight—what else is new? We had a meeting about F***'s memorial service. Everyone was up in arms. It's the same old story of there's only one way to worship God. If God's like that, I'll have no part of it. I came home from the meeting & completely broke down. It was the first time in my life that my father ever felt sympathy for something wrong.

February 28: My mother knows how bored I am. She and I are both worried that I'll give up & never even graduate. At this point, with almost five semesters to go, I'm at the peak of boredom Hank reached in his senior year.

March 4: Mr. Drummond told me he thinks it's amusing I get fantastic grades on my tests & no one really cares. Like my father, when I was in the 99 percentile in the nation—"Well, that's what you're supposed to get." Mr. Drummond said he's come to understand my quietness. Thank God.

March 17: I don't know if a lot has happened, but I feel as if I've been through a hell of a lot. I am more or less fed up with this place, although I don't know why. . . .

March 20: Tonight spring starts at 7:18. I've spent time

wandering through the fields & woods & thru the city & the more I wander the more restless I get.

March 26: I feel awful. . . . I've never felt so low. . . . It's such a beautiful day I want to get up . . . & run. I want only to get away from all of this domination. I think I'm losing my mind.

March 27: I haven't lost my mind yet. . . . I spent this morning walking & this afternoon playing tennis with J*** & reading. I don't understand why people tolerate me.

April 15: Today is the Vietnam Moratorium. No one is wearing an armband. It kind of died a not very violent death. . . . Talked to Mr. Drummond (who now calls me "JJ") (after Janis Joplin) (because of my hair).

April 19: . . . There's no one I want to be with. I *seem to be* best friends with J***. Really, I couldn't care less about J***. I'm bored with J*** or anyone else. . . . Whenever I talk to anyone, I have to react differently. The big problem is that I don't know who I am. . . .

April 24: Kip crashed one of the cars. *Dad's* car. Living here is like living on death row. The police told Dad he was probably doing 70 or 80.

April 26: I wish Kip were out of here. . . . My parents have grounded him until graduation. No phone, car, radio, stereo, or anything. I hate living here.

June 3: I've disregarded this journal as being . . . trite. . . . I'll never be a writer. . . . If I were going to be a writer, I would have strived to make this diary beautiful. . . .

When I closed the battered notebooks, I found myself wondering a little weirdly if she had any inkling how much of a boon her writings would be to all of us when she or I grew older. Had she reappeared at just this time because I needed her? Had I learned enough in seven years of therapy to help her with some of what pinned her down with such despair?

If I could have told her anything, I would have told her she wasn't crazy. I wasn't actually certain whether she would have found that a comfort or a disappointment. She was a voracious reader, but there was something in her admiration of great literary crazies that frankly made me nervous. What fifteen-year-old should pay so much attention to the suicide lore of great writers? She already knew the story of Virginia Woolf's death—but it would be another five years until I read a single word of her work, and four years more until I actually had some admiration for it. She read too much Fitzgerald; *Tender Is the Night* struck me as an unlikely favorite novel. And, for my comfort, she was far too taken with Zelda Fitzgerald's breakdown, with the fate of James Joyce's daughter, and, for that matter, with Seymour in the Salinger novels. It all made me a little nervous, although what I sensed in her was some admirable combination of resignation and bravado: If she was going to be crazy—and that fear was evident in her journals—then why not follow those who went down with pathos, wit, or high drama? Soon, however, I would be desperate for JJ's wildness and strength and weird brand of wisdom.

Like many people who have been traumatized as children, I often talked to my psychologist about "The Body"—which is to say, my body—as if it were some strange beast lurking on a faraway plane of existence. Even so, after four years of therapy, and of steadfastly refusing long-term medication, it began to occur to me, in some remote and terribly vague way, that I often felt groggy, or even ill, after I ate certain things.

My weight has fluctuated all my life. Ever since roughly the age of ten, I've been physically strong and active, but my adult weight has sometimes dropped as low as 111, when my ribs are visible through heavy sweaters, and has shot as high as 175, when I feel too humiliated to be seen in public. During those years, when my weight rose and fell, settling here and there for long periods of time, it always seemed to me that outside circumstances were somehow in control. The lowest weights occurred when I was reasonably happy, or when I had friends who were very fit. Higher weights seemed governed by factors I could never quite identify, never mind understand. I blindly accepted a variety of common wisdom about food: That I lacked character, discipline, and willpower. That I should eat three meals a day and skip all snacks, especially food at bedtime. That I should drink milk from time to time, bake my own whole-grain bread, and eat fruit and unbuttered popcorn for desserts and treats. I would turn out to be wrong on every count.

Of course, I repeatedly tried and failed to lose weight, and it was during one of these bouts, when I had cut my intake of sweets, milk, and breads, that I decided to "splurge" and have a sandwich and a glass of low-fat milk for lunch. I sat an extra while at the table, talking with some colleagues. I began to feel uneasy, stood up, and found that my chest was so tight I could hardly breathe. My peripheral vision was rapidly vanishing, too. I crept back to my office, closed the door, and within a few minutes was so depressed that I canceled the rest of my classes, headed home, and spent the rest of the afternoon crying hysterically.

But it was an odd kind of crying. It wasn't the painful crying that sometimes follows abreaction. It wasn't the crying that accompanies exhaustion, and it wasn't the crying that expresses grief over what has become of my life. Frankly, I felt as if I were on a barbiturate-induced crying jag.

The next time I saw my psychologist, I told him the story.

He stopped and thought. "Could be food allergies." He went over the principles of allergy and addiction, handed me a book, and suggested a little research.

Once again, I began to read, this time wading through books and articles written in the 1970s. Some of them claimed food allergies were the source of all ills—from schizophrenia to arthritis. Others viciously attacked food allergists because their writing was anecdotal rather than scientific. My therapist told me the drug companies had done a good job of squelching research into food sensitivities: "There's no money for the drug companies in a cure for arthritis." A nutritionist friend added that the food giants had also helped kill such research: "The conglomerates can't afford for the American public to give up wheat and sugar."

In the end, I decided that all that mattered would be what worked for me. Life seemed pretty damned anecdotal anyway. I settled on a simple plan: I would "challenge" any suspect foods, then methodically limit my intake of the culprits.

But first I had a week's vacation, and each day I was away, I treated all the kid parts I could muster to a different farewell treat: a cookie, an ice cream cone, yogurt, popcorn, and the like. On my return, I did the challenges: for seven days, I stopped eating wheat, sugar, eggs, corn, milk, and so forth. The first seventy-two hours were wild. I sweated. I coughed. I was anxious. I laughed and wept. Sleep was worse than usual. But by the seventh or eighth day, a remarkable change had taken place. My lows were not as low as I remembered them. I seemed less emotionally volatile, less in a constant wrestling match with moods and urges. What was more, I felt clear-eyed, energetic—and I did not crave food.

Still there were the challenges to get through: I had to return each food on the list to my diet and note all reactions, from coughs, sniffles, and sweats to irritability and hyperness. Milk nearly knocked me back to sleep. Gluten made it hard for me to breathe. Eggs triggered nausea and cold sweats.

What I eliminated from my daily menus were the common bugaboos for many Americans: milk, eggs, and the gluten found in wheat and other grains. The effects were profound and far-reaching. I lost twenty pounds in four or five weeks without any sense of deprivation. In fact, I was eating enormous quantities of food, but my metabolism seemed to have shifted into high gear.

I also had lots of energy—almost more than I knew what to do with. Several friends commented on the change in my skin and hair, and my eyesight became so sharp I sometimes felt like a cartoon character with X-ray vision.

Interestingly, despite the controversy in the literature, every health professional I knew confirmed the likelihood that I was indeed sensitive to certain foods. Tim added the list of foods to my medical records in case I was ever hospitalized, and my ophthalmologist told me that allergies were among the most common causes of blurry eyes. I wondered why no one had ever *said* anything, but both my psychologist and my nutritionist friend offered the same reason: most patients will not hear of such a radical dietary change.

People often have a horrified reaction when they find out what I am not allowed to eat, and they often remark on my "willpower." For me, however, knowing about my food sensitivities gave me a powerful tool in my struggle with MPD; my psychologist and I soon noticed that I had more energy, and therefore more capacity to have fun against the backdrop of the pain and misery of therapy. I also had more stamina: the abreactions did not take quite so much out of me. I seemed more cheerful and more clear-headed, and it began to seem to me that I could, by God, affect my own well-being.

At times, I was downright full of self-congratulation: See? I didn't need medication. All *I* needed was a quirky but balanced diet.

Two years into the regimen of food allergies, I was at home with a bad cold and a sore throat. I'd had far fewer colds and petty illnesses on my new diet, but this time I felt miserable enough to take a few days off from teaching. I slept a lot, and drank a lot of grapefruit juice. In one twenty-four hour period, I slid from despair to feeling alternately suicidal and full of rage. My frame of mind seemed downright dangerous. I was out of control and deeply frightened.

Through sheer good luck, my therapist and I were scheduled for our weekly phone conference. Unfortunately, we had one of those dreadful conversations in which I was fairly begging for him to help me while also instinctively attacking everything he said. I was so desperate and yet so reactive it wasn't possible for him to say anything that didn't infuriate me. The conversation, if it can be called that, went on for about ten minutes.

Finally he said, "Is it time for us to have a fight?"

I clung to the phone and began to sob. Then I took a deep breath and said, my voice flat and dead quiet: "I think there's something wrong with me." I paused.

He said nothing.

"Something chemical," I added.

He said, wryly, that if there hadn't been something chemical wrong with me earlier there probably was now: no one could be so despairing and so enraged without affecting their brain chemistry.

"Not *now*," I said. "I mean *before*. I swear I feel like I'm on drugs."

There was silence for a bit. "Jane," he said. "I want you to think carefully. Can you remember what you've been eating?"

"Nothing bad," I told him. "Just a lot of fruit juice."

"How much?" he said.

"Oh shit," I said.

Memories flashed before me: Gentle Mrs. White, slowly eating her full breakfast, each and every day. And the one day she did not, staggering around the kitchen bellowing at Mr. White. "It's her blood sugar," he had whispered. "You go on to the barn. I'll take care of her." Terrified, I had watched them both over my shoulder as I slipped out of the house.

"Blood sugar?" I asked my shrink, my voice a little horrified.

"I don't know," he said. "It's a possibility."

We decided I would cut the fruit juice, eat some protein, take some Xanax—and look into blood sugar as soon as I got over my cold.

I wish I could say that I dealt with hypoglycemia like a trouper, but I certainly did not. All the sullenness, all the resentment I had not felt about the food sensitivities engulfed me now. I had been through one major dietary upheaval. That was goddamn enough. This wasn't *fair.* I couldn't do it. I wouldn't do it.

"You'll do it when you're ready," said my therapist.

I felt trapped. On one hand, if I continued with my current diet, I continued to court blood-sugar related mood swings, and I already had enough problems. On the other hand, dealing with hypoglycemia was going to mean a lot of work and a lot of upheaval—and I already had enough work and upheaval.

Grudgingly, I headed back to the library. Fine, I thought grumpily, I'll just find some plan and do exactly what it tells me. Maybe it wasn't a new regimen I was objecting to—maybe it was just having to *think* about what to eat that was getting on my nerves. Session after session with my therapist was consumed by discussions of diet. His reading about MPD was of no help. Yes, he said, there was some interest in the relationships among MPD, body chemistry, eating disorders, and diet. But no one knew anything yet. Researchers were only just beginning to note the high correlation between a history of trauma and allergies, but there was no understanding yet of causal relationships. "Write about your experiences," he told me. "You know as much as anyone at this point." It's hard to sulk and feel flattered at the same time —but I managed that too and slouched back to my reading.

Hypoglycemia is a kind of medical chimera. It is either the cause of every ill and ache known to modern man—or a figment of ignorant and untutored minds. As a result, what's available to read is at best haphazard. And whatever one reads in one source is contradicted in the next. Eat a lot of protein; don't overdo the protein. Eat a lot of fat; get as thin as possible. Balance on the verge of constant hunger; always have a snack within reach. There were days when I toyed with the idea of calling my nutritionist friend and simply begging her to write me a diet. But I knew that she would just tell me again that, in the end, the best diets are formulated by educated patients. She would give me more to read, she would answer my questions, but she would never just tell me what to eat.

Tim, when consulted, simply confirmed a diagnosis of "functional hypoglycemia." He knew that I needed whatever boost I could get to carry on with my professional life and struggle on with therapy. He gave me some handouts, then folded his arms and regarded me. "You'll just have to experiment," he said. "If you keep at it, you'll figure out what works for you."

In the end, I came up with a variety of principles: I had to eat every three hours, in roughly equal amounts. I could have no sweets of any kind. I would try the extreme diet first and even eliminate fruit. Every meal had to include some protein. And I would eat substantial protein just before going to bed.

It didn't take long to incorporate the principles into my life. I divided up my meals, bought an obnoxious watch with a timer to remind me when it was time to eat, and loaded my glove compartment and office desk with nonperishable snacks. As recommended by one book, I even prepared all six meals the night before, on the theory that when one's blood sugar is low, one tends to be too stupefied to eat properly.

I wish I could say that it worked.

Granted, there were two major benefits: My sleep disorders decreased by 75 to 85 percent, since, apparently, a brain deprived of glycogen is more likely to have distressing dreams. And, during the day, for a while at any rate, my moods were more level.

In other ways though, my life spun out of control. I did stick to the schedule of eating every three hours, and I even avoided everything I was supposed to avoid. Sadly, though, I had to cut still more foods from my diet and that meant that all The Kids' special treats were eliminated: no granola bars, no whole-grain cookies, no fresh fruit. Soon I began feeling anxious as hell, and I started gaining weight. It's one thing to snack on fresh fruit or carefully measured whole grain snacks: it's another to snack on peanut butter, soy cheese, and nuts.

It's hard to say exactly what happened. I felt ill at ease. I was gaining weight. The Kids were miserable, I was miserable. And yet I could see that—even if only for the benefit of improved sleep—it was wise for me to be on this diet. Something was wrong, and I kept hoping I would soon see things differently, putting this slight additional problem into some perspective.

Finally, we came to the end of a school year. During the summers, I have more time to take myself in hand and accomplish major psychological tasks. I was absolutely determined to get on a strict 1800-calorie-a-day diet even if I had to count the sunflower seeds one by one. I would eat exactly what I needed to eat, and if The Kids had to suffer and be miserable and if I had to suffer and be miserable, so be it. Ploughing straight through this problem was the only thing I knew to do. I had done it before and I would do it again.

The Kids cried a lot during those few days and I felt like an ogre. Hadn't they given up enough already? But my psychologist and I talked about the fact that they had to learn there were other ways to feel okay than by eating. And I had to prove to myself that I had the strength to pull this off. For the first five or six days, I balanced my misery with a sense of grim virtue.

And then one day I came home from riding, walked into the house, and soon found myself, boots and all, sprawled on the couch. It's unclear to me how much time passed before I began to realize what was happening: my thoughts were caroming through my head at about a thousand times their normal speed. Ideas flashed by like skyrockets. One idea touched off another and

another and another. I felt absurdly powerful: I could think any
thought. I could get any perspective I ever needed on myself, on
those around me, on the world. I could think of a million things
to do—but I could do none of them because each was followed
instantly by another.

I lay there on the couch from the middle of the day until
dusk. Abruptly I curled up in a ball and began to tremble. Something terrible was wrong with me. In time, I dragged myself to
the kitchen, forced myself to eat, took a little Xanax, then passed
out on my bed. I felt as if I had had a glimpse of the inner lining
of the universe, as if I had seen the very turnings of the stars, or
as if I had witnessed the firing of each and every synapse in my
brain. I was utterly drained, and badly shaken.

The next day, I walked into my therapist's office and was
barely sitting down when I began to tell him what had happened.

His face softened and he simply looked at me for a long while.
His eyes take on a certain roundness when he is at his most compassionate. For a moment, he fingered the arm of his chair, then
said: "Well, it's not written anywhere that you can only have one
problem."

Quietly, he asked questions: about Hank's history, about other
family members, about past experiences with this phenomenon,
about any patterns I could discern. We sat and talked and, cau-
tiously, over the next few weeks, slowly came to a conclusion.

What happened next was even harder than finding out I am
a multiple. I'd had some suspicions of MPD, and even before that
diagnosis I'd had time to comprehend, time to grieve, time to
work on my repertoire of jokes about multiplicity. But this was
a fresh and shocking wound; I found it terrifying. It didn't seem
fair, and it didn't seem manageable. MPD is curable. I'd had no
idea what that meant. Curable meant: Be tough, work hard, have
faith, look at things head on, *you'll get there.* But this was not
curable. This was controllable, druggable. I could wail and I could
protest, but with every passing week, it was more and more un-

deniable: I have chemically induced patterns of euphoria, wired-ness, and rapid thought interspersed with crashes and depressions. In short, cyclothymia. And no amount of therapeutic courage would ever change that.

Soon after this second diagnosis, fifteen-year-old JJ first came back onto the scene. Within a week of her arrival, my therapist spent some time with her.

Her hands searched in vain for her long wavy hair. She examined her hands, her clothes. She stared around the office.

"Do you know where you are?" my therapist asked gently.

She stared at him.

He introduced himself, then identified the town and the state.

"That's cool," she said.

"I'm a psychologist," he went on. "We can talk about whatever you'd like."

She shrank back into her chair, and looked nervously at the door. "Is my mother out there?" she demanded, her voice frightened and sullen.

"No," he said. "You're here alone. Your mother is hundreds of miles away."

She stared at him. "Are you sure?"

"We can go out and look in the waiting room."

She thought a minute, frowned, then shook her head. Above all else, she would not embarrass herself.

"Do you know Paul and Evelyn?" she wanted to know.

"No," my therapist said, almost a little sadly. "I'm sorry I don't. They helped you a lot though, didn't they?"

"Yeah," JJ said. "They're my *friends*," she added sullenly, as if he might take exception in some way.

"They're good friends," he said.

"I'm not taking drugs," she announced abruptly. Clearly she had somehow gotten wind of the decisions that lay ahead in the treatment of cyclothymia.

My therapist paused. "What makes you think you'd have to do that?"

"I don't know," JJ muttered. "I'm just not going to do that."

"This is your first time here," he said gently. "Let's take our time."

She thought, she jiggled her foot, her hand went to her shoulder to smooth her long-gone hair. Suddenly her gaze fixed on the dog I'd brought to that appointment. He was dozing on the floor.

"What a great dog," she said. "Is he yours?"

"Mmmm, no," said my therapist.

JJ got down on her knees and stroked the dog.

"I wish I could have a dog," she said, sighing sadly. "My mother won't let me. I'm only allowed to have cats."

"Actually, mmm, that *is* your dog."

JJ's gaze never left the dog.

"Oh no," she said. "I don't have a dog. I'm not allowed. You're really lucky," she went on. "He's wonderful. Do you bring him all the time? To your . . . your . . . office, I mean."

He tried again. "Really," he said. "That dog lives where you live now. If you check during the week, I think you'll be surprised."

She gave the dog another pat, then got up off her knees. "You're really lucky," she said again. "If I could have a dog, I'd get one just like yours."

"Mmmm," said my therapist. "We're almost out of time. But you can come back again."

"Will you bring your dog?" she said. She gave him a pleading look. "Don't tell my mother that I'm here," she begged. Then her gaze narrowed. "I'm not taking drugs," she said fiercely. "I promised that I wouldn't anymore."

"I know," he said quietly. "I know."

"We're not takin' med'cine," The Kids began to wail at every opportunity. Clearly word was out within my system. As the weeks went by, my moods—my revolutions per minute, really—shifted erratically. I didn't mind the depression so much as I minded the days when I felt so wired I could barely concentrate. Often I felt as if I might jump out of my skin, and I would get more and more exercise in a futile attempt to wear myself out. For several days, I would have to force myself to bed, often lying in the dark with my brain humming along at an impossible clip. At these times, I seemed to think truly remarkable things, and once in a while, I seemed to do some important integrative work, leaping forward and grasping new concepts. But soon the crash would come, and in a period of twelve hours or so, I would go from feeling as if I had the world's fastest, although perhaps most impractical, brain to feeling as if life was entirely too much work to contemplate living one day more.

I couldn't seem to solve this problem in my usual way. The situation was too complex. It reminded me of a word problem in high school algebra with far too many variables. Given multiplicity, food sensitivities, hypoglycemia, cyclothymia, a gang of small children terrified of more med'cine, and a teenager stubbornly refusing drugs, find the calmest way to live while maintaining physical health. Again and again, I had the sense that a mind thinking in the same old way wasn't going to solve this one.

"It will take a leap of some kind," said my therapist.

"Give me a hint?" I said, my voice tinged with desperation.

He shrugged. "I have no hints," he said. "I just don't know. You'll find your own way. You always have."

For once, I thought, I just wanted him to tell me what to do.

One day, it occurred to me to simply go to my appointment and beg for medication. I didn't care about my scared and touchy selves. I didn't think I could take any more cyclothymia, much less any more fretting over whether or not to take medication.

I didn't do it, but I did go in and tell him what I'd been thinking. He smiled at the irony of my actually asking—never mind begging—for medication. And he knew me well enough to know that I had lofted the idea to find out his thoughts on the matter. I had begun to notice he'd been providing me with information, and encouraging me to read, but refraining from offering an opinion of any kind.

His opinion, now that I had deliberately asked for it, was utterly ironic. "Right now, Jane," he said, "I can't say I'd be in favor of medication." He paused. "In fact," he said, watching me with care, "I'm entirely opposed. It's a bad idea. For now, at least."

I was shocked.

He went on to explain that, while we could try Lithium for the cyclothymia, there was no telling what it would do to the integrative process. "You're making blinding progress," he assured me. "I don't want to jeopardize that."

I couldn't believe he thought my current state of misery and turmoil was progress in any way.

"Prozac is out," he continued.

I must have looked amazed.

He smiled. "You've fought me tooth and nail about Prozac for years. I've come to respect your decision. I think it's been the right one for you. There's a reason for your refusal. I can't say I completely understand it, but we'd be wise to honor it."

I slumped in my chair. I felt as if, in my struggle over these last years, I'd been plotting my own defeat.

Out of the blue, I said, "I haven't been an easy patient, have I?"

He began to speak, as if to reassure me otherwise, then he stopped and thought. "Honestly?" he said. "No. You've never been an easy patient. But you're doing what you have to do, and I respect that. It's okay."

I sat for a while, mulling.

"What am I *supposed* to do?" I said.

He looked at the calendar. "In one year," he said, "let's have this discussion again. Meanwhile, I want you to get to know the cyclothymia. And we'll have to get to know more about your experiences with medication."

I sighed. A year? At least I had a concrete answer. It was now my job to wait and think.

Grudgingly, I reexamined my history with mint soup and Librium. It might be true, I came to admit, that childhood medication had helped me cope. It allowed me to get some rest, helped me to attend school more often than I might have, and it perhaps decreased my problems in adulthood. Perhaps by sleeping away some of those long, drugged afternoons, I was kept, even for a little while, out of the path of my brother Hank. Perhaps the muffling effect of the sedative saved me from creating and later having to integrate even more selves.

I could also see that my early experiences with drugs, and my later promise to Paul and Evelyn, effectively protected me against the use of street and recreational drugs. I remember classmates drinking Robitussin at high school dances, smoking pot, dropping acid—and I actively wanted none of it. In college, far too many people "goofed" on one another—lacing joints and junk food with acid and other drugs. Drugs were everywhere, and although I mastered the etiquette of admiring clever pipes, creative roach clips, and hand-painted hookahs, I slipped away whenever they were in use. However, had I not had my early drug experiences, I can just imagine how seductive and soothing dope and other drugs might have seemed in my late teens and early twenties.

On the other hand, I'd missed a lot growing up on medication. Shortly after I entered this reflective period, I watched a friend's four-year-old daughter storm out of the kitchen because she could not have a cookie in the last ten minutes before dinner. She tore up the stairs, stopped at the top, and screamed that she hated her mother. Then she slammed the door to her bedroom. My friend looked at me and said, "I hope you're not horrified." I was, but not at her saying no to the cookie or at her little girl's outburst.

I was realizing that I'd completely missed one of the tasks of childhood: to feel a wide range of intense emotions, to learn that those emotions pass, and to learn how one is ultimately to behave when one feels the emotion of the moment. A few minutes later, Julie was sitting in her mother's lap, sniffling and giggling. But here I was, thirty years later, talking to a therapist two hours every week.

At the urging of my psychologist, I dug deeper and deeper into my own resistance to medication. The Kids were mad and scared, JJ adamant and hostile, but I held my own strong, and perhaps idiosyncratic, opinions, too.

On a simple and perhaps selfish level, I had to admit that I believed that medication would have dulled or blunted my perceptions. What I felt, I would not have felt so intensely. What I recalled would have more quickly passed from my mind. It was horrifying to admit, but I wanted all the pain and upheaval to be worth the while. I wanted to be a witness, as cognizant and clear-eyed as was humanly possible. I wanted to be fully present, fully aware, fully attentive to my own process. I didn't want it to happen behind my back; I didn't want it muffled, skewed, or softened. It struck me as a rare opportunity and one that, since I was stuck with it, I might as well pay close attention to.

I also believed I would have sacrificed a few weird but pronounced benefits to medication. Over time, it had become evident that my deep depression could be seen in two ways. Depression is a dark and dangerous illness. Nonetheless, depression seemed to serve a function in my process. It was as if I somehow went underground, burrowing deep into myself: brooding, mulling, molting. And each time I emerged from a depression, I was profoundly changed. I was often reminded of Persephone: while she is yanked underground, the world above turns lifeless, cold, and dreary. For me, each reemergence from depression was into an utterly new spring, and I could only guess that, while medication would have made those times less dark and less cold, it would also have dulled the brilliance of the next season.

Medication also, I was willing to guess, might have prevented me from discovering my sensitivities to foods, my hypoglycemia, and probably even my cyclothymia. Perhaps that would have been a blessing, but I knew myself well enough to know that I would have felt betrayed if I had finished a course of therapy and eased off medication—only to find myself suffering the vagaries of food sensitivities and all the rest.

Most important, and perhaps most revealing, was admitting that mine was a fight to discover and reclaim my own identity. I needed to be introduced to hacked-off parts of myself, I needed to go open-eyed into the dark corners of my soul, I needed to meet the monsters who also bore the name of Jane or JJ, and I needed to protect and nurture countless hurt and terrified children. I also needed to prove to myself that I was not weak and I was not stupid, and so it meant the world to me to undertake my therapy on the strength of my courage, brains, and intuition.

But I uncovered a host of troubling questions.

If I decided to take medication at the end of a year, how would I ever broach it to The Kids who had been punished with mint soup or to JJ, who fought the hard battle of dependency?

Why did I resent that Prozac was the current first choice of medication for dissociators? Did I feel belittled by its trendiness, its incredible commonness?

Would medication really mean a loss of self? In the quest for self, which is one definition of integration, would medication detour, deintensify or speed up the process?

Was I simply a coward, too frightened even to undertake a controlled trial of medication?

What did I really want, anyway? If I could have designed my

own medication, it would ever so delicately have removed the highest highs and lowest lows of cyclothymia. I did not want a medication that some writers claimed could revolutionize the self. I also wanted a private drug, one that would not be detected by my eagle-eyed colleagues in the nursing department, who often guess, over lunch, at the medication taken by students based on the merest shifts of affect or behavior.

And yet, when I began to read, much of what I came across alarmed me.

It alarmed me to read that childhood trauma is now believed to alter permanently the chemistry of the victim's brain. Was I therefore clinging not to myself but to some vestigial damage?

It alarmed me to read that the brain, like the body, is considered by some psychobiologists to lose its "biologic capacity for health" as it ages.

It alarmed me to think that my stubbornness and my fears—given the possibility that medication would prevent my descent into the deepest chasms of depression—was putting me at a greater risk for suicide. Was my refusal therefore the strange obverse of an addict's: ruining my life by refusing to take, rather than refusing to give up, drugs?

It alarmed me to hear my nutritionist friend—a person who never reaches for medication first—ask me gently whether I've considered that all this struggle without the buffer of a good drug could be worsening my health. Was I aware, she asked, that I might be shortening my life because of the terrible cumulative toll of my disorder and my therapy?

It alarmed me, and suddenly saddened me, to think of the added worry and burden I had caused others. One day, as I once again wrestled with the urge to kill myself, I heard my psychologist remind me, perhaps for the hundredth time, that I could reach him by phone twenty-four hours a day. And suddenly I wondered how hard my decision not to take medication had been on him and others.

I had few answers. All I seemed to know for certain was that the discovery of cyclothymia, and the decision that would someday be made about medication, had prompted the return of JJ at fifteen. I was in desperate need of her willfulness, her wit, her determination. I was teetering on a dangerous brink, harried by my fears and my dilemmas, and terrified of all that lay ahead of me. I felt completely crazy.

Instantly I leaped to reassure JJ that she, at fifteen, was *not* crazy. Multiplicity and cyclothymia are not craziness. An overload perhaps, even an absurd overload—but not madness. But, if she wasn't crazy, easy logic had it that I wasn't either. Overwhelmed, frightened, outnumbered, uncertain beyond belief—but not crazy. Sane enough, in fact, to finally admit that perhaps bravado, doggedness, grit, even a romantic belief in my own indomitable spirit might not be enough.

What would happen? I read and read, I pondered in my journal, I agonized, I lost sleep, I couldn't stop talking about medication. I kept wanting to line up my selves and tell them to grow up or else.

"Take your mind off it," my therapist finally said. "You should know that conscious thought will only get you so far. We said a full year had to pass before we'd make a decision. It's only been a few months."

I sighed. He was right. As usual, I was in too much of a hurry.

"How'd you manage without medication at fifteen?"

I frowned.

He reminded me that as a fifteen-year-old I'd had a lot of grit and determination.

I resisted the impulse to point out that I no longer was a teenager.

"So tell me what you did," he said. "I'm sure you didn't just sit around and *think*."

"I guess I found things to do," I said after a while.

"Like what?"

I shrugged. "I don't know. Friends, tennis, music, distractions."

"Getting any ideas?" he said smiling. "Personally," he said, "I'd vote for distractions. What was your major distraction back then?"

I thought a while, then blushed and shook my head. "I'm not sure I'm ready to talk about *that*," I said.

He stopped and thought, then gave me a shrewd look. "Talk about that?" he wanted to know. "Or talk about *him?*"

I sighed dramatically, feigning an exaggerated world-weariness. "Him," I said. "Of course." Then, facetiously, I added: "Drugs or sex. What else is there to talk about?"

MORE GIRL STUFF

 MY DISTRACTION WAS A BOY named Mark. It was spring of my senior year, and I met him, a freshman at the local state college, on a day I goddamn well didn't care what anyone thought about me. I had just been rejected by my first-choice college. Later I came to see that the Canadian university, where at least some of my courses would be taught in French, had probably done me a huge favor by rejecting my application, but at the time I was disappointed and quickly adopted a kind of wild, cutting humor. I couldn't afford to allow myself to care about the rejection and, as a result, when I met Mark, my usual compulsion of projecting personalities to suit those around me had been temporarily disconnected. I didn't care what the blasted college thought and I didn't care what anyone else thought, either. So Mark met a close approximation of the real me.

I hesitate here, knowing the risks and clichés of writing about one's first brush with love, and yet what happened between Mark and me would have enormous significance over the years.

As we began to date, I found it quite startling that someone could actually *like* me without all the effort I usually had to sink into relationships. Mark was not at all athletic, so he had no interest in swimming or playing tennis. Instead, we hung out, went to movies and concerts, drove around, walked a lot, and talked and talked and talked. Soon I began to glimpse the possibility that I might not be completely stupid. Mark was terribly bright —I could see that—and by reflection, although I felt inferior, it was clear I could keep up with him in perception, wit, and repartee.

Very quickly, my attachment to Mark brought the first adult confusion over sex. We were both virgins, but our physical intimacies steadily increased. And I was bewildered. I liked the physical contact and affection, I liked how we felt about each other, I liked the closeness and the laughter and the intensity of what was happening. None of it seemed sick, disgusting, or depraved. But, in a split second, I would switch from being affectionate and warm to terrified and watchful. And since Mark was attentive, he could read the quick surge of panic, the sudden rigidity of my muscles, and the abrupt fixed quality of my eyes. He was the first person to realize something had happened to me and, although I was vague and incoherent, he soon guessed it had something to do with my brothers.

I can only imagine how it felt to be a nineteen-year-old college freshman holding a nearly naked girl who, in a split second, changes from responsive to half-comatose, but Mark was careful and quiet, often trying to get me to talk. Despite the abrupt and predictable panics that forestalled intercourse, we grew increasingly closer until we finally decided that it would be a little ridiculous for me to go a thousand miles away to college in the fall. The separation seemed to us unbearable; maybe I could find a college a little nearer.

But then the end of the academic year arrived, and Mark headed to a distant city for a summer internship. The deal was that he would write or call first; he wasn't sure of a telephone or address. I meanwhile took my last high school exams, went to graduation—and waited.

At first, it was easy to explain to myself why there'd been no contact, but as the summer wore on with still no word, even after letters I'd written to his parents' address were neither returned nor answered, I drew my own conclusions, and, at summer's end, headed off to college a thousand miles away. I would gladly have slunk halfway across the globe.

One of the hallmarks of my life, and certainly one of my handicaps, has been my facility for drawing subconscious but powerful conclusions based on certain experiences or events. These conclusions are then neatly turned into promises I keep with a startling fervor, considering that I am seldom aware of either the conclusion or the promise on a conscious level. Only now can I see that I drew two simple and what would turn out to be disastrous conclusions from Mark's silence.

The first was that Mark was the only person who had ever really known what I would later come to view as a genuine internal self. But he had rejected that self, and that, I swore, would never happen again. No more self-revelation; no more rejection.

The second was that if I hadn't been so terrified of sex, he wouldn't have left. I would therefore shed, or at least disguise, my fear.

For a long while, the following years were shrouded in a traumatic haze. When my psychologist asked me to write a chronology of those times, I could remember where I went to school, what I studied, and what part-time jobs I had, but memories of men were mostly quick glimpses in the periphery of consciousness. With some effort, I managed to remember who I knew, and even jumble them into sequence, but beyond that, my recollections remain sickening and erratic.

Interestingly, from what I could tell, I was not promiscuous. Plenty of college classmates had far more boyfriends and lovers than I, and in far more rapid succession. Often I seemed glad to revert to my childhood refusal to see myself and those around me in terms of gender. Usually I was glad to be alone, because then my head seemed clearer and life seemed less confusing. But when I had a boyfriend or a lover, I remained true to my internal, self-imposed dictum: no man ever again so much as glimpsed my real self. Instead, when I met someone, I instinctively manufactured personae to match his requirements or to fulfill his expectations. This behavior would continue until my life changed course in some way and I suddenly had no need for my current companion, or until the man made some kind of move that threatened my real, hidden self. Abruptly, I would leave him.

In one way, I had enough power in my relationships to fulfill my promise: no one ever rejected me again. And yet, in other ways, I was completely powerless: I seemed a complete stranger to myself and to everyone around me. I didn't know I was multiple, automatically creating selves who hid my feelings, likes, dislikes, ambitions, heartaches, and opinions. All I knew was that my romantic past seemed to include half a dozen smitten and then angry and disillusioned men, whose interest in me I could never quite explain.

As to sex, I coldbloodedly set out to be educated and desensitized. What happened, I can see now, is that I created a self or selves who coped with sexual matters. I also know that after losing Mark I was bent on a course of subtle self-destruction. I hardly cared what became of me, and simply, within limits I can sense but have yet to discover, adopted the sexual tastes and practices of my partner. They were heartbreaking and pathetic years, and I dread their full integration into my everyday working memory.

I did see Mark again. I was home from college, and one evening Mark's old roommate called and invited me out for a drink. Jim and I had struck up an easy friendship, and, after some vacillation, I agreed to meet him. Just as I sat down in the little darkened booth, Mark showed up, too. We were stunned to see each other. Jim, it turned out, had staged this little reunion without telling either of us his intention.

I remember Mark stopping at the table, looking down at me, and bursting into tears. "I'm sorry," he said. "I'm such a coward."

After a few minutes, Jim fled in embarrassment. Mark and I

sat and talked. The old bond was still there, instant, palpable, and electric, but it was all too much for Mark. Recently I have learned that I share a trait with other multiples that I must keep an eye on: because of what I have survived, I sometimes respond with an intensity of emotion that is far too great for ordinaries. I can see now that I probably *was* too much to cope with: too fierce, too forthright, by turns too frightened and too bold, too needy and too giving.

Still, we saw each other from time to time. It seemed impossible to keep away from one another, impossible not to talk long into the night, but also impossible to resume a physical relationship. Neither of us was willing to take that risk. He wouldn't chance the intensity; I wouldn't chance rejection.

In the end, I packed my bags, headed to another region of the country, and resigned him to some sore and troubled corner of my memory. I thought about him sometimes, but never talked about him and never thought I'd hear from him again. A year and a half passed.

And then a letter, much-forwarded, arrived. Mark had been seriously ill. He was better, the doctors believed he would survive, but he wrote that the world seemed very different to him now. He missed me. He needed me—but he would understand if I couldn't or wouldn't come running.

In time, I wrote back, and, after a few months, spent a vacation with him.

He had lost weight, lost some of his vision, and lost every shred of his optimism. He was despairing and depressed. But I was there, bag in hand, and although almost twenty years have passed, I have yet to sort out what actually happened. It began well, ended badly, and somewhere in the middle his mental state and my multiplicity wreaked a lot of havoc.

Within hours of my arrival, we were back on a weirdly familiar footing, laughing not so much at old jokes but at new ones, comparing notes on our lives, talking about the week, about the huge gamble we were taking. But as the days passed, it would turn out that his medication left him impotent, and that his black despairing mood was so deeply frightening to me that I was soon projecting personalities. I can't say he knew I was a multiple, but he had to sense there was something false about me. I sensed it in myself, and sat up one night alone, drinking wine, wondering what on earth was happening. I desperately wanted to make him happy, something I now know is truly offensive to the genuinely depressed. I was also so afraid of his despair and of the possibility that I might lose him again that I was probably sending out close approximations of myself, airbrushed of anything that might offend him, yet ironically preventing genuine closeness and companionship. In the end, he threw me out on the grounds that he would ruin my life if I stayed. Certainly there were other reasons, too, but in the long run it didn't matter: he had rejected me a second time.

While I was in college, I was somehow protected from making permanent and potentially disastrous decisions by my determination to finish my degree before I did anything else with my life. But after graduation, I was somewhat lost, having practically no idea of where I wanted to live or what I wanted to do.

One afternoon, I had stopped at a store to pick up some cans of fresh tennis balls. While waiting my turn at the register, I stood mulling over a brochure about a new design in tennis shoes. Someone cleared his throat. I glanced up. A man standing next to me told me the new shoes weren't worth the money. He went on to say that he coached various sports at a prep school, and that they had tried the shoes and found they simply didn't hold up well.

A new clerk was running the register and in the long delay, while the young man laboriously rang up purchases, the prep school coach and I began to chat. We talked about tennis and about the weather, made a few tentative jokes, then when our purchases had finally been rung up, we went out and spent the rest of the afternoon drinking coffee.

Over the next weeks, we saw each other often: swims, bike rides, walks, and the like. I found him attractive; he was older, he seemed worldly, funny, bright, established, and, to my amazement, he seemed interested in me, a very green college graduate.

One evening, he invited me to a quick dinner at his apartment; afterwards, we had tickets for a play. I went to dinner, expecting to be taken to a play; sex was not in my plans for the evening. But Jack seemed somehow different, and after dinner, he mused that there were better things to do than go see plays. I felt what I had so often felt in childhood: powerless and stupid, as if I'd walked into an obvious trap I'd been too ignorant to foresee. And then I vanished. My worldly, sharp-tongued companion fully seized on my pliancy, and I got pregnant.

What began that evening, and what was to last the entire course of our relationship, was that I hardly ever remembered having sex with him. I simply panicked, switched off, and eventually came to, feeling dazed and disoriented. I have yet to untangle this part of my past: Why did I go back after that first evening? Why did I stay? How did I find the nerve to leave at the very end? I have no answers to these questions yet, but I have come to view Jack with disgust because, although he couldn't be expected to know he was dealing with a multiple, he should have recognized my passivity and amnesia and guessed something was amiss.

He was astonished when I told him I was pregnant, but he confided that in a way he was relieved; he was glad to know he was capable of fathering a child. I was a little stunned by his remark, and felt like a human petri dish, but he was quite enthused about the prospect of becoming a parent.

I was not. I was experiencing nothing short of sheer terror. The sources of that terror are only gradually growing clear to me. One very simply was that, having grown up in the house with no sex, it was absolutely unthinkable for me to tell my parents I was pregnant. I also felt more trapped than I ever had in my life. Suddenly I had to deal directly with my body and I had to deal with time; this was not a problem I could deny or outwait. I also suspect that my nonfemale selves must have gone into a tailspin. Very quickly I went from trying to adopt Jack's enthusiasm about having a child to planning to commit suicide. I was very close to killing myself, when I suddenly realized I could save my own life by having an abortion. It was either me or the pregnancy.

I made the phone calls, and in a strange surge of honesty, told Jack exactly what I thought: I could not have this child. If anyone tried to make me, I would kill myself. Somewhere deep inside, there seems to be a line I will not cross, a self whose needs I will not, in the end, violate. Jack was taken aback, but then admitted he was beginning to realize that perhaps he wasn't ready to be a father.

And so I had an abortion. I remember very little of it, except that the women around me were full of fear and sorrow. But I felt as if I were going to be freed from a death sentence.

Pure instinct drove my decision to have an abortion, but during the following years, as various friends decided to have their first children, that instinct never slackened: I recoiled at the mere thought of having a child.

From the time I was very young, my parents and my older relatives often talked about what it was going to be like when I had children of my own. Why have a daughter, or a granddaughter for that matter, if she is not going to bear children? Why indeed? On the simplest level, my childlessness has been a bid for psychic freedom. If I do not have children, in some small way I get to be myself rather than a female robot obeying the family dictates for my reason for being.

My mother, however, takes my refusal personally, and her anger is unrelenting. At one point, she was showing me some things she was wrapping as baby gifts for Kip and his wife Sally's first child. I commented on how odd it was that she was sending them a silver baby cup. We hadn't had such cups when we were young.

I picked up the little piece and examined it. "It looks old," I told my mother, and with a finger traced the heavily ornate monogram.

My mother snatched it out of my hands.

"Of course it's old," she said. "That was Kip's."

"Kip's?" I said. "How come I didn't have one?"

"What makes you think you didn't?" she snapped. She glared off into the distance. "Each of you four children had a silver cup. After a certain point, I packed them away. I planned to send them as a surprise when your first children came. Hank and Josh already have theirs. And now Kip."

She lifted the little cup and I reached out my hand to examine it again. My mother swaddled it in tissue paper and tucked it into the box.

I asked if I could see my own baby cup.

"That cup is none of your business," my mother told me angrily. "You never had children," she hissed at me. "There are plenty of family things I will never tell you."

But I also do not have children because I am afraid of them. As a child, I feared other children because of the things my brothers and the neighborhood boys did to me, but as I grew older I remained frightened of children for different reasons. For one, I couldn't stand it when they were upset; their screams and cries seemed to echo in the caverns of my skull and rake up and down my spine. In retrospect, I'd guess that I was connecting the outside sounds with the tamped-down memories of my own early childhood—but I avoided young children because I felt anxious and fearful in their presence.

Now, although I have come to like children—a few particular children, anyway—I find that I am still anxious when around them. I cannot seem to avoid comparisons between the child before me and what was happening to me at that particular stage in my own history. It horrifies me to see how very young and vulnerable the ages of three, four, five, and even older truly are, and I am often forced to reassess my own sometimes too-harsh judgments of my behavior at those ages. I don't think I could endure the heartbreak of watching a child grow up under my roof.

Years ago, my brother Kip gave me a hard time about my attempts at writing. According to him, anyone who wants to write has far too much ego for her own good. I was stunned. Sitting at a desk in an empty study tapping away at a piece of writing that might or might not get published requires far less ego, to my way of thinking, than bringing a fragile and dependent child into the world and thinking you are going to be a good parent. I wonder that anyone has that kind of confidence and courage; I do not.

My relationship with Jack ended violently. He was bent on controlling me, successfully building on my natural feelings of inferiority and striking down any parts of me he disliked or found threatening, but he also saw me as a means of support. He quit his coaching job in a rush of anger when he hadn't liked his schedule for the following term. He gave lessons here and there, and tried to land a job as either a golf or tennis pro, but soon I was working extra hours to pay the bills. It had been I who had bought another car when ours died, I who signed the lease on the little house we were renting. I went through the days with the help of a cast of selves, but whenever I was truly present, I was miserable and suicidal. Once again, my deep, too often hidden, protective self emerged. We had reached the line I would not cross.

"I'm throwing you out," I finally told Jack. "I can't take any more."

"You can't," he sneered. "There's another half-year on the lease. Just how do you plan to get me out?"

"I've arranged to pay the penalties," I said. "Two days and I'm gone. And you are, too."

It was an extreme move: to leave a house I liked, pay a lease penalty, and move to another state to rid myself of a lover, but I was willing to do it. It was time to get on with my life; I had decided to start graduate school. Jack stalked out of the house and roared off in my car. I called a friend who was standing by and asked her to come over in a few hours so I could safely pack my things.

But I underestimated Jack. All too soon, he roared back up to the house, stormed into the bedroom, smashed my head against a wall, and raped me. If I needed confirmation of my decision, he readily provided it. But he moved out and so did I. Interestingly, he would wheedle me for the next year, angling to come live with me again, telling me he loved me and it would all be different.

But I had learned.

Sometime after I moved away from Jack, I met the man I eventually married. He differed enormously from Jack. He was hardworking, charming, polite, thoughtful, even deferential. I couldn't believe my good luck; my friends couldn't either. But within two years of marriage, the charm evaporated. He was drinking heavily, getting into legal scrapes, and quitting jobs.

When I began to see my psychologist, my husband told me very bluntly that people changed when they went into therapy, and that if I changed in any way he didn't like, he wouldn't hesitate to leave me. He was angry when he said it, and it had been meant as a threat, but what I heard instead was the first whisper of freedom. In the end, a major reason we divorced was that, while each of us was clearly staggering under the burden of enormous problems, only one of us was willing to turn and face what needed to be faced.

In the years since our divorce, I've heard that his pattern has remained the same: he charms some woman to smithereens, then gradually his facade slips, eventually the woman throws him out, and he tells anyone who will listen that he'll never have anything to do with anyone like *her* again.

I do not recite this pattern as a point of ridicule; it was my pattern too for many years. Each time I escaped from a situation, I would tell myself "Never again," but I tended to look not to myself for change but to the men around me.

There was one final relationship, which lasted for a year or two, after I split up with my husband. I was aware that I had been sexually abused, that I had been raped as an adult, and that I was a dissociator. I didn't know I was a multiple, but I knew I'd been through enough in my life, and I adopted a new guiding principle: I would never do anything if I felt uncomfortable or coerced. The rule was perhaps extreme, yet it marked my first deliberate step toward changing myself. Since I had a pathological reflex to please those around me at all costs for fear they might kill me otherwise, I needed a stringent and inflexible guide to protect my soul.

What I found in this last relationship was that, for the most part, I could protect myself when around someone else. It took a lot out of me, to be able to say something as simple as the fact that I was too tired to go out and wanted to get to bed early. It took even more out of me on larger issues. Did I want to go and live with him? No. Why not? I couldn't say, didn't know in any conscious way, but my gut told me it would be a mistake. The same was true for any situation involving physical contact. There were times I craved affection, wanting to be held, wanting an arm around my shoulders—but then sometimes in half a minute I would feel as though I would scream if he so much as came within six feet of me.

It was probably good for me to have the chance to sense my own needs and emotions in the presence of someone else, and it says much for this man that I felt safe enough and comfortable enough to do so, but I can't pretend that it was fair to him. I felt bewildered and frightened of my own sudden and violent shifts —which would later make sense when I learned I was a multiple—and I often worked myself into a state of exhaustion trying to remain consistent and recognizable. For him, my sudden turns and shifts were not only bruising but confounding. He commented often on my "moodiness," and once even asked whether I might be a multiple. In the end, when I began to realize I would soon have to decide between continuing to change in therapy and trying to find some level of stasis so that our relationship might survive, it was an easy choice. We had had some wonderful times together when I was feeling well, and since I readily admitted I was the one who needed to get out of the relationship, we were able to part in a gentle and humane way, with, I suspect, no small amount of relief on his part.

What always struck me as I reviewed my history with men, even before I found out I was a multiple, was that my relationships, however awful they would turn out to be, did improve from one to the next—if one excluded Mark, the very first.

But after I was diagnosed as a multiple, I deliberately gave up the whole idea of having an intimate relationship. New alters and new memories were continually emerging, and I, the so-called host personality, was in a near-constant state of flux. I couldn't imagine finding someone flexible enough, and perhaps brave enough, to spend a lot of time with a woman with such variable moods and presentations. Besides, what I needed most were simplicity and stability, and men, in my experience, had never provided either.

PAYING FOR IT

My DIVORCE BROUGHT WITH IT a peculiar blessing: without the erratic spending habits of an alcoholic, my finances stabilized and then improved. Even during the first year of therapy, all was well. I had a college-sponsored policy with Blue Cross and Blue Shield. After I had met the deductible, the policy paid for full battery testing and for weekly one- or two-hour sessions. Still, after two years of therapy, as it became clearer that I was not simply an easily curable nervous wreck but had deep-seated problems, I became increasingly aware that my mental health benefits were actually quite limited. There was a difference between benefits for outpatient meetings with my psychologist and benefits for inpatient hospitalization. The annual maximum for outpatient care was $5,000, the lifetime maximum was $10,000, and as I scrutinized my policy, I felt my first waves of fear.

I was a person with genuine, serious problems—problems which, in a sense, had been foisted off on me when I was very young—and yet it seemed to me that I had few resources. I worried often about what would become of me when the money ran out, especially as, at stages, I felt only marginally functional. My therapist often suggested hospitalization, or at least a substantial leave of absence from the college. But I refused hospitalization, although in retrospect I see the dangers I courted by insisting on living every single day outside the sanctuary one might find in a good psych unit. I always felt I should save my medical leaves for true emergencies, because if I ran out of sick leave my next option would be to take a leave without pay. At that time, in the mid to late 1980s, the seemingly constant news reports on the correlation between homelessness and mental illness did not exactly escape my notice. And so, as long as I could still feed myself, drive a car, and find my way to class, I was determined to keep on going for fear of what might happen if I didn't.

But before I reached the maximums on my mental health coverage, my insurance situation changed. I live near the intersection of three states. Those of us who live here cross borders constantly and without much thought as we buy groceries, see dentists, shop, go to the movies, and so forth. As it happened, my therapist was in one state and my college in another. One afternoon my therapist greeted me with the news that my insurance would no longer cover my appointments; he and other mental health providers had been notified that my insurance company would only reimburse providers within their state. I was stunned and frightened; as a policy holder, I had not been informed directly that my coverage had been curtailed.

This maneuver succeeded for a very simple reason: nearly everyone seeing a psychologist places a higher value on confidentiality than on a public fight. And what patient who needs the attention of a mental health professional in the first place has the wherewithal to fight with an insurance company? In my case, although I felt furious, my therapist and I decided that a lawsuit, or even an inquiry, would attract too much attention to me personally. After much discussion, the first of many along these lines, the deciding factor was that the financial costs had to be balanced against the psychological toll.

And so I did not fight. Instead, we filed the paperwork and requested a continuation of my case. Our first application was denied. We filed an appeal, divulging still more of my record, and the appeal was denied, too. Later, at a meeting of providers from neighboring states, my state's representative from Blue Cross and Blue Shield would admit, probably by accident, that not a single initial request for continuation, and not a single appeal had been granted.

Still, there was no public outcry, frankly not even a single notice in the press. Straight medical patients might have been more vocal, but the mentally ill are easy targets.

My own therapist dealt with the situation in two ways. The first was that he took steps to get licensed in neighboring states. The second was that he repeatedly reassured me that he would still take my case, and would charge me only a token fee. We settled on an hourly rate of ten dollars—embarrassingly low but, for me, affordable—and, agreeing that we would stop talking about my insurance company, we went back to work.

Five years into the therapeutic process, the question of insurance ambushed us again. I had been diagnosed as a multiple that autumn, and throughout the winter, as I struggled to come to terms with having the disorder, I began to think about the possibility of spending the following summer in residential treatment. Frankly, I hated the idea, just as I had first hated being sent to summer camp, but it seemed to me that it would speed things up a little if I devoted a three-month stint to very heavy work. My psychologist and I believed my inpatient benefits were still intact, and so I began to contact hospitals and to look into programs.

My first choice, far and away, was Ridgeview outside Atlanta. My psychologist talked with their staff on the phone, I read the literature, and both of us were impressed by their patient-centered philosophy which allowed multiples to work at their own pace. The hitch, of course, turned out to be insurance. After a call from the hospital to my insurance company, I was turned down for lack of funds. My outpatient and inpatient benefits had been combined, and there was very little money left. The Ridgeview representative said she was terribly sorry and wished me luck elsewhere. Well, Ridgeview is a private hospital, but it still hurt to be so summarily excluded. Sometimes I found myself wondering where the multiples on Ridgeview's extensive waiting list got their money.

I looked into two other programs as well, and what I learned was that all programs have their hard, unyielding edges. One program was so regimented that it was clearly not for me. The literature clearly indicated that all patients would participate in all activities—no matter what. Having been treated that way as a child (You will do exactly what I say every minute of every day), I didn't think it was an approach that would help me to get better. Although my psychologist tried to explain that the program had probably been designed that way to foster the research of its director, it struck me as a kind of boot camp for multiples.

That program and another, however, did offer a reduced fee if one was willing to participate in ongoing studies. I suppose depending on the kinds of trauma one had experienced as a child being a subject was fair exchange for treatment. But so much of the formative abuse I had undergone as a child had taken place either at the hands of doctors or at the hands of my brother Hank, who saw me as a guinea pig or specimen, that I decided to forgo residential treatment.

"Okay," said my therapist, on a day that I was fuming about having been shut out of long-term treatment, "so you're not going."

The irony wasn't lost on either of us that I, who had refused local, short-term inpatient treatment, was throwing a mild tantrum because I couldn't spend three whole months in the hospital.

"Why don't you try to make daily life a little easier?" my therapist said. "That's half the reason for going to the hospital in the first place."

I scowled. Almost from the very beginning of the process, I had resisted spending money on anything that struck me as unnecessary. Every step of the way, I had had to be convinced that my health and well-being were worth an outlay of cash.

My first concession, at the start of therapy, had been to join a gym. I had been part of a faculty fitness program run by my college, but it had folded shortly before I saw my therapist for the first time. "Join a gym," he'd said. "Join a good one and get there nearly every day."

"It costs too much," I grumped.

"Figure it out," he said. "A buck a day, maybe a little more . . ."

"Fine," I said, and vowing I would blame my impending bankruptcy on my shrink I skulked off to the gym.

Soon I had to admit that I was feeling a little better, and ever since, I have hung on to a gym membership for the very simple reason that an hour of serious exercise nearly every day helps stave off depression. When I begin to skip workouts at the gym, I begin to fail. At times, when I think about economizing, I think about finding some other way to exercise, but between the vagaries of the weather and of my teaching schedule, it is either miserable outdoors when I would have time to walk or run, or it's already dark. A buck and a half a day seems a fair trade for the convenience and the safety.

But money became more complicated, and more unnerving, after the diagnosis of multiplicity.

The first odd expenditure was the result of my psychologist's insistence that The Kids needed a stuffed animal. He always filled me in on what he had discussed with them. "What they'd really like," he told me, "is to have Homer back."

I shook my head. Homer was the large, floppy stuffed dog I had had as a child. I had no idea if he was packed away in my parents' attic or if he'd been thrown out, but I certainly wasn't going to contact my mother and father and ask them to look for him.

My therapist smiled. "It would give your parents something to think about though, wouldn't it?" Then he said I'd better think about getting a new one for The Kids.

I can't say I was happy about it. I insisted it was ridiculous. I was thirty-five years old; I had no children; I didn't need a stuffed animal.

"I'm going to suggest you go home and talk it over with The Kids. It would really help them."

I was no sooner in the car than The Kids set up an internal uproar. They wailed, they begged, they pleaded.

"Fine," I said, and turned the car around and headed to a store that I knew had a wide selection of stuffed animals. I had about three dollars in my wallet, but I would just go in there, find a teddy bear or something, throw my credit card at the situation, and get this over with.

The shop was crammed; a menagerie of animals overflowed the shelves and counters. I grimly headed toward the teddy bears. I couldn't believe I was doing this. I scanned the shelves. "So?" I asked The Kids.

There was silence.

I picked a large gray bear off the shelf, and glanced at the price tag. I couldn't believe what it cost.

The Kids glowered at the bear.

Please don't like this one, I thought.

We don't want a dumb bear with a dumb look on his face, they muttered.

Thank god, I thought, and shoved the bear back onto its shelf.

Suddenly there was a voice at my elbow. "Looking for anything in particular?" It was a young clerk, probably a local college student, neatly dressed in a shirt and tie.

I studied his face. Had he been able to hear The Kids?

"I, um, need to buy a gift," I said.

"We have a wide—"

I cut him off. "I'll know it when I see it," I said.

We don't want a dumb bear . . .

The young man didn't flinch.

"It's for an extremely particular child," I added, hoping to shut The Kids up.

The clerk laughed. "You know what?" he said. "I think half the adults in here really are buying something for themselves. No kidding," he said. "We had a lady just this morning . . ."

I wandered off, and in time, The Kids seized on a lion that was sprawled rather elegantly along a top shelf. *There he is!* they said, as if spotting an old friend at the bus station.

I told them I wasn't sure I could afford it, and indeed, when I took the lion down, I saw that the price was just under two hundred dollars.

We want him, The Kids insisted.

I muttered some nasty things under my breath about my shrink, then put the lion back. The Kids began to cry, and I offered them a deal. They could have the lion on the condition that they wait an entire week. In the meanwhile, we would go somewhere every day and look at other possibilities.

We don't want a . . .

"I know, I know," I told them. "No dumb bears."

Three days and four toy stores later, in a little place some twenty miles off my beaten path, we found a stuffed badger. The Kids fell in love with it, and I breathed a little prayer of thanks that it cost far less than the two-hundred-dollar lion.

Badgers, I told The Kids, are solitary animals but fierce when they are threatened. This particular badger looked smart and watchful. What was more, I added, I didn't think many kids had a badger of their very own.

They clung to him with pride, grimly hanging on to him all the way home in the car, making it difficult for me to drive, and every night thereafter they made a comfortable spot for Badger in bed. Whenever we left home, they found room for him in the suitcase.

Badger, fortunately, was a one-time expense, partly because The Kids project their feelings onto him and, just as they had once wanted to be an only child, they are quite certain he will not countenance the presence of another stuffed animal of any kind. But as time went on, I found money sifting through my hands in other ways. There were the books and publications about MPD and related subjects. There were the expenses of the diet: soy milk costs more than cow's milk, arrowroot more than cornstarch, alternative flours more than wheat. There were other things for The Kids: we went through a lot of coloring books, and also have a pile of tapes that help The Kids to fall asleep. There was the reward system for the diet change and, from time to time, there were regular allowances for other selves paid out to different banks and stashes around the house. There are all the expenses related to having dogs, because my youngest parts, and even my teenagers, seem to benefit from having pets; I admit I, too, like not only their companionship but also their slumbering but sharp-eared presences in the night. And, when I go to conferences, I always pay the extra fee for a single room because I need a place for trance work, a haven for my shifting selves—and a home for Badger.

The steadiest expense, of course, is the therapy itself. Ten bucks an hour is a mere pittance to pay someone with the skills to treat a patient with MPD. But that fee hides other costs. One is that, because I can afford to pay my therapist so little, he in turn can afford to devote limited time working with me. I see him in his office ninety minutes a week, substantially less than some clinical writing recommends, and I consult him on the phone for half an hour a week. In case of crises or calamities, I can reach him by phone at other times as well.

Mostly, I feel grateful for this arrangement: I can rattle off a list of local clinicians who would have closed out my case the minute I ran out of insurance.

But other times, I can't help but worry. Because he is being paid so little, I feel as if I should somehow be a "good" patient —which is not entirely in my nature—and I feel guilty every time I am stubborn, grumpy, or belligerent. I worry, too, because his children will be heading off to college in the coming years; it would make sense for him to raise my fee, but I'm not sure what I'd do.

And then there are the times I feel flat-out sorry for myself. I can't help but feel my lack of funds translates into lost years of my life. Like most multiples who succeed in the therapeutic process, I undertake much of my work independently, but it is still hard not to believe that the less time I have to spend on intensive work, the longer the process will take. And, the longer it takes, the longer I will have to live with the symptoms of the disorder and the disjointedness of the work—and the less time I will have to live later on in some state of integration.

By now, I have several automatic responses to my money worries: I do what I can to speed along through the therapeutic process, I at least try to be a good patient, and I buy the occasional ticket for the local lottery.

I also often think about finding a better job. My professorship gives me a nice title but little money: after fifteen years of college teaching, I make only a few thousand dollars a year more than a first-year high school teacher in our local school district. But each time I consider making a move, I wonder what I would do without my acquired stature at the college, which is a great disguise for my disorder. On bad days, I can't picture myself sorting out the politics and the unwritten rules of a new institution, and I can't imagine giving up the cushion of my four months' accumulated sick leave or doing without my long vacations which I devote to the most disruptive phases of the therapeutic process.

The new health-care package at my college offered a brief glimmer of hope: we were promised "unlimited lifetime" mental health benefits. Unfortunately, one must see a counselor assigned by the insurance company; there is no patient choice and no concern for the significant vagaries which contribute to a good working relationship. What's more, the list of counselors seems very limited; mine was not offered the opportunity to participate. Even worse, colleagues who are clients in the system all report the same thing: at their first session they are told that they are eligible for ten hours of treatment at the listed fee in each calendar year. That's it. If a case can be made for true debilitating illness, another ten hours, at a higher fee, will be granted. Twenty hours, however, appears to be the annual maximum. One friend told me he figured it this way: he had twenty hours to get better or to prove he *couldn't* get better.

Without the agreement I have with my therapist, I would be forced to participate in my college's new plan. With only ten to twenty hours of psychological care a year, my ability to function would be significantly jeopardized. Either that or I would soon be living in poorer and poorer housing as I tried to pay cash for qualified care. If my therapist billed me at his full rate, I would owe him three-quarters of my take-home pay, and in my more melodramatic moments I try to imagine what life would be like in a rented room with a washbasin and a hot plate in one corner.

Too much time spent thinking about money always teaches me the same thing about myself: I am remarkably naive.

As I was growing up, I learned that when I was ill or in need of professional help it would be available to me. There was never any question of finding good doctors, specialists, or medications. I feel sheepish, ignorant, and extraordinarily middle class but, until now, I have never been in the position of not being able to afford what is easily proven that I need. But now, whenever I hear a news analysis or report on proposed health care reform, I listen —usually in vain—for two elements I have come to see as crucial: a solid but flexible mental health benefit, and some mechanism that effectively allows patients to appeal the decisions of insurance companies.

On nights when I find myself lying awake and worrying about money, I try to tell myself to forget it. There is little that I can change. Besides, I have a job, I have a psychologist, I can pay my monthly bills, and I am getting better. What's the point of all this worry?

That question had its answer on July 26, 1992.

I was on my way to the gym that morning, then I planned to head to the college to check the off-term mail. Idly I drove along, thinking through the day and listening to the morning news. Then a particular report caught my attention. I listened sharply for a moment. The Americans with Disabilities Act had just become law. I swerved my car off the road, and sat shuddering and weeping. Just that one time, for just that little while, under the bright promise of this new law's protection, I allowed myself to feel every gut-wrenching fear I'd ever had about what would happen to me if I were not able to keep my job or to foot the bills of my disorder.

SETTING OUT

 ONE AFTERNOON, I was having a conference with a student. As we were finishing, she mentioned that she was struggling with a term paper for her psych class. She wanted to write it about adults who had been sexually abused as children.

"Well, that's a good topic," I said offhandedly. "There must be loads of source materials."

The student shrugged, then said the real problem was that, as part of the assignment, the professor required that she interview someone involved with the topic and include a case history.

I had been in therapy for seven months. I didn't know it, but the first small jolt of reconnection was about to hit.

"How," the student mused aloud, "would I even find someone who was sexually abused?"

Inside, I heard a voice say: Well, *I* was . . .

Then other voices kicked up a panicked chorus.

The next thing I knew, the student was saying, "Ms. Phillips? Ms. Phillips?"

"I'm sorry," I told her. "I'm not feeling well."

She guessed it was probably the flu that was going around. She'd heard it was hitting very suddenly. Anyway, she said, getting up, she thought she'd better find another topic for her paper.

"Probably a good idea," I told her.

I went home, wept, hammered my fists into my pillow, and, the next day, white and shaky but not from the flu, I told my psychologist with enormous difficulty that I had suddenly realized that that childhood assault had actually happened. What's more, I realized, it had happened to me.

"To *me*," I whispered, and then did little but cry for the rest of the session.

Again and again, I tested the truth of this realization that had come roaring out of nowhere: *I* had been that young child who had been seized and flung down on the floor. That had been *my* arm that had been wrenched, *my* head that hit the clothes dryer. Worse, that had been *my* brother and he had certainly meant to do me harm.

"Everything is different," I said at one point, and found myself reaching out to touch the things around me as if to somehow reorient myself to the physical world.

"Everything will always be different from here on out," my therapist told me. Then we just sat. When the hour was up, he smiled gravely and said, "Welcome back."

Years later, my therapist would often express his regret that it had taken him so long to recognize my multiplicity, especially since, although he viewed himself as something of a free thinker within his profession, he had adhered to the then-standard professional belief that multiplicity was a rarity and that it might indeed be caused by a patient's response to the therapist's actions and expectations. There is no way, of course, to change the timing of my diagnosis. But now that an opposite professional trend seems to be under way—the rapid and immediate diagnosis of multiplicity—it seems to me that I was almost lucky, because I had the chance to experience the fundamental principles of the therapeutic process and the chance to gain some confidence in myself before I was identified as a multiple. It was as if, before setting out on a perilous voyage, I had a few first tastes of dirty weather, made my first stabs at navigation, and had the chance to find my sea legs.

In the weeks that followed that first jolt of reconnection, I often picked at the mystery of this first recounted trauma. How could I not have remembered being cornered in the laundry room? Where had this memory been? It spooked me that something so significant could have been so successfully hidden from my conscious view. I began to think of the memory itself as a solitary bead that I had found in some deep corner of a pocket or hidden in the bottom of a drawer. The odd thing was that the rest of my life, the events that I had remembered all along had already been neatly strung onto the bead-thread of my life story. And so this stray bead was startling. I knew it was mine. I knew it matched the others; yet it presented me with only awkward choices. For a while I kept it separate. I fingered it, studied it at all hours of the day and night, looked at it in natural light, held it up to all the other beads to find the place where it might fit.

In the coming weeks, when I was often distracted and unnerved by other memories of Hank's behavior, I sometimes told myself that getting better simply meant finding my other lost bits of time, examining them, getting to know their heft and their significance, then working them somehow into my history. Perhaps, I told myself, I could be a kind of emotional archaeologist, discovering and sequencing my own history.

It was a nice illusion while it lasted. A string of beads is such a tidy, linear object—which time and memory, I soon learned, certainly are not. And therapy would never be as methodical as archaeology; our findings would be scattered and chaotic, the layers, the shards, the quadrants impossible to distinguish.

In the coming months, scrap after scrap of my sexual history fluttered in the forefront of my consciousness. I could not bring myself to talk about them, but I couldn't stop them, either. At night, it was increasingly difficult to fall asleep and almost impossible to stay asleep. During the day, I was so distracted I had to struggle to concentrate on my classes. I began to think of time as the floor of a diabolical funhouse: at any moment it could give way, tilt me, tumble me, send me flying down some chute into some other part of my life. When memories came to me, they were not memories, those things we recreate or banish with at least some semblance of will in order to represent the past. When I woke screaming in the night feeling a hand on my throat, when I startled awake feeling a hand groping up my skirt, I was not recalling the past: I had been dropped back into it. The present, the time frame from which I had been jettisoned, did not exist. All that existed was the original moment, and the sensation, the terror, the humiliation, the powerlessness.

Finally, I sat late one night at my kitchen table and wrote down everything I could recall about sex. I hoped that getting it all on paper would allow me to stop remembering it. I also took a vow that night: I swore that I would always try to tell the absolute truth, even when I found it sickening. The whole project took me until after midnight, and then, feeling drained but desperate and in dire need of sleep, I took the letter into town, forced myself to mail it to my psychologist, and staggered home to bed.

A few days later, I slunk into his office feeling bitter and ashamed.

"Do you want to talk about this?" he said, briefly lifting the letter from his desk.

"No," I said.

"We won't if you don't want to," he said, smiling. "But it really helped me to get the background."

I harrumpfed.

He sat back in his chair and mused. "Sex," he said, "has caused you nothing but trouble."

I glared at him. "I thought we weren't going to talk about it."

He shrugged. "We're not," he said.

I scowled out the window and resumed my silence.

After a few minutes my therapist began to muse again. "It's interesting, though, isn't it, that—"

"*Please,*" I said.

"Sorry," he said, then closed his eyes and folded his hands.

There were times to talk, but there were also times to be silent and to wait. Both he and I would have to learn this; for him, it would be the hardest lesson of our work together.

My sleeping patterns grew steadily worse. I screamed in the night. I woke every forty-five minutes, I woke at three in the morning and didn't go back to sleep, and after truly scouring nightmares, I simply got out of bed, got dressed, and huddled on my couch waiting for the sun to rise.

More and more our sessions centered only on the question of sleep—or my general lack thereof. My skin was growing more and more pale, and my hands were acquiring something of a tremble. At times I was so exhausted it seemed almost too much work to breathe.

"How did you sleep when you were a kid?" my therapist asked.

I gave him a blank look. At first, I remembered only that grim prayer about dying in my sleep and the occasional privilege of having my cats sleep at the foot of my bed.

But then the rest of it came slowly back: the funny stories told about my walking and talking in my sleep, my terrible fear of allowing myself to sleep because of what might happen if I did, my parents' impatience with children who did not go to bed and *stay* there, the nights when, as punishment, I would not be allowed to have the cats on my bed. Some nights, I forced myself to stay awake until everyone had gone to bed, and then, in the belief that if I couldn't be found I couldn't be hurt, I slept in some odd cubbyhole in the house: on the floor in closets, in my laundry hamper, behind a chair in the living room. Other nights, I simply prowled the house, sometimes rehearsing my suicide, sometimes standing noiselessly in my parents' bedroom angrily watching them sleep and knowing what would happen if I woke them.

Our discussion prompted me to try the old childhood trick of sleeping somewhere else when I felt too frightened to be in bed. I made my way to the couch or to an upholstered chair on the deck; sometimes I even sprawled, with my sleepy but gleeful dogs, on the living-room floor.

But that was all that I would try. My psychologist made suggestion after suggestion: self-hypnosis, keeping a written record of each night, relaxation, hypnosis in the office, even calling him at home at two A.M. when I could take no more.

"I'm okay," I said, week after week. "I can tough it out."

Sleep just couldn't be worth all this effort. There was no way, I believed, that I could overcome the terrors of the night, and each evening, as the sky gradually grew dark, I grew increasingly anxious, knowing I would have to get through another night.

Finally, one week, my therapist shook his head angrily.

"Jane," he said. "You don't seem to acknowledge *my* responsibility here."

"Yours?"

I dug my hands under my thighs to steady them.

"If this keeps up," he said, "I'll have to think about having your driver's license pulled."

I shrank back in my chair.

"I can't *sleep!*" I said, feeling the surge of nastiness that comes over me when I feel threatened and exhausted. "I'm *sorry.*"

"Jane," he said. "What if you're in an accident?"

I wanted to make my *So what?* face, but didn't. All I needed was another lecture on why I wasn't supposed to kill myself and I would probably just go home and get it over with.

He turned his chair away from me, and I saw his shoulders fall. "Since you won't let *me* help you," he said, fed up and a little weary, "go and do some reading. Find your own way out."

We were near the end of the session. "Fine," I said, getting up and stalking out. "I will." And in something of a huff I went to the library.

Not only did I learn about sleep, but I learned one other principle I would need as I set out toward integration: I am so removed from certain ordinary experiences that I have no idea what I am missing; I certainly don't know what I need to ask about or learn.

What I read first were books and articles on normal sleep, and I admit that I was stunned. I'd had no idea, actually, why human beings slept. Before my reading, sleep had seemed like some peculiar human tradition, a nightly test of bravery I inevitably failed. Why anyone in her right mind participated in this trial I had no idea. What perfectly sane person would strip off her clothes, turn off the lights, and willingly give up consciousness?

What I learned, however, were things probably every schoolchild knows: sleep is a physical need. Somehow, in the midst of my fears, I had neglected to learn that it is only during sleep that the body replenishes its hormones and thus shores up its immune system. Only during sleep can the body right its balance of depleted chemicals, heal its wounds, and recover from its illnesses.

To my surprise, I also learned that good sleep begets good sleep. I'd had no idea that my sleep deprivation, because of my bad nights, very nearly guaranteed that following nights would be just as bad or even worse. The more tired I was when I went to bed, the more likely I was to suffer those weird and lifelike nightmares when I first dropped off to sleep. Throughout the rest of the night, I was no doubt experiencing an ongoing cycle of REM deficit and rebound, triggering still more hellish dreams. Worse, sleep deprivation was probably also causing me to remain for longer periods in delta sleep, but those longer periods of the deepest of sleeps were the breeding ground of sleep terrors—those blind, pitch-black wakenings I supposedly should have outgrown in childhood.

If other people could go to bed and sleep at night, I decided that I could learn to do it, too. I established a regular bedtime, and planned to stay up late no more than one night a week. I addressed the question of safety and comfort, installing new locks, putting a flashlight near the bed, and buying flannel sheets and a new comforter. My therapist and I worked on some contingency plans. What would I do when I had nightmares? Under what circumstances would I get out of bed? How many bad nights would I have in a row before taking a day off to sleep on the couch during the safety of daylight hours?

Every night, I grimly headed off to bed right on time. I hated it, but gradually the new strategies worked. My sleep was, and remains, quite disturbed from time to time, but it began to change from a problem with its own potentially serious conse- quences to an indicator that there is trouble afoot somewhere in my system.

One night I went to sleep very tired, fell asleep, and woke within minutes screaming because of a horrific nightmare. I sat up, blinked groggily, then dug down a little deeper under the covers. "Hypnogogic hallucination," I mumbled to myself, and then woke up again, laughing this time at the utterly casual way I identified and accepted what had once so thoroughly frightened me. I knew I finally had the problem licked.

I had been in therapy for two years when some colleagues and I took a group of students on a field trip. The week-in, week-out nature of therapy was often wearing, and I could think of nothing better than hopping on a bus with a group of language majors. We would spend a few hours in the art museum, then after some free time, meet for dinner at a French restaurant and go listen to a chamber orchestra. The trip, I thought, would give me a little break from all my internal turmoil and travail. What I got, in- stead, was a reminder of the relentless nature of the therapeutic process. One did not simply get on a bus for the day and leave it behind.

The day began well enough. We arrived at the art museum, and a lively curator gave us a witty but insightful tour. Afterwards, as the students went their own way for a few hours, I wandered back through certain galleries.

I was reminded of a field trip I'd once taken in a humanities course when I was a college junior. We were visiting an art museum and then had tickets to a play. At the museum, it had turned out that because of my current rabid interest in art history, I knew more about some of the paintings than my professor did, and, as I was something of a favorite student, he gladly turned the commentary over to me. After a while, my fellow students wandered off, and, for the next hour or so, the professor and I had roamed quite amiably, alternately discussing paintings and my future.

As I was leaving the museum, I was remembering that afternoon, a little wistfully since the professor was now long-dead. I was musing with some affection over the cheek I must have had to have taken over like that when I caught sight of a tall young woman striding along with long flying hair, a dramatic hat pulled down over one eye, and a portfolio under one arm.

Suddenly I saw myself again, in my last college years: my hair was long and streaming, too, and I had sauntered everywhere as if driven by some ferocity of purpose. I had even worn my grandmother's cast-off, calf-length mink, and had had a hat with a marvelously theatric brim.

I stood and watched the young woman dodge her way across the street, and I thought she looked quite stunning and perhaps a little daunting. And then, across the chasm of dissociation, there was a jolt of reconnection: My god, I thought, I'm a woman, too.

If multiplicity works by assigning various tasks and pieces of information to separate parts, integration takes place when tasks or information are somehow shared. For me, this sharing began during the first years of therapy, when I knew I was a dissociator but did not know about my multiplicity. The process of integration seems to have no "logic," and it takes place in its own time, although looking back to that moment on the stairs of the art museum, the connections can perhaps be reconstructed: I am in a nostalgic mood for myself as a twenty-year-old college student. By chance, I see a young woman of a similar age. She catches my eye because of her appearance and her seeming sense of purpose. Without deliberate thought, I note the similarities between her and my old self at that age: the stride, the hair, the hat. But then the connection somehow reverses: the young woman on the street is decidedly, undoubtedly female, feminine, womanly. Idly, I check my old self-image and find something there I have never seen before: femaleness. It takes only a pulse-beat for the connection to shoot back in time: I was not just a child when Hank assaulted me, but a little *girl*. And the same connection abruptly reaches forward to the present: as I stand here on these art-museum stairs, I am a *woman*. Nothing more, nothing less.

The rest of the trip was a nightmare. I spent the afternoon sitting in a bar. I found a window seat on a busy street, sipped a glass of wine for hours, and examined everyone who walked by. How on earth, I wondered, did anyone get through the day with the enormous burden of their sexuality? I tried not to think about everything that had happened to me only because I *was* female. I felt tricked, duped, exposed. How could I not have *known?* How was I ever going to survive? And why *now?*

I limped through dinner, fending off comments on how quiet I was, and later I was grateful for the hush and darkness of the concert hall. That night I cried for four straight hours in the darkness of the bus, but I didn't know which was the worse tragedy: having been born a girl or discovering that fact, in this visceral, undeniable way, at the age of thirty-one.

———

Integration, I was learning, raised frightening and far-reaching questions; some of these would challenge my most fundamental beliefs about myself and about the world. Recalling a string of unpleasant, even damaging, childhood events was only the beginning. Unless I was willing to examine all answers to the questions that came surging up from my subconscious, therapy was useless. And, unless I was willing to act in some new way, seeing a therapist two hours every week was merely self-indulgent.

In the months that followed the sighting of my feminine self on the art museum stairs, I changed in a disturbing way: I suddenly found other women absolutely fascinating. I watched my women students, I watched my women colleagues, I watched the women at my gym with a compulsion that scared me half to death. I could barely take my eyes off them: how they talked, sat, moved, dressed, did their hair. I was fascinated by the range of behavior I saw in women: the student who might come to class one day in suit and heels and the next day in jeans and track shoes or a friend who might painstakingly do her nails, and then within the hour go out and weed her garden. I wanted to ask why people were piercing more holes in their ears, how they had learned to be so expert with their makeup, how they knew what to tell their hairdressers. Certain women I found incredibly attractive during this time, and I gnawed incessantly over the question of whether or not I was gay.

One afternoon, my therapist allowed me to read through the answers I had given during my initial testing. In the margin, next to my response to an apperception image of a half-naked woman lying on a bed with a man standing nearby wearing a tie, someone had written, in a large, confident script, "Is she gay?"

"I didn't write that," my therapist said.

I nodded. He had not administered the tests; obviously the note had been made by the psychologist who had.

I shifted in my chair, made a face, and took a deep breath. "Well, but do you think I am?"

"Gay?" he said. He smiled and cocked his head. "Well, do *you* think so?"

"I don't know," I said, then thought. "Probably not, anyway."

"What does your gut say?"

I laughed. "Well, okay, my *gut* says no." I paused. "Definitely no."

He laughed, too. "I'd be surprised if you were," he said, then added, carefully hedging his bets: "It wouldn't be the end of the world, though."

I will admit that I was relieved. I did not *want* to be gay. I am not a homophobe, and have several friends who are gay; in fact, it is the quality of their lives that led me to hope so desperately that I was straight. Although in some ways society seems more accepting, too many of the gay people I know lead their lives either in fear of discovery or with a kind of tiring bravado. My life seemed hard enough without that.

It took a while, but it finally came to me that I was passing through a belated stage of adolescence, when girls do indeed study one another and sometimes develop crushes on other girls they admire. My perception suddenly shifted, and I realized that women I was worrying about feeling attracted to were women I admired. I didn't want to be *with* them; what I wanted was to *be* them.

I decided to study all the women that I chose. I had not been paying much attention to the question of womanhood all these years, and I had plenty of lost time to make up for. For quite some time, I went on watching women the same way one might wander through car dealerships scanning the new models. I was scouting prospects, trying to see what kind of a woman I might want to be, and taking notes on what I might need to learn.

In the end, the question of sexual orientation quietly receded. Later, when I learned I was a multiple, it became clear how complex the issue of sexual orientation can be. Most multiples have alters of different genders, and if executive control is determined by whatever alter has access to the body at the moment, what happens to a male alter in a female body? What's *his* orientation? And is it his? Or is it the host's? These are fascinating questions, but in the end they are distracting and irrelevant to the process of integration. In the future, the question of sexual identity would reemerge, but for the moment, I knew what I needed to know about myself.

At the end of one summer vacation, I came out of a depression with a new insight into myself and my life: I was smart, perceptive, full of ideas and opinions—and yet I never spoke up at the college. As my mood brightened, it seemed clear that this would be the year I would become a more active participant in the faculty discussions and debates.

Well, okay, said my psychologist, but take it easy.

We were beginning to learn that I never take anything easy, and at the beginning of that academic year, within minutes of my first opportunity, I was launched on some point or other about which I had strong and genuine opinions. The problem was that even as I spoke I heard the sound of a cocking gun and a whispered threat: "You're gonna die, Jane." The safety goes *click-click.* "You're gonna die." *Click-click, click-click.*

I had been through enough to know the voice was Hank's, and that it was rising from my memory as if I'd tripped some invisible audio switch.

I toughed out the meeting, kept on talking, then rushed back to my office. As I sat with my head down on my desk, I realized that it wasn't my stupidity that kept me from speaking out at meetings: I didn't express myself because I was afraid of dying. But just how reasonable was that fear? At the time, I had a cloudy understanding of the concepts of "past" and "present." So instead of being able to understand the simple fact that I was thirty-five and not ten, and that my brother was sitting in some far-off boardroom, not here, I attended every meeting at school that semester mentally frisking everyone in the room, determined to prove that I could participate and not be killed. I was careful to be the first at meetings, eyeing people as they came through the door: "Well, whadya think?" I'd ask myself. "Does he have a gun? Does she? Does she?" Nope, nope, nope, I told myself, and after long months of assessing the likelihood of getting shot at academic meetings, I gradually taught myself to relinquish the fear.

It came to me that the vigilance of the traumatized comes, in part, from the need to guard against both the past and the present. If something happened once, I seemed to believe, it could happen again, and my "job" as it were was to maintain a constant vigilance not only against what might happen to me right this minute, but to guard simultaneously against everything that had ever happened to me in the past. I had five years of practice, in dozens of situations, painfully separating the past from the present and working up the courage to test the difference between reality and my perception of it. Once the diagnosis was made, I needed every scrap of faith and confidence I'd acquired to continue in the process.

Trust was the one thing I failed to acquire. From the very beginning of our work together, my therapist pointed out that it would help if I could bring myself to trust him. He explained trust, offered examples of it, made promises of what he would and would not do.

I can't even pretend that I believed him. I trusted no one, I had ample reasons for trusting no one, and I wasn't going to trust him either. I almost hate to recall the lengths to which he went in order to foster trust. There were a few extra-long appointments which helped me to get to know him better, although I still considered trust out of the question. He wrote on more than one appointment card that I could reach him by phone twenty-four hours a day. I never called. He did his best to remember and follow through on the slightest things, from how I drank my tea and how I liked my chair turned to even small remarks I'd made in preceding weeks.

Nothing worked. I didn't trust him, I wasn't necessarily interested in trusting him, and frankly I felt he wasted a lot of valuable time talking about it. I liked him, though. He was smart, and bright, and usually compassionate. He listened with almost uncanny care, but he could be witty and irreverent, too. On the other hand, sometimes I was afraid of him, and sometimes he just didn't seem to understand me at all. At times, all that kept me from skipping my appointments was a promise I'd once made to myself that no matter how humiliating, how painful, or how frightening it was, I wouldn't abandon the therapeutic process.

That vow, however, and all I learned in the first five years, was just enough to carry me into the rough wild seas of treating my true disorder. He was right, though: trust would have eased the voyage.

MIDDLE PASSAGE

WHEN I DISCOVERED I was a multiple, I did three things: I took a week off from teaching and spent it moping; I looked into long-term treatment, and I asked my therapist to stop sitting in his chair.

"I can't believe I'm going to ask you this," I said.

"Try me," he said, leaning back in the old oak chair he'd once told me he'd bought at a country auction.

"Well, um, I—"

He let the chair fall forward, and rested an elbow on one arm of it.

I pointed to the chair that matched the one I occupied: a soft upholstered thing that rocked and swiveled. "Well, I, um, I'd like you to sit over there instead."

He shrugged, paused, and after an odd musing look, stood up. "Over here?" he said, turning the chair so that it faced me, then sitting down.

I let out a long breath. "Yes," I said. "That's better." I bent over and put my head down on my knees. I felt about to faint. "It's so stupid," I said. "I'm sorry." I inhaled carefully. "I just felt as if you were coming *at* me. I felt so . . . so . . . overpowered."

He thought, nodded, and halfway laughed. "You've never been a good patient."

I sat up and gave him a startled look. I'd tried, over the years, not to be *too* wayward.

184

"What I mean," he said gently, swiveling his new chair back and forth like a little kid on a soda-fountain stool, "is that I've always had to back off so you don't feel as if you're being *treated.*"

I nodded sadly.

"How do I get better if I can't stand treatment?" I said. I'd been reading what a monumental task lay ahead of me if I wanted to resolve my multiplicity.

He sighed, then gestured around the office. "Anything else you want while we're at it?"

I looked around, then bit my lip. "Well, I—" I stared up at the ceiling, feeling foolish and trying not to cry. "It's so stupid."

"It's okay," he said. "We have to start somewhere."

"Right," I said. Then I asked if we could turn off the floor lamp and the desk lamp and, while we were at it, close the blinds partway.

Again, he thought, shrugged, and did as I asked.

The atmosphere was more muted now, and I sank back in my chair. "Light kills my eyes," I said.

"So," he said, "start there."

"Light?" I said. "What about it?"

Was the light bothering me, he asked, because I was trying not to dissociate?

I was baffled.

"Most multiples say it's easiest for them to dissociate or switch looking straight into light. So I thought you might be having to fight to maintain consistency."

"Uh-oh," I said. "Then I got it backwards. Bright light makes me vigilant. I *never* switch in bright light."

He considered that. "The hospital," he said. "Three years old, blinding light?"

I started to laugh. "Not only that," I said, "when I became a multiple back then, I hadn't read the literature. I'm bound to have some of my symptoms inside out."

He laughed, too. "Probably," he said, then went on to say that as far as he was concerned all multiples were different, and that each one had to find her or his own way to integration.

Information, we decided, was the best place to begin. I needed some solid references. He sent me to the medical school bookstore to buy a copy of Frank W. Putnam's *The Diagnosis and Treatment of Multiple Personality Disorder.* A few days later, when we were scheduled for a check-in on the telephone, I raved about how terrific the book was.

"I'm glad you've gotten started," he said.

"I read it last night," I told him.

"Last night? All of it? It took me *days.*"

I started to laugh. "Yes, but *I* was reading about myself. Speeds things up considerably."

What helped me most in Putnam's writing, in addition to the information on patterns in the systems of multiples and the carefully detailed treatment strategies, was Putnam's overall respect for his patients. It was disconcerting yet consoling to read descriptions of mysteries I'd sensed, but had never quite unearthed, about myself. Still, there was both a wryness and a warmth in that text I've never come across elsewhere, and I felt better about MPD, having seen the disorder through Putnam's eyes.

"Putnam" became a kind of collaborator in our work. The book gave us a shared frame of reference, offered a pool of ideas and possibilities for treatment strategies, and provided a gentle way for us to nudge each other in one direction or another. "Perhaps you should reread Putnam," my therapist would say when I was being especially wrong-headed or seemed unusually lost. "Well, *Putnam* says," I'd remind my shrink when I wanted to take exception to something he was trying to explain.

Our first goal, it was clear, was to uncover as much as possible about the players in my private system. Since I was still resisting directed hypnosis, we decided I would spend some time in a trance at home each day, working independently to map my system.

The task was fascinating. I spent hours inventing charts, then sketching and resketching them. I added parts, moved them around, slipped in and out of trances, checking my information and trying to discover who was linked to whom in the system. I had to scrounge for larger and larger pieces of paper, and dig through drawers looking for colored markers. When I was finally satisfied, I painstakingly made two clean copies.

At my next appointment, I presented my map to my therapist with as much pride, I suppose, as an explorer might present a chart of some new territory to the main underwriter of an expedition.

We pulled up chairs and rolled it out.

"Good Lord," he said, leaning back a little.

What lay before us was a color-coded chart of about a dozen selves. Since there were no individual names within the system— no hidden Marys, Mikes, or Lucilles—each part had been given its own title and had been assigned its own color. Arrows indicated pathways of co-consciousness; bars indicated amnesia barriers.

I looked at the chart and felt suddenly chagrined. It made sense to me, but no wonder he seemed so taken aback.

"Maybe you can explain it," he said after a minute. And for the rest of the session, I pointed out my selves and the links and barriers between them. At the end of the session, he rolled up the map and kept it, and, in the following weeks, it was evident he had studied it with care.

The problem with the map—and with maps in general—was that it was soon outdated. Other selves appeared, co-consciousness developed here and there, still other selves seemed to vanish. From time to time I drew other maps, but I never again labored with such diligence. In time, my "maps" devolved into casual lists of whatever parts I could sense were currently distinct presences.

I still balked, however, at the idea of sitting there in the office and having my therapist "call out" selves as he chose. Putnam and other writers insist the multiple must agree to this procedure as part of the treatment method, but somehow I could never see the difference between my parents or brothers forcing me to assume a particular self and my therapist forcing the same response.

We compromised. After doing a little warm-up in the office, I would slump deeper in my chair and start my own self-hypnosis. He would join in quietly with the suggestion that "The Adult Jane" should step to the rear and that whatever other part wanted to should come to the fore.

And step to the fore they did. Over the next three years, part of nearly every session was devoted to this kind of work. The Kids were frequent visitors, checking in with their worries and with endless tales of exploits with the dogs. Teenagers appeared and talked about drugs, about Mark, about life at home. My therapist met angry parts, scared parts, parts caught in frightening moments. Young women in their early twenties showed up, too, wringing their hands or stroking their neck in the aftermath of rape. He never insisted on names, but always asked for some identification: an age, a fear, the year. And then he sat and heard them out, talking through whatever seemed most urgent to them at the moment, telling them who he was and offering them the chance to return to the office during future appointments.

An especially significant group of visitors were the so-called Internal Self-Helpers. Most multiples seem to have these parts who offer advice and information to the therapist when the process goes awry or bogs down. My therapist was always very careful after any session to tell me whom he had seen and what the main topic of discussion had been, but he seemed particularly careful to give me detailed accounts of the appearance of these internal guides.

When they showed up in the middle of the non-trance part of the session, I would suddenly feel as if I were about to faint. Nearly always I put my head down, muttered something about feeling as if I were going to be sick, and then, in a while, I would find myself sitting in some other part of the office—in his desk chair or on the windowsill. My therapist would be looking thoughtful and bemused and, after giving me time to reorient myself, would tell me that an Internal Self-Helper had just appeared. Then he would explain to me what had just been explained to him. Sometimes it was the suggestion that he give me time to reach a deeper level during the trance work or that some other technique might work. My helpers sometimes explained issues that would need to be discussed in the coming months, identified clandestine selves, or simply clarified points he did not quite seem to grasp.

These self-helpers were spooky in a way, but they also made good sense: it was as if they had paid attention while I had been building the elaborate protective labyrinth of my system and as if they could most easily provide the clues as to which way we should turn next in exploring and later dismantling that same system. That my therapist was always careful to tell me of their appearance and of their advice made a significant contribution toward integration: his acknowledgement of, and respect for, these helpers taught me that I could help heal myself and that I had power over my multiplicity.

One afternoon, I sat fidgeting in my chair, then got up to pace back and forth across his office. It had been a year of direct work on MPD. He sat, as he did every week now, in one of the "client" chairs and watched me stalk back and forth. As was often the case, I felt stupid and embarrassed. I knew I'd be miserable until I said something, but I was also determined it was stupid to speak up.

"Jane," he said finally. "Why don't you just *say* it? We've been working together a long time."

I sighed. "You'll be mad," I said.

He shrugged. "So?" he said. "I'll be mad. I've been mad before." He paused. "Or maybe *you're* mad."

I turned and scowled at him. Some days it drove me crazy that my therapist sounded like, well, a therapist.

"You just don't *understand*," I said, with sudden fury. Then I held up a hand. "Don't say it," I pleaded. I would scream if I heard one more platitude about anger.

"I didn't say a thing," he said.

Suddenly I sat in my chair and folded my arms across my chest. "I sound just like an adolescent," I said, laughing nervously. "This is awful."

"Maybe you *are* an adolescent."

I clenched my teeth together to keep from blowing up. Angrily, I reminded myself I'd once vowed always to tell the truth to my therapist.

"Give me a minute," I said, then sat breathing quietly. "Or I'll turn this appointment into a full-scale debacle."

He laughed quietly. "You can if you want. You know how."

"Shut *up*," I said. "Please. I'm sorry. I don't want a fight."

I sat concentrating on my breathing. I'd been in therapy for six full years, and by now I knew I sometimes dealt with fear by backing him into arguments about something different altogether and then holding it against him that he was too busy arguing with me to talk about some far more sensitive issue. I'd also learned that, as a multiple, it was almost instinctive for me to "send out" an alter, or at least behavior that could distract from the issue at hand. Yes, I was picking fights and acting like a thirteen-year-old because what I had to say was embarrassing and frightening.

Finally, I sat looking at my hands. "We've been meeting a long time," I said. "But sometimes I feel as if you just plain don't understand."

I saw a watchful quiet take hold of his face.

"Jane," he said, "if you think you need to see—"

"I don't want a new therapist," I told him, and made a face.

I thought I saw him relax.

We'd been through that once before. My process had so bogged down that we had agreed he should send me to someone else for a while. But the woman he had sent me to had met me at the door with papers I was to sign agreeing she could use my case for research. Ten minutes into the appointment I realized she had begun tape-recording the session without my permission, and her suggestion, when I told her that multiplicity left me feeling too squeezed for time, was that I take a forty-five-minute bath each night, that I let my alters have complete freedom during that time, and that, when the three-quarters of an hour was up, I tell my internal selves that they were to go "down the drain" until the next evening. The Kids cried all the way home from her office, and I did, too. I never kept my second appointment with the woman, and couldn't wait to see my own therapist again.

"What I want," I said, "is in Putnam. And it embarrasses me to want such a textbook thing." I gave him a pleading look and desperately wanted him to simply guess what it was.

"Putnam covers a lot of ground," he said.

I took a breath. "What I want," I finally told him, "is to meet another multiple. I just think that—"

"I think that's a great idea," he said.

"I was afraid you'd say that," I told him.

Another multiple, I felt, might understand me in some way he never would. I was suddenly desperate to meet a kindred spirit and to compare notes and perhaps have a few laughs about living with such an odd disorder. On the other hand, another multiple might understand me *too* well. I feared feeling vulnerable and exposed.

"I'm not sure what can be arranged," he said. "It shouldn't be another one of my clients. But I'll make some calls and maybe I'll have something for you in a week or two."

I began to sputter apologies and explanations. I hated that he had to go to extra effort; I wasn't sure it was a good idea. "Besides," I told him, "I might chicken out."

"Let me take care of the contact, and then you can decide for yourself."

Ten days later, I was standing in my kitchen looking at a name and a phone number written on a piece of paper. My therapist had called a few colleagues and one of them, in turn, had a multiple who had reached the stage of wanting to meet one of her own kind. It was decided I would be given her first name and phone number and that I would call her when I was ready.

I had had the number for two days, and finally that evening I had vowed I would call before I went to bed. I must have taken the phone off the hook and replaced it a dozen times. Finally, I dialed the number in a rush, and after the first ring a soft voice answered.

"Hello," I said, suddenly wondering how on earth to identify myself. "This is, um, *Jane*," I said. "I—"

"*Jane*," she said, as if we had already fallen into some code of placing extra stress on the only name we had agreed to exchange. "This is *Marcia*. I've been waiting for you to call."

The arrangement had been that we would chat on the phone and then, if it seemed a good idea to both of us, we would meet face to face and see what happened.

It was strange getting started. What did one say? So, I hear you're a multiple, too? How many kids do *you* have in your system? Since I'd read that multiples seem to have an uncanny knack for reading one another's words and shifts, I felt especially nervous. I feared giving away too much about myself and feared saying the wrong thing.

We went with So-I-hear-you're-a-multiple-too, and quickly segued into some desultory talk about how rotten it was and how hard the therapy was. We talked about this and that, and then she told me who her therapist was.

I suddenly felt unnerved. Her therapist was a man who'd made a substantial name for himself because of his work with sexual abuse survivors; he often lectured and offered workshops. For some reason, I blurted out that I'd been a multiple for three, maybe four years before I was sexually abused.

The phone line fell eerily silent.

I refrained from clicking the phone hook and calling "Marcia? Marcia!" as if I were in some old movie.

The truth was, I knew that shocked silence, the horrible moment after some blow has fallen, and I felt quite frightened: I *had* said something wrong.

Finally, Marcia's voice came over the line again. She sounded stunned. "That happened to me, too," she said and began to cry.

I clung to the phone.

"But my therapist doesn't want to hear it. He says when I bring it up, it's only because I don't want to talk about the sexual abuse. I don't even know if he believes me."

I hesitated. "I believe you," I told her. "If that helps any."

Her crying grew much quieter. "You have no idea," she told me, "how much I needed to hear someone say there's more to this than sex."

And she had no idea just how grateful I was, right that minute, for my flexible, eclectic therapist.

Marcia and I went on to talk of other things. She told me about her support group and encouraged me to join, but I heard so many stark confidences during the week from students that I had no interest in spending two evenings a week doing the same. I told Marcia that I pretty much devoted my free time to having fun, if I could.

"Fun?" she said. "I'm not nearly well enough to have fun."

I pondered that. How well did one have to be to have fun? My own therapist insisted that learning to have fun was critical to the therapeutic process.

After a few more minutes, we hung up. Marcia wouldn't mind having me join her group, she said, but other than that she didn't feel ready to get together with me. I breathed a silent prayer of thanks. There was something altogether too weighty about her presence on the phone. Once again, I thought ruefully, I was glad to be following my own course, and glad to have my flexible, sometimes irreverent therapist as my guide.

After my talk with Marcia, it began to dawn on me that my therapist tended to ignore labels such as "physical," "sexual," or "emotional" abuse. In fact, he hardly ever used the word "abuse." We ignored the dogma of the treatment of abuse victims or survivors and examined the salient episodes of my life in terms of meaning and developmental effects. When I underwent my appendectomy at the age of three, what would that experience have meant to me at that age? How would I have seen, felt, and thought when I was three? What conclusions did I draw about the world, the people around me, or myself? What developmental tasks were distorted, derailed, or delayed? What did I need to learn in the present to make up for what I had missed learning all those years ago? What did the wounded three-year-old self need so that she might heal and resume her suspended growth?

Soon my time was taken up with two major tasks: learning as much as necessary about human development and getting a more conscious and deliberate knowledge of each of my selves. Again and again my therapist sent me to the library or spent some time explaining developmental behavior at certain ages. Although I began to feel far more crazy than I ever had before, it seemed to me that I had to "honor" my disorder. Being half a dozen ages all at once was often frustrating, but when the wishes of one self clashed with another I sometimes felt overwhelmed.

More than one restless teenager agitated for contact lenses and pierced ears. If the system had included only them and me, I would probably just have given in. But we were not alone in the system, and each time these requests were made, I said no. Contact lenses were out of the question because The Kids had already had too many unpleasant and painful experiences inflicted on their body. Piercing ears fell into much the same category. I refused to ask The Kids to endure physical pain solely for someone else's pleasure. But another objection soon arose. The Kids admitted that The Teenagers had been working on them, trying to convince them how wonderful it would be to have earrings. But The Kids had a little surprise of their own.

"We would say okay to earrings," they confided. "But The Boys wouldn't like it."

"The Boys?" I asked them.

"Oh yes," they told me. "There are boys in here, and they definitely don't want earrings." The Kids giggled, then vanished. And that was that.

More serious trouble started whenever my parts broached the question of weight. The Kids' only concern was that they got to eat their daily quota of snacks. Older kids, however, wanted to starve back into the thin, athletic, boyish, flexible body they once had. They liked to eat, but every time they resurfaced in a middle-aged female body, they panicked and insisted their *real* body must be around here somewhere. There were parts who feared having any female attributes that might advertise them as a sexual object; whenever given the chance, they cast their votes either for starvation or for suicide. And the young woman in her twenties had an all-too-common reaction to being raped: her weight shot up a full forty pounds within a short time after the attack, and when she too increasingly became a presence, she read the numbers on the scale each morning and fretted that she did not weigh nearly enough.

Often I wished I could be a total autocrat, and just choose a weight and tell them all to pay close attention: there would be no more haggling and no more behind-the-scenes maneuvers. It was this kind of relentless conflict that made me long for integration.

Similar battles were fought over clothes. Jeans and turtle-necks? Skirts and flats? Suits? Sweats? Or what? I never had clothing in my closet to please everyone, and I selected clothing for any given day by pure default: I never wore anything that any part found frightening. Fortunately, the range of attire for women is quite broad, although I wondered whether safety and comfort would always take precedence over either taste or femininity. My best guess was that even if my less feminine parts faded considerably during integration, I had become so accustomed to clothing that had comfort as its prime feature that I would never change. It will always be easier to teach in trousers: one can sit on the desk, rest a foot on a chair, or stride at top speed across campus when late for a meeting. And how much simpler it is to pull on trousers than it is to mess with slips, pantyhose, and shoes not quite designed to be worn on the human foot.

Parceling out the meager twenty-four hours in any given day proved the most difficult quandary of all. On the most fundamental level, there was the list of what had to be done to maintain basic physical health and mental stability: the preparation of six small, hypoallergenic, hypoglycemic meals; an hour of exercise to stave off depression; an hour of trance work or journal writing; and eight to ten hours of sleep. Beyond that were an hour of commuting and eight or so hours of college work and the question of when to see friends, when to take showers, clean the house, walk the dogs, and on and on. I spent two hours a week in contact with my therapist, and an additional hour and half driving back and forth to his office.

I was happiest and calmest in the summers when I did not teach. How I loved the peace and quiet of routine, and how I loved to go to bed at night having accomplished what needed to be done. The days of summer seemed infinitely beautiful to me; get up, walk dogs, read or write, exercise, cook, see friends, meditate, write in journal, sleep. I had friends who often asked what I had done lately for "excitement." I have never craved excitement; I crave the slow routine of one long day after another.

How I managed during the academic year was very simple. I spent half my time scheming about ways to get everything into the day: I made lists no ordinary mortal could complete. I talked constantly about time with my psychologist, who often must have felt as if he were as much a time management consultant as a therapist. And I took care of whatever was in the worst condition at that moment. If student papers were piling up, I cut short on sleep, skipped the gym, and got to work. But after I skipped the gym a couple of days, I decided that no matter what else I did I would get there first—even if it meant tearing into school moments before a class. When, because of all of the preceding, I hadn't managed to trance out or ponder in my journal, each of those in turn became the current crisis-driven priority. The situation was maddening and exhausting. My days were crammed and seldom left me with a sense of satisfaction.

I understand that it is recommended that multiples who have jobs continue to work because of the value of a "reality referent." I understand the concept and, in fact, frequently used my colleagues and students in benign ways to test out new things I had learned. The problem, however, was that I was caught in an impossible time crunch between being a multiple and being a college professor. I never felt completely rested—except during the summers or when I was forced to take some medical leave—and I never had any down time. I could never imagine that people actually found the time to watch television or to read trash fiction (two activities I associate with being too ill to do anything else), and I am still dumbfounded when I encounter boredom in those around me.

In order to "save" time, I tried to establish as much coconsciousness as was possible and safe. My youngest selves appeared most often when I drove or puttered around the house. I would listen to their chatter and talk over everything with them from the impending death of their favorite dog to why we had to go to school or what they wanted to eat for dinner. Seldom did they get special time set aside for them alone, although they were always thrilled to go riding or walking and occasionally to the grocery store. Once in a while, they did seem to need time out in the benign sense: time to do nothing but curl up on the couch or sit on the floor petting dogs.

Other parts were treated in similar ways. It was easiest for them to appear while I was working out or driving. (Teenagers, however, I fended off while driving. They were terrifying when allowed to get their hands on the wheel.) Often while I was dozing off at night, parts appeared, and occasionally I could listen in on conversations among various selves.

At times, however, parts required special favors and expenditures of time: The Teenagers couldn't believe how far it was to the nearest major city and occasionally needed to be taken there just to walk city streets again. They, in fact, were prone to boredom and often pined for excitement, and occasionally I gave in to them. Other parts required time to pursue private interests: part of me still loves to play the flute. Others crave time in shopping malls (not a personal favorite), and still others are happiest playing handyman, pounding nails and painting whatever needs it.

Sometimes I compared my life to that of a professional woman with a family. I too, although secretly, was concerned with the welfare of children, teenagers, and assorted "family" members. But there was a major difference: I could not arrange separate outings for my selves. I could not send my younger selves out to play or drop The Teenagers at the mall. Nor could I encourage my internal carpenter with a few minutes of chat and the occasional snack—I had to be out there, too. I had all the concerns and interpersonal demands of anyone with a family—with the added complication that we shared one physical being.

Most of the time, my parts accepted that they were required to get along. I grew up sick of fighting and brutality, and my parts also seemed to long for peace and harmony. Sometimes there were jealousies and hurt feelings, but as often as possible we collaborated, cooperated, compromised. I am reminded, at times, of one of the classic methods of team building: give strangers a problem they must solve together and they will get to know one another in the process. The daily scheduling dilemma has been our team builder.

Now and again, however, the team approach to time failed. And when it did, it failed on a grand scale. One symptom was uncontrolled switching. If a part had been fended off too long, or had been offered too many promises that, for one reason or another, I had not been able to fulfill, I found myself engaged in an exhausting struggle for executive control. The longer the struggle continued, the more difficult it was for me to see, breathe, or think. In time, I learned to maintain one clear, genuine, consistent central personality for longer and longer periods, but when I was forced to do so for too long—usually because of external circumstances—I began to suffer.

If I managed to maintain during the day, I was likely to pay at night. Just as I was on the edge of sleep, a part would surge to the forefront. I tended to think of this as "power-switching," because it was accompanied, according to my therapist, by a surge of adrenaline, and because the switch itself was a kind of internal, although temporary, coup. On bad nights, after periods when I had not been able to schedule enough time for alters, the surging and switching continued for hours. Each neglected part in turn surged to the forefront, hung around, talked, thought, remembered, complained, schemed, then as it faded was replaced by another neglected and aggrieved part of the system. There were long periods of time when I tolerated this behavior—and lost literally whole nights of sleep, lying there wide-awake, transfixed by self after self, each energized by adrenaline and pent-up emotion, while I, and my body, grew more and more exhausted.

In time I learned. I knew what this switching meant—everybody needed more time—and yet I also knew that this kind of switching took too great a toll. I learned to apologize to my parts, promise to do better, then get up and take a tranquilizer. It was always with some reluctance that I did this, but anarchy, in the end, was bad for everyone. I needed my sleep in order to wring as much time as possible from the next day.

All my life I have had several notable quirks that had to do with time. Whole chunks of it sometimes disappeared. When I was in school, I sometimes didn't hear assignments—truly had no idea, for instance, why all my classmates had done some project that I had never heard about in the first place. Often I was unable to recall simple things. When someone called on the phone and asked, idly, what I'd been doing, I had no idea. How was my weekend? I didn't know, couldn't even recall the weekend. What had I read lately? No clue. I'd even guess that if I had been abruptly blindfolded I probably couldn't have said what I was wearing. Like all multiples, I learned my dodges and my evasions. I passed myself off as absentminded or abstracted. I discovered that people who asked about my weekend really wanted to tell me about *their* weekend.

When I was finally diagnosed as a multiple, these quirks suddenly made sense; each of my selves had its own part of our story, and its own sense of time.

Imagine projecting a movie to a roomful of people. Imagine that they range in age from three to thirty-eight. Imagine that some of those people are dead asleep and do not know a movie is being played. Imagine that a very young one spies on the whole thing, but pretends to be asleep. Imagine that some of them catch only a few minutes, or the parts that interest them. Imagine that at least one part watches the whole thing, but does not speak. Imagine that there are scenes some watchers interpret one way, that others interpret the opposite way, that still others do not understand at all. Imagine that some parts hear a phrase or see a gesture that repeats and repeats in their minds.

This roomful of varied movie patrons is a kind of model of how I experienced time. Not only did I have sealed-off traumatic memories, I had a wild range of perceptions of that time: my internal five-year-old, who tried to miss absolutely nothing, understood things differently than did a more grown-up part. And parts that were not consistently engaged missed whole scenes, even whole decades. Other parts, required to remember, sat quietly but explosively in their seats, waiting for the movie to end so they could get up, go out into the street, and *tell* somebody what they'd seen.

When it came to time, I had to struggle to learn one frightening concept after another: concepts any ordinary learns without much thought.

One day, a student came into my office. She was livid. I sat and invited her to sit, too.

Just the day before, for at least the twentieth time, my therapist had explained that, for ordinary people, emotions pass with time. Healthy anger, he insisted, served an immediate purpose and then began to fade. I did not believe him: I had a self whose full-time job was to contain my large reservoir of rage and other selves who felt constant fear. Emotions didn't pass; neither did time as far as I was concerned.

The student slammed her notebook on my desk. I glanced up and realized that I happened to be facing the clock. The student launched into a tirade about the fact that she had never worked so hard in all her life as she was in my stupid course which she didn't even need for her stupid major and all I ever did was write stupid comments on her translations and her tests and give her stupid C's. Her face was red, she shouted until the tears came, she even stamped her foot.

I tried to look as if I were listening. Mostly I was watching the time. How short *was* anger?

Just under three minutes, as it turned out. Then the student's voice dropped, and she began to cry, even thanking me for passing her the tissues. After four minutes, she was asking for advice, and after five she was apologizing and telling me she felt like a jerk.

I told her it was okay, and offered some obvious advice about it being better not to wait quite so long before coming in for help.

Inside, though, I was fairly chortling. Intense emotions *did* transmute. My student's anger faded, turned to something else. I still wasn't sure what happened to time. I certainly didn't believe it simply passed.

Privately, I believed the past still existed. The Teenagers in the system wandered the house in search of long-gone favorite clothes and trinkets, and often The Kids, when they were feeling bad, told our therapist that they missed their kittens or would like to ride their bike or sit in front of the fireplace roasting and eating popcorn.

"We want to go *home*," they sometimes pleaded.

"I'm sorry," my therapist told them steadily, "but it's not there anymore. You live here now."

The Kids would squirm and sigh.

A year ago, when I made my annual visit home, The Kids were fired up with expectation. I could hear them mentally listing all the things they intended to bring back with them, and all the things they wanted to look at while they were there. Instead of being fatigued from the long drive, they grew more and more eager as we drove through town and out toward my parents' home.

Trouble started the minute we pulled in the drive: the swimming pool had been bulldozed and covered over. We got out of the car and picked our way across the lawn. When The Kids were three years old, and their mouth and cheek were bleeding, they had had to climb the three concrete steps of the back porch. That porch was gone now; we stepped up onto an expansive redwood deck. The kitchen door they had pounded on had been replaced by sliding glass doors. I rapped on the glass, then stood for a moment looking over the yard. The swings were gone. The huge oak The Kids had loved to climb in later years had been cut down; a fragile ornamental of some kind had been planted in its place. Even the kitchen in the old house had new skylights and a graceful bow window.

The Kids were profoundly silent.

"Come in!" my mother called.

We stepped into the kitchen. The stove and refrigerator were in the same place. The Kids remembered those. The floor, the countertops, the tablecloth, even the phone on the wall were foreign.

I heard my father's footsteps coming down the hall. My mother stepped out of the laundry room.

Who are they? The Kids whispered to me.

"Those are my parents," I whispered back.

I hugged my mother and my father.

They're not my *parents,* The Kids whispered back in horror.

They stared at my mother and father the whole time we were there. I tried to get them to see the resemblance between the parents they knew and the parents sitting here with us. They either couldn't or wouldn't.

At one point, I excused myself from the conversation and on the pretext of using the bathroom walked through the house, showing The Kids around. I had seen the changes gradually take place over the years, but The Kids were stunned. The bathrooms had been entirely redone and were now different colors. The living room furniture was far from what it had been thirty years ago. Silently The Kids took in what was missing: their favorite chair for hiding in, and hiding behind. I walked them to the doorway of my brothers' old rooms; Hank's was now a guest room. I could feel The Kids heave a sigh of relief that he had somehow been eradicated. But then I stood them in the doorway of their old bedroom. It was now the bunkroom for my nephews when they visited. There was not one scrap of evidence The Kids had ever lived there. They stood transfixed and silent, then told me, close to tears, their meaning different now, *We want to go home.*

I visited with my parents a little while longer, said my good-byes, and, exhausted, pulled away from the house. Since I would have to beat my way through city traffic to get to my hotel, I decided to pull over somewhere and rest. I stopped and bought a cold drink, then, after some thought, I walked over to the town park.

I sat under a tree on a little grassy knoll, opened my drink, and nervously looked around. I was too tired, I thought, to run into anyone I knew. Across the way were the baseball diamonds. Kids skidded up on their bikes for the practices and scrimmages, and parents pulled up and dropped off more kids. Everything seemed the same: the bleachers, the good-natured taunting, the colorful caps, and the gloves dangling from handlebars. The late afternoon crowd was making its way out of the swimming pool. I found myself watching closely, wondering if I would see anyone I knew. I closed my eyes for a minute and thought about what a rough day The Kids had had.

It's not there anymore, they kept telling themselves, as if they'd just gone home to find the place had been bombed out or razed.

Well, they needed to know that, I thought to myself.

Casually, I opened my eyes, and the world around me looked different, too. I didn't recognize a single sponsor spelled out on the back of the softball shirts. The music coming from the pool parking lot was not what it had been twenty years ago. I studied the faces of the swimmers and the sunbathers hauling towels and beach bags and whining children, and realized that, except for relatives, I didn't know a single person in this town. My old high-school chums, in their bell-bottoms and their army jackets, would not be turning up. I could walk down the block and blast tennis balls at the backdrop but none of my buddies would come by for a game.

For a moment, I felt as if I'd walked out on a ledge that was giving way beneath me: I would fall, there was nothing to support me. Then the past simply fell away, and while I sat there in the park, with rap blasting instead of rock, time neatly divided itself into the over-and-done-with-past and the right-this-minute-present.

That night I called my therapist as planned so that I could check in.

"It's over!" I told him. I was jubilant. "I finally realized it's over."

"Mmmm," he said, his voice low and cautious. "What's over?"

"The past!" I told him. "It's *finished*. I finally got it! Time *divides!*"

I heard him inhale, then pause, and I remember his exact words: "Thank god," he said.

Time suddenly seemed less of a trap, less dangerous. There was no longer an invisible membrane through which I could slip and thus find myself reliving past events. Many of the flashback triggers seemed suddenly defused, and my memory was finally not so much a mine field through which, ironically for my own good, I was forced to stumble so much as it was an old trunk I could rummage in at will. It possibly still hid some nasty surprises, but it also held many of the answers to my mysteries. I had discovered an essential truth: my past belonged to me; I did not belong to it.

For nearly all of my seven or eight years of therapy, one aspect of time troubled my therapist: he couldn't understand my relentless haste. All along we had known that we were, in essence, following the lead of my subconscious. After my diagnosis, since he did not call out alters but allowed them to appear in their own time, he set neither the sequence nor the pace of our work. The sequence did not bother him, but he frequently remarked that he thought

I was going too fast and he often speculated that there must be some reason for it or at least some way to slow me down. He was concerned that the process seemed to take too much out of me, and he worried that I was perhaps not resolving issues as thoroughly as necessary—that I might be leaving things half undone and therefore need to return to them later in order to integrate.

I've been in a hurry all my life. As a child in school, I was competitive, but not necessarily with my classmates: I was trying to keep up with my brothers. I had also always been something of a perfectionist and sometimes I suspected that even in therapy I was trying to beat some kind of record or trying to prove yet again that I was smart. But then one day it finally came to me that I wasn't trying to race other multiples to the finish line of integration; I was trying to beat my own death.

One afternoon, years before, I had picked my way along the cracked, narrow sidewalk of the highest bridge in the city. Halfway across I stopped, leaned against the railing, and pretended to look north into the heart of the city. My coat hung open. I wore no hat. Sleet clumped in my hair and melted down my neck. It was my twenty-third birthday. Below me lay two options: the river and the railroad tracks.

Traffic roared back and forth behind me on the bridge. The vibration and the bounce rose through the soles of my feet. The river was the least messy of my choices. I stepped a little in that direction, then peered straight down into the water.

I remember that I looked up at the steel gray sky, pushed my freezing hair away from my face, then looked back down at the water. For a moment, the world hung silent and suspended: there was no roar of traffic, the river's currents seemed as if they had been painted on a canvas.

I sighed, then thought, Okay. I'll give it one more year. On this day, one year from today, I will choose again.

The river rushed once more far below me; the bridge rumbled with cars and trucks. I stood a while longer, grieving for a thousand reasons I could sense but could not name. Then I turned away from the river and headed home.

Every year on my birthday I relived this moment. Every year I stood on my figurative bridge and decided once again whether I would grant myself one more year. During the rest of the year and during therapy, my days were not so rushed and crowded that I did not sense a deep yet articulate fear of living a wasted life and dying an early death. The idea made me feel helpless and full of sorrow.

Paradoxically, although I was often suicidal, I believed that any death would be an early one. After all, my youngest self was three or four. How old would that self be in five years? In ten? Sometimes I wondered how old I would be if I counted up my parts and averaged their ages. Significantly younger, I would guess. And yet the years kept passing. If I looked at the actuary tables, I had yet to reach the probable halfway point of my life, but I had lived so long fearing death that the *tick-tick* of clocks sounded a lot to me like the *click-click* of the safety of my brother's gun. Each turned page of a calendar brought me another month closer to my own death. Every day, every hour I was alive seemed a miracle; every minute seemed like one less that stood between me and my grave. I lived so long with a brother who desperately wanted to kill me, and with my own impulse toward self-destruction, that it frequently surprised me to be alive at all.

During this time, it occurred to me that a violent death was not my necessary end, and I spent some time actually thinking about how and when I would like to die. I imagined myself outdoors in a garden at high summer, sitting in a well-cushioned wrought-iron chair set half in the shade of some old, stalwart tree. I wanted to be old, but strong and hearty until the end. I did not want to die abruptly—say, of a heart attack while hiking—because I wanted to have some time to talk, to think, to remember before finally letting go.

Strangely, imagining a better death changed my view of time. Imagining an expanse of days stretching into old age meant I'd begun to sense something about time I'd never sensed before: that if time divides into past and present, perhaps it also reaches forward into the future.

TOWARD JUST-ONE

ONE AFTERNOON DURING my appointment, my therapist excused himself to take an emergency phone call in an adjoining office. My mood was oddly buoyant, somehow surreal and remote. In his absence, I got up and wandered around the office, examining the lamps, the view from the window, the rank of reference volumes on the shelf over his desk.

Idly, I took the *Diagnostic and Statistic Manual* back to my chair and browsed through it while I waited. I didn't look up MPD, as I had already done more than once. Instead, I let the book fall open here and there and read snatches of description and diagnostic criteria.

I heard the door open, and glanced up.

He apologized again for interrupting the session, but I waved him off and continued reading the little block I had begun.

Halfway into the room, he realized what I had in my lap and abruptly stopped. He looked wary but wryly amused.

"And what do you think you're doing?" he asked, half as if the *DSM* was off-limits to patients, even though he himself had handed it to me more than once.

I slapped the book shut, then looked up at him and grinned. "Oh," I said with exaggerated casualness, "shopping for a new disorder."

He laughed and took the book from me. "You have enough problems," he said.

"But I'm so tired of being a multiple."

209

And I was. Two and a half years had passed since my diagnosis as a multiple, and I had begun to resent everything I read about the disorder because MPD on the page was a whole lot more fascinating and dramatic than the weird and tiring texture of my life. Where, I asked him, were the fusions bathed in light? Where were the explosive revelations that would change my life for good and all? When was *I* going to get to say, "I was born at thus-and-such an age on thus-and-such a day in the office of my therapist"?

He smiled sadly. "Lots of luck," he said. "You're already here. I think you're it."

I sighed and made a face.

One morning, a few weeks later, I was sitting in my office, reviewing a set of lecture notes. Often my therapist had pointed out that I spent too much time on my teaching: I was too thorough when I read my students' work, too compulsive about planning the details of my classes. On this particular morning, it came to me that I had not only written this set of notes, but that I had been over them before. I stared out my office window and let myself wonder. Exactly how many times *had* I worked on this set of notes?

There was a kind of internal shuffling, a realignment in the way I viewed my selves, then the answer surfaced: three times. My therapist and I had known for some time that I had a layered personality system, with nearly identical and almost interchangeable selves standing in for one another.

What I had been doing at the college was submitting nearly all of my work to this triumvirate for review. Dizziness swept over me. No wonder my students always commented on how thorough I was, and how organized, when I usually felt as if I wasn't quite sure what I would say or do next when standing in front of a class.

I put my notes away, went to the cafeteria, dawdled over coffee, and forced myself to meet my students "unprepared." The class went just fine, and later that day, while driving home, I grumbled at myself, growing angrier and angrier at all the time I had wasted over the years.

The next time I saw my therapist, I announced that I had made a decision.

I can only imagine how it feels to be a therapist listening to one's longtime patient warn that she is about to say something he very well might not like and announce that she doesn't especially care what he thinks. But I was feeling oddly hostile and defiant.

"So, mmm, what's up?" he said. He was smiling, but watching me quite closely.

I pulled my jacket tight around me, then dug my hands deeper into my pockets. I suddenly felt silly. But then, in a flash, I was mad again.

"I've decided," I told him, "that multiplicity is causing me entirely too many problems." I told him about my trio of teaching selves. I said I'd finally realized how much time I spent worrying about whether I was projecting the right personality at the right time. I was tired of always having to scramble to remember things, tired of the anxiety I felt each time the phone rang, because once I answered I would have to undergo a series of rapid-fire switches, looking for a part who knew the caller.

He listened to me with care, nodding, even laughing at some of my descriptions.

"This is a breakthrough," he told me gravely. "This is important. What you've come to realize is that multiplicity is the problem now. It is no longer a solution—although it was when you were a child."

He beamed at me. I scowled back.

"That's not the breakthrough," I muttered. "It's too much work to be a multiple. It's harder for a multiple to get through the day than it is for an ordinary person."

He nodded. "That's what I was trying to say," he assured me.

I moved to his vacant desk chair, spun it briefly, and stared off into space. "But what I've *decided* is the breakthrough," I said.

His voice turned flat and cautious. "And what's that?"

"I've decided not to do it anymore."

He grew still. "Do what, Jane?"

Suddenly I laughed. I realized he thought I was talking suicide. "Nothing bad," I said. "I've just decided I'm not going to *be* a multiple anymore."

"I don't think—"

"What I mean," I said, "is that I'm going to stop dissociating. *I* am going to be here from now on. *I* am going to be in charge of my life."

He sat back in his chair and regarded me in silence.

I grew a little bit defensive and insisted it wasn't a so-called flight into health, when all the parts submerge and one part carries on in a vacuum. It was just that life had grown too complicated; there had to be a simpler way to do things. And maybe I could prove to myself that I was strong enough and tough enough and smart enough to live in the world without a crowd of walk-on selves to help me out.

He remained silent a while longer. I was scowling, angry that he didn't seem to believe me, or didn't seem to think I could pull it off.

"I know it's not the complete answer," I told him. "I know I'm not *cured* or anything, but it's a step. Right? It's a step."

He gave me an amazed smile. "I haven't said anything because I don't know what to say. I believe you. Life as a multiple is a mess. But I've never heard of anyone just deciding to stop dissociating. It's quite the leap," he warned.

"Well, I'm not promising anything. I just want to try. I have to do something. This whole business is driving me crazy."

He asked how long I'd been able to maintain.

"Two days," I said. "With deliberate trances."

He thought and nodded. "Try it," he said. "If anyone can do it, it's probably you."

Suddenly I was nervous. "Don't hold me to it, though," I said. "I'm just going to try."

He smiled. "It's your idea. I'll help if I can. How's that?"

I nodded, then sat for a while gloating, yet fearing the task I had set for myself.

I can't say that it worked completely, but suddenly my new resolution did focus my attention on my own inclination to switch. Sometimes I have wondered at what point multiplicity becomes a habit, switching not because one has to and not even because there is a real reason to switch, but just because that's what one does, what I did. I was more focused on my own presence in my life, and I found that I had a little more time because I was not doing things three, four, even six times in a row. Not only had I reviewed my teaching three times, I often repeated other actions, from locking the doors at night, to drafting my annual budget. On the other hand, because I had to remain consistent, I also grew tired much more quickly. Not only was I unaccustomed to being out in the world for any length of time, I was also probably missing the regular fixes of adrenaline that personality switches provided me. I slept long hard nights during these first weeks and months, and I took a lot of naps. I still switched, but over time I grew confident that all my switches were internal or private—taking place where only I could hear them, unless I was with my therapist. And because I had fewer fears that I would be exposed as a multiple, I soon began to feel more resilient and more confident.

A few months later, I was standing in my bathroom, already in a nightshirt and bare feet. I was getting ready for bed, cleaning my teeth, and thinking about very little except how nice it would be to get a long night's sleep.

Suddenly my eyes caught in the mirror, and in a flash I had dissociated into the mirror. When I was younger, many of my selves had come to me via my bedroom mirror and, back then, I often longed for someone special to look into my eyes and actually *see* me. This person would recognize my one true self—something I could not do—and would coax that self to life.

All these years later, there in my bathroom mirror was the same intense look: the expression of profound longing, the desire to be given life. My childhood fantasy came back to me, then abruptly shifted: I was no longer waiting for someone to come along, recognize me, and bring me to life.

My back and arms rippled into gooseflesh. I stared into the mirror, back through time and selves and my own history. I dropped my toothbrush. And then I began to cry and laugh and whoop. It had taken years, and it had come as a terrific surprise to my grown-up self, but the moment was every bit as significant and intense as I had once longed for it to be. Only now I knew that *I* was the person who would see me first, *I* would coax that shy but hopeful self out of the glass, *I* would rescue the lonely, yearning younger selves.

During these times, weekly work with my psychologist continued as usual. We talked over the daily incidents in my life, he checked up on how I was sleeping and how much exercise I was getting. Was I still following my diet? Where was I in the cycle of cyclothymia? We talked about my internal progress. I still checked in on the phone once a week between appointments, and, when I was in the office, we carefully planned how we would spend the time.

Often we returned to the fact that the process of integration was so erratic and unpredictable. We seemed to verbally capitalize the word, referring to the Process the same way one might refer to the Trinity or the Bermuda Triangle. What was happening was difficult to dissect. My process was not remotely linear, not entirely logical, not completely conscious, and not always scientific. It seemed oddly paced, unpredictable, and disturbing, yet it also was profoundly beautiful and usually seemed somehow exactly right. At times, I often sensed that I was glimpsing the darkest aspects of human behavior and the strength and majesty of the human spirit. The weeks and years were tedious and wearing, but the time was marked with blinding revelations that I could barely articulate, which soon vanished from my conscious mind yet which changed my life forever.

One day I asked my psychologist if he knew what was going to happen next.

He grinned at me and shrugged. "No clue," he said.

I made a face. I had been looking for reassurance.

"But," he said, "I usually know where we are, and I can always tell you where we've been."

I thought for a moment. That was more than I could do. To me, my process often seemed to ricochet as crazily as a ball in a pinball machine, dropping for long periods into various deep slots from which I could not seem to retrieve it, then caroming to the top of the board and rebounding here and there for extra points, earned partly through sheer doggedness and partly through sheer luck.

What remained consistent, though, was the work we did with The Kids. We often reserved the last fifteen to twenty minutes of the appointment for them to come out and talk to my therapist. At times it seemed frivolous to me. Since they had been freed from the expectation of turning into either a boy or a girl, they focused on other things. Sometimes it seemed to me they were focused on nothing at all. Some days, at their insistence, we took along one of the dogs, and The Kids and my therapist simply sat on the floor, petting a dog ecstatic to have so much undivided attention. My therapist asked them about certain things he knew were happening in daily life, and taught them various skills. Often they would say, "We don't feel good," an expression that could mean practically anything, and over time they learned to distinguish between whether they were sad, frightened, or angry. They were sometimes able to tell the difference between emotional and physical distress, although they themselves never felt physically ill. The Grown-ups, they would confide, had a sore throat or some other illness.

Although the work they did with him seemed to have no substance, I could certainly see the ways in which they were changing. Early in the process, they had often insisted that Badger go with them to appointments, and so I had lugged along a knapsack with Badger stuffed inside. There was a period of months they had dragged along favorite books, and had sometimes coaxed my therapist into reading to them. They had clung to him when allowed to do so, hanging on to his arm, his hand, even the front of his shirt. But over time, these things gradually gave way. Badger, according to them, no longer wanted to come along. He was feeling okay, they insisted, and didn't mind staying home. The books suddenly seemed too young for them, and they gradually acquired the habit of judging certain things as being for "babies"—certainly too young for them. They lost their frantic craving for physical contact, and over time even their speech improved.

It was perhaps this last I noticed most, and found most fascinating. I could literally hear them mature. They pronounced certain words more clearly, their sentences grew longer, more complete, and more complex, and they gradually acquired a sense of humor. Instead of a constant, tearful, brooding presence, they gradually became fun to have around. They often saw the funny and absurd side of things, and they saved up hilarious stories to tell our shrink. Time they spent with him was often taken up with much giggling and silliness.

For years, my therapist had told me how much he liked The Kids, but it took me a while to discover, to my surprise, that I too had grown fond of them. Sometimes I wondered who they were, really, and where they had come from. Certainly I recalled nothing like these funny, exuberant selves from my original childhood. My therapist's quiet speculation was that they had gradually evolved into what I might have been like as a child under different circumstances, and he often told me that children who are diagnosed as multiples most need, not intensive therapy, but a warm and nurturing environment where they will gradually and naturally shed their disorder as they grow.

A year passed. I finally did have a consistent adult self who went out into the world, and I realized that the focus of my work had shifted from recollecting the past to acknowledging my selves, to facing some horrifying questions about the present and the future. Who was I, really? How on earth was I to cram all these selves into one person when the time came? When I looked back, I wondered if I had gone through my life as a complete stranger not only to myself but to everyone around me. I wondered, for instance, if I had ever had anything remotely resembling a genuine relationship with another human being. I had had some close, deep ties over the years, and sometimes I wondered if all of them had been false. Had I ever had a real friend? Could I ever separate pathology from identity? At what point did my disorder end and my self begin? For answers, I searched the behavior of the people around me, and what I saw confirmed what my psychologist had often said: mental illness is not behavior different from what is found in the rest of the population; mental illness is only its more extreme manifestation. I discovered that I was not the only person wondering who I was and whether anyone really knew me.

One day I was sitting and chatting with my therapist. It seemed to me that I had, right that minute, no burning issues; instead, our talk ranged freely.

"It's interesting," I said, apropos of nothing, "that The Kids

are getting to grow up without ever having to be a boy or a girl."
I paused, then laughed. "Which means, I guess, that *I* get stuck
with that job."

"What job?"

"You know," I said. "Turning into a woman." Suddenly I was
squirming like The Kids. "The rest of the way," I said, trying to
appear nonchalant.

He nodded, waited.

I laughed nervously. "I can't believe I said that."

"Well, you did," he said.

"But *me?*" I said. "Why do *I* have to talk about gender if they
don't?"

He smiled. "Oh, I don't know," he said facetiously. "So you
can set an example? Because you're a grown-up?" He turned serious. "It actually makes good sense for you, and not The Kids,
to do this."

I started crossing and recrossing my legs. Always a bad sign.
Then I smiled hopefully. "Well, I've done my best to evade this
question for a good thirty years." I stopped and thought. "And
for eight straight years of therapy, too."

"Yes," he said. "And look where that got you."

"So," I said, shrugging and still trying to joke, "what's the
big deal? An extra self here, an extra self there . . ."

"Jane," he said.

Abruptly I got up out of my chair and stood by the window.
I pressed my forehead to the sash, stared down into the street, and
began to cry. I fought to keep my shoulders quiet, and for a long
time I just stood there, utterly still, tears streaming, my back
turned firmly toward him.

He was silent.

In time, I took a good deep breath, then another and another.
I blotted my eyes. Finally I turned halfway from the window,
folded my arms, and leaned against the sill.

There was a long silence.

After a while, I said, "Do you remember that dream?"

He exhaled carefully. "Yes," he said quietly.

I knew he did. "That" dream was a dream I'd had during the first year of therapy when I'd begun the habit of writing down my nightmares and sending them to him for discussion. But that dream I had refused to talk about, although we often referred to it obliquely, and had even given it a title: "The Dream of the House of Women."

In the dream, I stand in line to use a women's restroom in a very crowded restaurant. When my turn comes, I step through the door marked WOMEN and find myself going down a ramp into a building that is half cattle shed, half prison. It is dark and horrifying and filthy. The air is rank. All kinds of filth squelches underfoot, and soon I find that this prison-barn is home to many women. They are captives here, in the pitch-dark and the stench. They know no other life. They wear everything from dowdy Victorian clothes to rags to raunchy lingerie, and everywhere I look I see women engaging in grotesque sexual acts and blithely carrying out bodily functions. I watch a woman give birth to a baby in the dirt, see another slash her wrists. Women rock themselves, touch themselves, threaten one another, shriek as if they are raving mad. More than one cackles at my evident horror and naiveté. It is like a three-way cross among Hieronymus Bosch, hard pornography, and some Third World disaster. I wander through, mute, sick, and terrified, thinking all the while that this is, in fact, what it means to have been born a girl. By the end of the dream, I have toured every square inch of the place, have recorded every detail, and have found a way out into the light. Once I am outside, no one believes what I have seen in that fetid darkness.

The next time I saw my therapist after sending him the dream, I had stoutly refused to discuss it. "I got out," I kept telling him. "In the end, I got out."

"Yes," he'd said. "You did. But some day you'll have to go back in."

Never, I had said. Never, never, never.

Now I looked him hard and straight in the eye. I didn't speak.

I watched him appraise me—my presence and my mood. He nodded. We both knew what I was thinking.

"It's almost time to go back in there," I said. "I can't believe I said that, either. But it's true." I stopped and thought. "It's no place for The Kids."

He nodded again, watched me carefully, then touched the arm of his chair with a fingertip. "It could be argued," he said, "that The Kids have already been there."

I let a dozen images from childhood flash through my mind. "Yes," I said. "You're right. The Kids have already been there." I closed my eyes for a moment and steadied myself. "I wouldn't want to be a girl, either."

I turned away and looked bitterly out the window. I knew I had not approached the dark, perilous heart of what it meant to be a woman; I had been circling the perimeter, and I knew from the past that true resolution comes only from pursuing a hazardous course straight into the center of my fears.

"Whenever you're ready," he said.

I turned.

"To go back in," he added.

I nodded, then sat back down in my chair and hid my face in my hands.

"Soon," I said. "I'll be ready soon."

It was a lie. I wasn't ready. I grew increasingly anxious and felt more overwhelmed by the day. Although I had been warned not to, I couldn't help listing everything that I believed needed to be done before I could integrate further. The list was so long that the only possible option seemed to be a total collapse. I worried about my health, the diet problems, the weight problems. I had a major toxic reaction to some food that required immediate medical attention. My cyclothymia was ratcheting my moods so wildly that I went for days seeing little reason to sleep, then, after a freefall into depression, went for days seeing little reason to be alive. I seemed to have no sense of self, no sense of who I was or where I was headed. During this time, my department entered a period of major restructuring, and my hours committed to college work dramatically increased. The Kids and other selves still demanded considerable attention, and all the while I gnawed almost constantly over the questions of who I was and how on earth I was going to reconcile myself to being a woman. I didn't want to reenter the House of Women, and I didn't want to have anything to do with getting to know The Boys. When I found the time, I worried about my continued refusal—which bordered on inability—to take medication that might at least ease the cyclothymia if not quiet the tendency to let the worries repeatedly tear at my conscious mind. There had to be a solution, and I knew from past experience it was going to have to come soaring out of the bizarre left field of my subconscious. "Hurry up," I wanted to tell it. But my subconscious works in its own time and in its own inscrutable way.

The answer came at the end of a long day at the college, followed by a round of errands and grocery shopping. I was rushing home, trying to make time, thinking about all the chores that still lay ahead and telling myself that I would have to rush through them because The Kids were tired and needed a break from all hustle and the hurry.

Suddenly I hit the brakes. It wasn't just The Kids who were tired and fed up with the day. So was I. I paused and checked inside myself. The Kids, I knew, would be furious that I would have to carry in the groceries and put them away, put the dogs out and then feed them, and throw something together for supper before we could flop down on the couch. Suddenly I realized that I felt what The Kids felt, that we were all part of the same being. That didn't change what had to be done that evening, but it certainly changed how I saw it.

In the coming days, I tested and retested this theory. When I caught a teenager pining for Mark, I paused and thought, "Do I miss Mark, too?" When someone was tired or mad or restless or disoriented, I checked to see how I felt. It was nearly always the same.

Gingerly, I pushed the idea a little further. If I had alters in order to feel certain things, or to carry out certain functions, I posed a very frightening question: Why were there boys in the system?

More than a year had passed since The Kids had given their giggling report on the presence of The Boys and, ever since, I had wondered when I would get to meet them and what they would be like. I imagined the hundred ways they could derail the whole progress toward integration. How did one come to terms with womanhood if one had to first acquire a group of boys? But one evening, as I was distractedly washing dishes, instead of wondering if they were going to demand, say, basketball shoes, or want to take up some new sport, it came to me to wonder *why* they were there. What purpose did they serve?

I stood washing and rinsing silverware, then abruptly dropped everything on the floor. The answer was both breathtaking and simple: Boys had power.

There were boys in the system because boys are strong and smart. Boys didn't have to do the household chores I loathed; boys got to do whatever they wanted. Boys weren't expected to be polite and neat and quiet. Boys had freedom, boys had lives to lead. Never mind the basketball shoes.

I didn't finish the dishes, but gingerly made my way to the couch and practically slipped into a trance before I was safely off my feet. My internal universe broke completely free of the laws that had once held it together. It was as if the stars and planets were suddenly wandering loose and without pattern.

Suddenly I had another answer to my therapist's early question of how I managed to survive: I had developed parts who never acquired a feminine identity but who adopted every power trait that could be observed in the boys around them. I would never know their likes and dislikes, and I wasn't sure how many identifiable external traits they even had. What mattered was that they had learned ways of living and of carrying themselves I had desperately needed as a child and still needed as an adult. The Boys, I could see as I lay on the couch and let revelations go spinning through my mind, were exactly what I needed in order to feel safe turning into a woman: from The Boys, I could acquire freedom, strength, and brains. They taught me I could set my own course, I could lead a life, I could decide what kind of a woman I wanted to be.

I entered a strange and exciting time. Just as I had once had to acknowledge the existence of my various selves as separate entities within myself, I now had to look beyond the distraction of their identities to their central reason for being. My system remained layered and complex; I still heard voices and sensed a wide range of urges and opinions. But now I saw my selves less as alters, less as individuals, and more as force fields. I studied the function of each part; some existed in order to remember, some managed certain emotions, others represented certain stages of development. Fortunately the academic year came to an end, because I entered a kind of free fall. I realized that, despite my skewed sense of time and the gaps in my contiguous memory, my whole constellation of selves had traveled together along the time line of my life, and that, even though my perception of my life was fragmented, my life itself had not been. After age thirteen, I had turned fourteen;

after high school, I had gone to college. Life had been orderly: my perception of it, even my experience of it, had not.

I soon seemed to be shifting from one hour to the next. Again, I found myself reaching out to touch physical objects, as if to orient myself to this new world, or as if to anchor myself in some way. I was excited but profoundly disoriented, and a little frightened that I might disappear altogether.

I am not sure where this fear sprang from, perhaps from the simple act of dissociation when one's self does disappear. I suspect it also came from popular myths and misconceptions about personality disorders, as if one could turn into Mr. Hyde and stay that way forever.

My therapist gave me a simple yet challenging assignment that I will probably return to for many years: he asked me to make a list of characteristics I believed I would never lose. In a week of sifting through my history and through the daily evidence of my likes and dislikes, I was able to come up with only three: I love animals. I need to spend a lot of time outdoors. I thrive on physical activity.

It seemed a paltry list, yet it anchored me. I believed I could weather anything if I knew I would not lose, or need to sacrifice, those three parts of my life.

Everything else, I thought, was up for grabs.

My therapist shook his head. "You have more than three stable characteristics," he told me.

"I do?"

He nodded.

"Well?" I said, dying to be told who I was and have it over with.

He shook his head.

I sighed. "I know, I know," I said. "I have to find them for myself."

As the weeks wore on, I gradually added a trait here and a

trait there: that, despite everything and often naively, I tend to see the world in terms of goodness, as if I can simply will the things around me to be as I believe they should; that I have a sense of humor and a sense of the absurd. It is a little like working on a life list such as birders keep, only my core personality traits are the focus of my search. At times, I'm fairly certain that half the people around me know more about me than I know about myself.

I tested my new level of integration and resiliency in a peculiar way: I decided to do a trial of medication. As with so many revelations, it simply came to me while I was doing something utterly mundane—like vacuuming—that I no longer feared that medication would obliterate my awareness or my very self. In fact, the more I thought about it and about my earlier idea that I would try medication for the cyclothymia after I had reached full integration, the more I realized that I had it backwards: I ought to try medication when I was laboring with two mental illnesses rather than waiting until one of them was resolved.

It was another four days until my appointment, and my psychologist was away from his office for the day, but he had given me a phone number where he could be reached. He was usually careful that I knew how reach him whenever that was feasible, although I seldom called him.

This time I did. I left a message, and he returned my call almost immediately.

"I'm okay," I rushed to tell him, knowing that extra calls from me first triggered in him the possibility that I was suicidal.

"Good," he said, and his voice relaxed.

I apologized for interrupting him, then rushed to tell him I'd decided to do a trial of Prozac. Since I'd already read everything I could get my hands on, I quickly sketched out my plan: I would do an eight-week trial and no matter what, barring awful side effects, I would stick it out. I figured three to four weeks for the medication to kick in and four weeks to see what the effects were.

"I'm glad," he said again and again. "Good, good, good. I'm glad."

We quickly discussed the logistics, which was why I had interrupted him. If I was going to do it, I wanted to get on with it, and I knew he'd have to contact a doctor. I was between doctors at this point, having yet to see my new one, but having lost my coverage with Tim.

"Who do you want me to call?" he said.

"Tim," I said. "I trust Tim."

"Good," he said. "I'll have something for you when I see you in a few days."

Although Tim's schedule was solid for a month, my therapist talked to him about my decision and Tim simply carved out an appointment for me in his schedule.

Three days later I was sitting in his office.

"I don't prescribe this medication without a specific goal," he told me gently.

I nodded. My therapist had told me Tim would want to talk over not only the side effects of the drug but my reasons for taking it. "You don't need to tell him everything," he had warned, reminding me of the need to keep my diagnosis private.

I took a deep breath and told Tim I was cyclothymic.

He nodded, seeming not in the least surprised. To him, it probably explained some of my mysterious appearances in his office when he could find nothing wrong with me.

Then, without pausing, I went on: "I'll tell you the rest of it if you promise not to put it in my file."

"Sure," he said. "Okay." He put his pen down on the desk.

"I also have Multiple Personality Disorder."

I watched him closely and all I saw in his face was compassion and surprise. I went on to tell him I'd had it since childhood, had known about it for four years, and that I was suddenly in a period of enormous breakthrough but that it was taking an incredible toll. Although I'd fought off the idea of medication for years, I told him multiples were often hospitalized during periods of upheaval.

"Given the choice, Jane," he interrupted, "I'd take Prozac any day over going to the hospital."

I laughed. "Me too," I said. "Me too." And I thought how much I was going to miss having Tim for a doctor.

We turned to the business of going over the potential side effects. He explained that his preference was that I take it for no more than six months, although he did have patients who had been on it for two or three years. He went over the dosages, then after writing the prescription, got down to the problem of my record.

"What's your official diagnosis?" he asked.

"I don't really have one anymore," I said.

He gave me a puzzled look.

"I ran out of mental health benefits years ago," I told him.

He sat back abruptly in his chair, straightened his tie, then said, quietly, "My god."

I nodded and shrugged. "Just use depression," I told him. "All multiples are depressed. Or even cyclothymia. I don't care about documenting that."

He hesitated, then wrote briefly in my file before closing it.

"Call if there are problems," he said. "I want to see you in a month, no matter what."

He opened the door, then stopped me for a moment. I thanked him for squeezing me into his schedule. He waved off my gratitude, then looked at me a moment longer. "Good luck," he said quietly.

I began the medication the next day. For the next ten days, I grumbled to my therapist about the side effects: mostly about the incredible thirst and the nausea.

"It's your call," he said, again and again. "It's your call."

"Eight weeks," I always answered. "This drug has eight weeks to prove itself."

Then I ran directly into a conundrum neither of us had anticipated.

I had been having one of those weeks during which everything seemed to fall apart: my telephone died and required the presence of a repairman crawling around the house and doing some rewiring; one of the dogs got sick; the horse I was riding was laid up with an injury; and my car went to the garage for routine servicing and didn't come back for five days. These were the kinds of externals that drive anyone crazy, especially when they happen all at once; for me, as a multiple, these circumstances would normally have stirred up a chorus of voices and had me living every minute in extreme vigilance.

The opposite happened. I was driving a borrowed car on some errands, then was headed to my appointment. All the errands went badly. My dry cleaning had been lost: could I come back for it? I checked in on the horse: he was still in pain. The borrowed car stalled out at every other intersection. Yet I was absurdly calm. It was summer, and I stopped, as planned, to eat my lunch at a favorite spot by a river before going on to my appointment.

I unwrapped my food and was about to eat when I noticed a shocking thing: the world was quiet. I cocked my head. Actually the world was not quiet. I could hear the river, and the summer songbirds, and the rustle of the breeze and cars going by on the nearby road. What was quiet was the inside of my head. There was absolutely nothing going on in there. I was simply, quietly present and aware.

I had been sensing moments of this quiet for the past few days, but this internal peace stretched on and on. The world seemed bright and slow and crystalline—almost enchanted. I slowly ate my lunch, then languidly packed up my things and headed to my appointment.

We began with chat, but from the look on his face, I knew my therapist could tell something was changed.

Finally I said, "I'm afraid to say too much about this, but it's, ah, well, it's completely quiet in my head."

"Quiet?" he said. "How quiet?"

"Absolutely, one hundred percent quiet." I told him about eating my lunch all by myself next to the river. I was practically glowing. "It was wonderful," I said. "I can't tell you. It was so wonderful."

He caught his breath, then exhaled. Soon we began to talk.

I realized that, in the past, the only way I had been able to achieve quiet had been to let one self obliterate the others. When I was vigilant and focused, I banished all but the present self and therefore remembered only scraps of what had happened. When I was relaxed, there had been nearly constant talk and chatter in my head. Off and on all week, I realized, I had been both quiet and fully present.

"Is this it?" I asked.

"I don't know," he said gently. "It's the beginning."

"Will it last?"

He hesitated.

"Don't answer that," I said. "I shouldn't have asked."

"Just enjoy it," he said. "And know that, if it disappears, it also will come back."

I was practically exuberant. "I'm going to turn into a real person yet," I told him.

He laughed. "You are a real person," he said. "You just haven't quite figured that out yet." Then he asked how I was feeling otherwise.

"You mean grief?"

We had often talked about the fact that integration wasn't necessarily going to be entirely joyful.

"None," I said. "Not yet, anyway." I shrugged.

"Let's take it all as it comes," he said.

After some discussion, we decided we would do no dissociative work that day. Why disturb the natural direction I seemed to be taking?

"Say hello to The Kids if you see them," he told me at one point.

"I will," I said. "I will." And for the first time, I felt a wash of sorrow.

The quiet didn't last. Voices came and went, and at particular times of the day it was noisier in my head than at others. Still, there was more quiet than there ever had been, and I found myself marveling at how much easier it would be to teach, or to do nearly anything, without the constant accompaniment of my internal crew. I also began to wonder why on earth I was taking Prozac. There wasn't a chance that it had kicked in yet, but I felt so dramatically better that I had no idea what to do about the medication. Stick it out for the sake of the trial? Or give it up so I would have the pleasure of knowing just how much of the peace was the result of my own nerve and hard work over the years?

My therapist said that, on the basis of my current level of dissociation, he would have vetoed the idea of starting Prozac. But we both admitted we had yet to learn the extent to which the cyclothymia was causing problems. For a while, at least, I decided to continue the medication, especially since it had yet to take effect.

At my next appointment, things were still pretty peaceful, but after some discussion, we decided that we would do a little trance work so that my therapist could talk directly to The Kids.

As usual, they began by wriggling and squirming, but they soon settled down.

"How are things?" my therapist wanted to know.

They fell silent, shrugged moodily. "Stuff is different now," they told him, a little subdued.

"Different how?"

They squirmed. "You know," they said. "We're not around so much. You know."

"No, I don't know," he said. "Where are you if you're not around?"

"With The Grown-ups," they said promptly.

"Oh," he said. "What's that like?"

They shrugged. "It's okay." They pulled on their bangs. "It's maybe better."

"Are you scared?"

They thought. "Nooo," they said, dragging it out. Then they began to scuff their feet together. "Well, we're not scared. Except for Badger."

"Badger?"

The Kids broke down. "Who will take care of Badger? He doesn't like to be all by himself."

"Poor Badger," he said. "What do you think we should do?"

The Kids leaned toward him and said with a certain fierceness, "Make The Grown-ups promise they will always take care of Badger. You make them *promise*," they insisted. " 'Cause we're worried about Badger."

"I will," he said gently. "I'm sure The Grown-ups will be good to him. You know," he added, "I kind of miss Badger myself. He hasn't come to see me in a long time."

"Badger grew up," they said. "He didn't need to come anymore."

"You're growing up, too," he told them, and studied their face with care.

They grimaced, then burst into tears again.

"We're not hardly going to come either, anymore," they told

him, crying and sniffling. " 'Cause we don't have to come as much as The Grown-ups."

"That's sad," my therapist said, telling me later he felt a little like crying himself. "I'll miss you a lot."

The Kids nodded sadly. "We'll miss you, too," they said, and cried some more.

When it was time for them to go, they reminded him one last time: "Don't forget about Badger. Tell The Grown-ups," they said. "Don't forget."

"I'll tell them," he said quietly, and, as he had so many times before, he eased them back beneath the surface.

For a few days, I saw and heard nothing of The Kids, and all I felt was a kind of relief. I was glad to have the quiet. My therapist said he guessed that they had finally had enough parenting: They had learned that the world was safe and that they would be well cared for, so they could yield the necessity of their near-constant presence.

One morning I went to the gym and, without much thought, had a pleasant workout. It came to me that it was the very first time in nine years that I hadn't had at least some level of anxiety attack at the gym. I had often wondered why terror and panic struck while I was working out, but I had always refused to give in to it and had simply forced myself to return again and again. On this particular morning, I was surprisingly relaxed, and guessed that The Kids, who had absolutely loathed the gym, had been responsible for the fear.

I was headed to the locker room when the thought crossed my mind that I still had time to get in a quick swim. The Kids, I recalled, had always liked to swim; while at the gym, I had generally bribed them with the promise of at least ten minutes in the pool. Then I realized that, for the first time, I was thinking of The Kids in the past tense. I hurried into my suit, pulled down my goggles, and swam half a mile, weeping with every stroke. I missed The Kids profoundly—their silliness, their jokes, even their moodiness and their strident opinions. I couldn't believe I had worked so hard to be rid of them, and suddenly I was desperate for them to come back.

I talked to my therapist on the phone that evening.

"I miss them too," he told me. "But you and I have to remember that The Kids were ready to integrate, and that we have to let them go. We can't force them back because *we* miss them or because we think we need them."

"I know," I said.

"I'm sorry, Jane," he said. "There will always be signs of them if we pay attention."

I dreaded going to bed that night. What would I do about all the things that belonged to The Kids? Did I leave their tape player in the drawer? Did I leave Badger on the closet shelf? What about the night light?

Finally, I could put it off no longer. I had done half a dozen unnecessary things, but I had to get up in the morning.

I cleaned my teeth, then went into my bedroom. It seemed almost spooky, it was so empty without a gang of tired kids, either in their silly or grumpy state. I pulled on a nightshirt and, out of sheer habit, opened the bureau drawer for the tape deck.

"You guys want stories tonight?" I asked as I had asked every night for years.

There was no answer.

I shut the drawer, then sat on my bed and stared at the closet door. What about Badger?

I got into bed and lay there for a while, feeling horribly alone. Then I remembered the promise my therapist had extracted from me, and, overjoyed to have a reason, I got up, pulled Badger down from his shelf, and climbed back into bed.

I lay with Badger on my chest and studied him. I couldn't

believe how worn he'd grown over the past four years. His plush fur was dulled, his ears bent and crooked, his middle a little squashed. I stroked his head and back.

"What an ace you've been," I told Badger. "You took good care of The Kids for quite a long time."

The implacable eyes stared back at me.

It made me smile to think that, instead of turning into either a girl or a boy, The Kids had simply integrated.

I touched Badger's paw. "Whoever thought it would come to this?" I said. "It's just you and me, Badger." Then I started to laugh. Had the Kids been wise enough to know I would need Badger too? I began to giggle at the thought of having my very own stuffed badger without the excuse of a gang of internal kids. And then my breath caught for a moment, and I laughed again and cried a little too: in my own laughter I could hear the high and happy notes of The Kids, giggling themselves silly, and I reminded myself that I would always have to celebrate the things The Kids had added to my life.

Exactly three and one half weeks after I began to take it, the Prozac kicked in. For the first twenty-four hours I slept; I was too lazy and too stupefied to do much else. The next day I had to teach. All day, I squinted at those around me as if I couldn't quite hear them. I cried all the way home, and cried off and on for the next few hours. I kept an eye on my watch; I was more than ready for my weekly check-in.

"The Prozac kicked in," I blurted out. I don't even know if I said hello first.

"How is it?" my therapist said.

"I feel so awful," I told him. "I just feel so . . . so . . . *awful.*" I couldn't find another word.

He asked me to describe it. I told him about the sleep, and about feeling stupefied and dazed. "I swear I'm hemorrhaging IQ points," I added. "I feel as if I'm getting dumber by the minute."

He laughed. "You IQ will come back."

"I feel so *awful*," I said again. "I know I said I'd do this for eight weeks, but I feel—"

"Exactly how long has it been?"

"Forty-eight hours," I told him. "I know I said I'd do this for eight weeks, but—"

"Jane," he said.

"I know I said I'd make it a fair trial," I went on, "but—"

"*Jane*," he said again.

"What?"

"There's an easy solution," he told me.

"There is?" I said. "I know I said I'd—"

"*Jane*," he said. "Just stop taking it. It's that easy."

"Can I?" I said. "Oh, thank goodness. Just like that?" And I babbled on.

My head cleared over the next few days, and the physical side effects took three more weeks to subside. In the end, though, I was glad to have tried the drug; I had finally answered what my therapist called "the Prozac question." Although I had taken it at the wrong time during my therapeutic process, I could understand the drug's usefulness in certain cases. I also understood that I am definitely not a good candidate for long-term medication. I was utterly delighted at the return of my own wayward mind— even with all its quirks and oddities.

A few weeks later, I walked into my therapist's office with a piece of paper.

"You're not going to believe this," I told him.

He shook his head and laughed. "By now," he said, "I'll believe anything."

I flourished the paper. "I," I announced, "have made a list."

He nodded.

I pulled it close to my chest and laughed nervously. "You'll never guess what it's a list of."

He shook his head.

"They're my goals," I said. "I've made a list of what I want."

"All *right*," he said.

"Nine years," I said. "It only took me nine bloody years to answer your stupid question."

He laughed. "If it took that long, I'd be inclined to say it was a good question."

I glanced down at the list, then had the sudden urge to tear it into pieces.

"There's a problem, though," I said, suddenly close to panic. "I'm afraid to tell you what's on it."

"Just like the old days," he said.

"No," I said, "it's not that bad." I took a deep breath and trust the paper at him. "In the old days, it would have taken me months to do this."

He took the paper from me, then held it up. "You sure?" he said before he began to read.

I couldn't stand sitting there and watching him read my list. I felt horrifyingly vulnerable and exposed. I got up, I paced, I tried not to watch him. As I had so many times before, I stood at the window and stared first down at the street, then across the valley to the opposite hills.

The paper rustled behind me.

I turned.

"It's a good list." He was nodding thoughtfully.

I sighed with relief, then picked my way back to my chair.

My therapist watched me for a moment, cocked his head, and asked, "How are you feeling?"

"Scared to death," I admitted. "Also dizzy. Or, no, more like seasick. Actually, I feel as if my brain is turning inside out."

"What about the volume?"

I looked out at the sky and took a few long breaths while I listened. "Well," I said, "I can't say it's quiet. But it's not— Well, it's not as loud. And it's certainly not as *frantic*."

He paused, then quietly asked about The Kids.

"Gone," I said promptly. "But here, too. You know."

I smiled to myself. *You know* had been one of their favorite phrases. Even some of their speech had been woven into mine.

My therapist lifted the list. "Can I read this to you?" he said.

I clapped my hands over my ears, then pulled them away. "Go ahead," I said. "I'm tough. I can take it."

He looked at me over the paper. "You don't understand," he said. "You've only begun to integrate—and there's a long way to go—but this is the first unified document I've seen from you."

"This is hard for me," I said. "Remember, I'm still here and all that."

And so were all my demoted selves. My mind seemed like a hushed and expectant audience in a darkened theater. I could sense their presence, sense their breathlessness, their wealth of conflicting fears and expectations, but I could not distinguish the individuals among them.

"Okay," he said. "I'll summarize."

I sagged with relief.

He spoke softly: "You still need to get through physical integration. We also need to discuss womanhood and identity." Suddenly he laughed. "And we still need to talk about your mother."

"See?" I broke in, laughing too. "It was bound to come to this. I'm going to see a shrink to talk about dear old mom."

Abruptly we both turned serious.

He held up the paper. "It's a good list," he said again. "One way or another, it represents all of your remaining—"

"Force fields," I finished for him. Then I held out my hand for the list. "I'm taking it home," I said. "Not that I don't trust you or anything . . ."

We both laughed.

I examined the list again.

"It seems ungodly long," I said.

"It's okay," he told me. "The end of integration is said to be roughly the sixty percent mark in the process."

"We've come a long way though, haven't we?" I heard the old tinge of desperation in my voice.

He hesitated.

"I think you can answer that for yourself now," he said.

I stopped and thought. "Have we had this conversation before?"

"Yes," he said. "Only now you're able to remember it."

I smiled ruefully. "Makes a difference," I said.

"Yes," he said. "It does. It certainly does. And do you remember what else I said back then?"

I scowled.

"I also promised not to abandon you," he reminded me.

I stopped and thought for a moment, then smiled gratefully. "You know," I said, "I think I'm finally ready to believe you." After a moment, I took a breath and asked, "So . . . where do we start?"

He shrugged, then gave me a quiet grin. "Anywhere you'd like," he said. "Anywhere you'd like."